White
Sea

Lake
adoga

Ural Mountains

n o

S i b e r

Volga

Oka

Moskva

Ural

Don

Donets

Volga

Aral
Sea

Sea of
Azov

Crimea

C a u c a s u s

C a s p i a n   S e a

Kura

Araks

lack Sea

tolia

Kizil Irmak

Taurus Mts.

Ceyhan

P l a t e a u

o f

rus

Orontes

Tigris

Euphrates

M e s o p o t a m i a

a

Jordan

P e r s i a n   G u l f

Atlas of
European History

CARTOGRAPHY
BY
THE CLARENDON PRESS
OXFORD

Atlas of
European History

edited by

EDWARD WHITING FOX

Cornell University

with the assistance of

H. S. DEIGHTON

Pembroke College, Oxford

NEW YORK

OXFORD UNIVERSITY PRESS

1957

© OXFORD UNIVERSITY PRESS, INC. 1957

LIBRARY OF CONGRESS CATALOGUE CARD NUMBER: 56-11113

MAPS DRAWN AND PHOTOGRAPHED BY THE
CARTOGRAPHIC DEPARTMENT OF THE CLARENDON PRESS
AND PRINTED IN GREAT BRITAIN BY
MESSRS. COOK, HAMMOND, AND KELL, LONDON
MANUFACTURED IN THE UNITED STATES OF·AMERICA

TABLE OF CONTENTS

Preface . . . . VI–VIII
*EUROPE . . . . Front Endpaper
*THE HOLY LAND IN BIBLICAL TIMES 1
    Inset I   The Empire of David and Solomon in the 10th century B.C.
    Inset II   The Divided Kingdom in the 9th century B.C.
*CRADLE OF CIVILIZATION 2–3
*GREEK COLONIZATION AND ALEXANDER'S WORLD 4–5
    Greece at the time of the Persian War, from 500 B.C. (*p. 4a*)
    Greece at the time of the Peloponnesian War, 431–404 B.C. (*p. 5a*)
*ANCIENT GREECE AND ITALY. Inset: The Peloponnesus 6–7
*ROMAN EMPIRE AT THE TIME OF TRAJAN: A.D. 98–117 8–9
 ROMAN EMPIRE AFTER DIOCLETIAN: Administrative Divisions . . . 10–11
 THE BARBARIAN KINGDOMS A.D. 453, A.D. 481, A.D. 511, A.D. 565. . . 12–13
 BYZANTINE, ISLAMIC AND FRANKISH EMPIRES: About A.D. 800 . . . 14–15
    Inset I. Extension of Frankish Authority   Inset II. Partitions of the Carolingian Empire
*MEDIAEVAL ENGLAND AND FRANCE 16–17
    Insets: Extension of Royal Authority in France:
      I End of the 11th century. II Mid-12th century. III 1328. IV 1420. V 1453.
*THE MEDIAEVAL EMPIRE: during the 10th and 11th centuries 18–19
*THE EASTERN MEDITERRANEAN AFTER THE FIRST CRUSADE: at the end of the 11th century   20
    Inset: After the Fourth Crusade (early 13th century)
*ENGLAND AND THE BALTIC: in the later Middle Ages 21
*MEDIAEVAL EUROPE: Centers and Routes of Trade 22–23
*SPAIN AND PORTUGAL: at the end of the 15th century 24
    Insets: Reconquest from the Moors:
      I Early 10th century.   II Mid-11th century.   III Mid-12th century.   IV Late 15th century.
*THE FAR EAST: The objective of European explorations 25
*THE GREAT EXPLORATIONS 26–27
 EUROPE: 1490, 1560, 1560 (Religious Situation), 1648. 28–29
 PRINCIPAL COLONIAL EMPIRES: About 1600 30–31
*RENAISSANCE ITALY: 15th century 32
*BRITAIN AT THE TIME OF THE CIVIL WAR: 1642–1644 33
*CENTRAL AND SOUTH-EASTERN EUROPE: 1648–1683, as seen from Constantinople . . 34–35
 EUROPE: 1721, 1789, 1812, 1815. 36–37
*THE AMERICAN COLONIES AND THE NORTH ATLANTIC: on the eve of the Revolution . 38–39
 CENTRAL EUROPE AND ITALY 1806 40
 CENTRAL EUROPE AND ITALY 1815 41
 CENTRAL AND SOUTH-EASTERN EUROPE AFTER THE CONGRESS OF BERLIN . . 42–43
 PRUSSIA AND THE ZOLLVEREIN   HAPSBURG EMPIRE 1878: Distribution of Languages   44
*EUROPEAN RUSSIA IN THE 19TH CENTURY 45
 COLONIAL EMPIRES ON EVE OF FIRST WORLD WAR 46–47
 CENTRAL EUROPE AND ITALY 1929 48–49
*WAR IN EUROPE: 1939–1945   Inset: The Rhine 50–51
 WAR IN THE PACIFIC: 1941–1945. 52–53
*GREAT BRITAIN AND FRANCE: 1955 54–55
*AFRICA: 1955   Inset: Africa and the East 56–57
*UNION OF SOVIET SOCIALIST REPUBLICS: 1955 58–59
 EUROPE: 1914, 1924, 1940, 1950. 60–61
*THE FAR EAST 1955 62–63
 WORLD, POPULATION 64
 WORLD, PHYSICAL . . . . Back Endpaper

THE GAZETTEER . . . . i–xvi
MAP EXERCISES

* Physical map

V

PREFACE

ALTHOUGH human history unfolds within the two dimensions of space and time, the geographic factor has all but been allowed to disappear from the European history courses now taught in most American colleges and universities. One important explanation of this development is the lack of a suitable historical atlas, and the publication of the present volume was undertaken expressly to fill this gap. Equally important in the decision to undertake such an ambitious project, however, was the conviction that not merely a new atlas, but a completely new kind of atlas, was required.

If map study has dropped out of history courses because no atlas was available, the lack of an atlas must to some extent be attributed to a growing reluctance on the part of students and teachers alike to accept the burdens of teaching and studying the cartographic context of history by the traditional methods. However much history courses may have suffered from want of geography, students of history have often suffered more from the meaningless feats of memory that were imposed upon them in the name of map assignments.

The spatial dimension can be successfully restored to the college course in European history only if students are provided with an atlas which will help them to understand the need for maps in the intelligent reading of history and at the same time aid them to assimilate methodically an increasing amount of cartographic information. The best of the older historical atlases were compiled not only by—but apparently only for—experts, with a resulting quantity of detail irrelevant to undergraduate courses and productive of little but confusion and distaste in the minds of students.

The first requirement for this atlas, then, was that it should provide only the information which would be useful in following the standard university courses and that this information should be portrayed as simply and clearly as possible. The method by which this aim was approached was to compile lists of geographic references in the current textbooks (in European history) and to build the maps directly from these lists. This means that any college student of European history should be able to find here all the cartographic information necessary to a careful reading of his text and to find it unencumbered with esoteric details.

In order to help him see the more obvious relationships between the largest topographical features and the historical narrative, many of the maps are presented on a physical rather than a political base. This emphasis on the structure of the area under consideration should give the student a frame, essentially unchanging, within which he can fit the less stable man-made features: states, roads, or national boundaries. Quite simply this means that the student who takes the trouble to memorize the location of these features—primarily the major rivers—will have a system of reference within which to set a large part of the geographic information which he will need to assimilate in the course of his studies. For this reason the rivers, and to a lesser extent other physical features, have not only been emphasized but deliberately presented as a formal pattern; and the supplementary exercises have been designed to relate new phenomena to this underlying structure.

In an effort to keep the maps simple and yet to include all information essential to a reading of European history, place names that appear on one map have often been omitted from others even where they might be expected to appear. It was hoped that the ability to see names clearly would more than make up for the occasional necessity of referring backward or forward a few pages to locate specific places.

With maps thus simplified, and place names accordingly easy to locate, it did not seem necessary to provide the traditional system of co-ordinates with the gazetteer. Places names are identified by page numbers and a brief description of their location rather than with traditional pairs of numbers and letters; Thus following " Paris " the reader will find: (Lutetia): NW France, on the Seine just below the confluence of the Marne R," rather than such symbols as " E 6 " or " 2 E 49 N ". If occasionally this adds slightly to the effort involved in finding a given place, it should add substantially to the student's knowledge of the physical setting in which the narrative of his text is unfolding.

Simplification and clarification of the maps have never been sought at the expense of essential accuracy; in fact continual care has been taken to insure that the atlas should conform to the best standards of modern map making. In many cases, however, particularly in maps dealing with periods preceding the last two or three centuries, a too detailed accuracy could become seriously misleading. The boundaries of feudal territories, for example, were not only notoriously unstable, they would often be difficult to establish at a given date. But if the precise boundaries of Aquitaine or Saxony would be meaningful only to the most erudite, the general location and relative positions of the more famous duchies and counties of western Europe are necessary information for even the beginner. For this reason, such unstable or ill-defined territories are shown either without boundaries or with boldly drawn approximate boundaries that avoid any implication of precise and firmly established frontiers. The same general method was used in the case of mediaeval trade routes where place names and river systems have been emphasized. If the exact route would be not only difficult to establish but variable, there is little doubt that the bulk of trade flowed, if not always on the water surface of the rivers, at least along roads and paths following their valleys.

Another problem of accuracy arose in the case of known geographic changes. The harbor of Miletus, for example, which played a part in the history of ancient Greece, has long since silted up, leaving the town site five miles inland. Although it might seem that an historical atlas should show the coast line as it existed at the period represented by the map, the practical obstacles to this are virtually insurmountable. If it is known that a harbor existed, knowledge of its exact shape is scant and unreliable, and the more historians try to reconstruct this kind of geographic detail (or, similarly to establish previous conditions of soil or climate) the more they realize that the results will be fragmentary and inexact at best. Since to draw maps from such information is hardly practical, it was decided to present all historical material against contemporary maps and to indicate by notes, where necessary, the few known and significant changes in topography.

Finally, every effort has been made to maintain in the mind of the reader the realization that he has before him, not merely colored diagrams, but accurate representations of the surface of the earth. To this end physical maps have been used to an unprecedented extent, most of the maps have been presented without the traditional margins (to suggest the continuous character of the surface under scrutiny), and a few have even been turned from the conventional

alignment to bring into view a particularly significant segment of the globe, so that the North is no longer at the top of the page. If the earth is the stage on which men act out their destinies, an historical atlas should provide—in its maps—a setting for the actions which fill the pages of history.

Only one who has been involved in the preparation of an historical atlas will fully understand the range and extent of obligation to countless others for suggestions and assistance which such an undertaking inevitably incurs. To acknowledge all would be impossible but I cannot fail to express my gratitude to those—collectively and anonymously—who have preceded me in the field and whose atlases I have consulted constantly. I must also acknowledge my obligation to the authors and publishers of the leading contemporary textbooks in the modern European history field; it was on a canvass of these books that the selection of subjects and details for this atlas was based.

During the formative stages of this work the Publishers and I consulted a large group of scholars and teachers with great profit, and, at our own request, specific suggestions were made by the following:

Professor Robert G. Albion
Professor Paul Alexander
Professor Frederick C. Barghoorn
Professor William C. Bark
Professor Julian Boyd
Dr. John C. Campbell
Professor Elmer H. Cutts
Dr. T. K. Derry

Professor William E. Diez
Professor Wallace Ferguson
Dr. Moses I. Finley
Professor Myron P. Gilmore
Professor J. M. Wallace-Hadrill
Professor Edgar Johnson
Professor Solomon Katz
Professor Thomas C. Mendenhall

Professor H. B. Noss
Dr. Harry M. Orlinsky
Professor Richard Pipes
Professor A. William Salomone
Professor Henry F. Schwarz
Dr. Theodore Shabad
Professor Raymond P. Stearns

Personally, I wish to express my gratitude to all members of the Cartographic Department of the Clarendon Press and particularly Mrs. Mary Denniston, Mr. Stanley Knight, and Miss Alison Shaw. Also I wish to thank Miss Mary Alice Boothroyd and Mr. Peter Czap for editorial assistance and Mrs. Phyllis Bell and Miss Elizabeth Kohl for secretarial help. It would be impossible to conclude without mentioning Major Thomas H. Thomas whose interest in historical geography kindled mine; and finally I must acknowledge the encouragement of my wife and children which made it possible for me to complete this atlas.

EDWARD WHITING FOX

Ithaca, New York, 1956

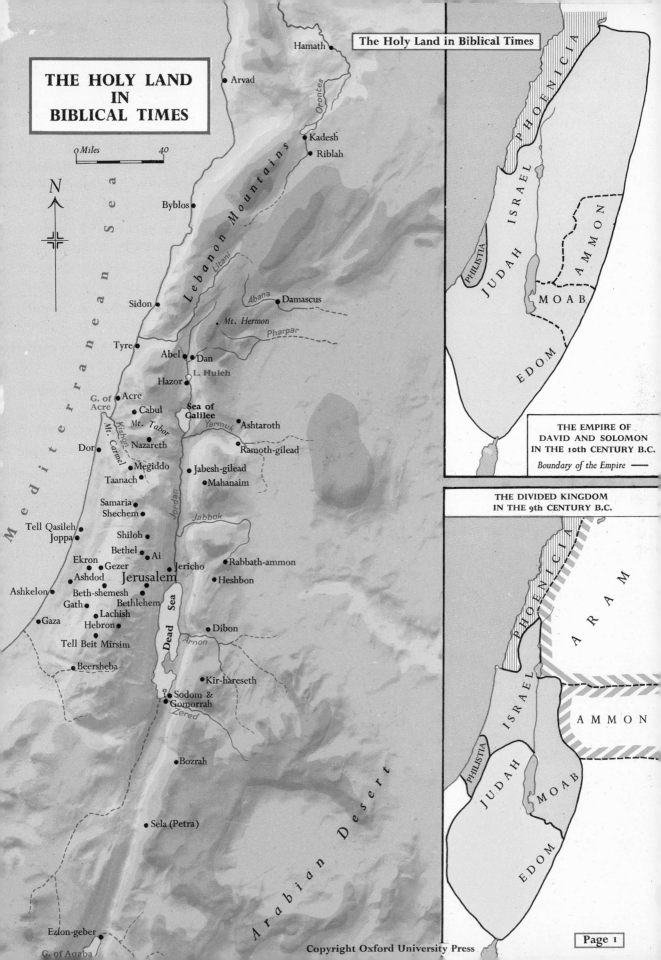

THE HOLY LAND IN BIBLICAL TIMES

The Holy Land in Biblical Times

0 Miles 40

N

Mediterranean Sea

Hamath
Arvad
Orontes
Kadesh
Riblah
Byblos
Lebanon Mountains
Litani
Sidon
Abana
Damascus
Mt. Hermon
Pharpar
Tyre
Abel
Dan
L. Huleh
Hazor
G. of Acre
Acre
Cabul
Sea of Galilee
Mt. Tabor
Ashtaroth
Yarmuk
Kishon
Mt. Carmel
Nazareth
Ramoth-gilead
Dor
Megiddo
Jabesh-gilead
Taanach
Mahanaim
Jordan
Samaria
Shechem
Jabbok
Tell Qasileh
Joppa
Shiloh
Bethel
Ai
Ekron
Gezer
Jericho
Rabbath-ammon
Ashdod
Jerusalem
Heshbon
Ashkelon
Beth-shemesh
Gath
Bethlehem
Dead Sea
Gaza
Lachish
Hebron
Dibon
Tell Beit Mirsim
Arnon
Beersheba
Kir-hareseth
Sodom & Gomorrah
Zered
Bozrah
Sela (Petra)
Arabian Desert
Ezion-geber
G. of Aqaba

THE EMPIRE OF DAVID AND SOLOMON IN THE 10th CENTURY B.C.

Boundary of the Empire ———

PHOENICIA
ISRAEL
JUDAH
PHILISTIA
AMMON
MOAB
EDOM

THE DIVIDED KINGDOM IN THE 9th CENTURY B.C.

PHOENICIA
ARAM
ISRAEL
PHILISTIA
AMMON
JUDAH
MOAB
EDOM

Cradle of Civilization

H I T T I T E S

CILICIA

Tarsus

Carchemish

Hara

30°E

35°N

MEDITERRANEAN SEA

Cyprus

Ugarit

Hamath

S Y R I A

Orontes

Balikh

Kadesh

Byblos

Anti-Lebanon Range

A R A M

Litani Lebanon Mountains

Sidon

Damascus

Tyre

• Mt. Hermon

Acre

L. Huleh

Sea of Galilee

Yarmuk

Mt. Tabor

GILEAD

C A N A A N

Jordan

Jabbok

Jericho

Heshbon

Jerusalem

AMMON

Dibon

Transjordan Plateau

Dead Sea

Arnon

Beersheba

MOAB

Avaris

Zered

GOSHEN

Pithom

NEGEB

Bozrah

ARABAH

Memphis

Sela

A R A B I

E G Y P T

Ezion-geber

Sinai Peninsula

Nile

Gulf of Aqaba

Beni Hasan

Tell el Amarna

Red Sea

0 Miles   150

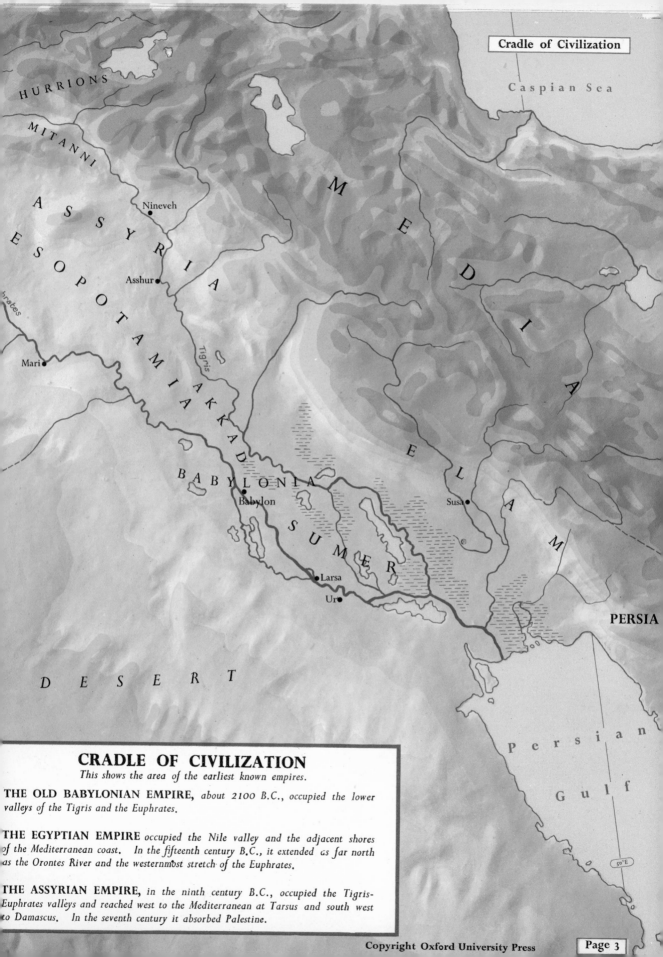

HURRIONS

MITANNI

ASSYRIA

MESOPOTAMIA

Caspian Sea

Nineveh

Asshur

Tigris

Mari

Euphrates

MEDIA

AKKAD

BABYLONIA

Babylon

SUMER

ELAM

Susa

Larsa

Ur

PERSIA

DESERT

Persian

Gulf

50°E

CRADLE OF CIVILIZATION
This shows the area of the earliest known empires.

THE OLD BABYLONIAN EMPIRE, *about 2100 B.C., occupied the lower valleys of the Tigris and the Euphrates.*

THE EGYPTIAN EMPIRE *occupied the Nile valley and the adjacent shores of the Mediterranean coast. In the fifteenth century B.C., it extended as far north as the Orontes River and the westernmost stretch of the Euphrates.*

THE ASSYRIAN EMPIRE, *in the ninth century B.C., occupied the Tigris-Euphrates valleys and reached west to the Mediterranean at Tarsus and south west to Damascus. In the seventh century it absorbed Palestine.*

The Greeks

THRACE

Strymon

MACEDONIA

Thasos

BOSPORUS

Byzantium

Propontis

PERSIAN EMPIRE

40°N

Vale of Tempe

THESSALY

Artemisium Prom.

Aegean Sea

Lesbos

LYDIA

Ambracian Gulf

Thermopylae P.

Delphi

EUBOEA

Eretria

BOEOTIA

Thebes

Plataea *Marathon Plain*

Athens

Corinth *Salamis*

Isthmus

Aegina *Sunium Prom.*

Troezen

Delos

Sparta

Naxos

Sardis

Ephesus

Samos *Mycale*

Miletus

Halicarnassus

Rhodes

20°E

30°E

Persian Empire	
Area of Ionian Revolt	
Neutral or Medizing states	
Greek Allies	

GREECE AT THE TIME OF THE PERSIAN WAR from 500 B.C.

0 Miles 150

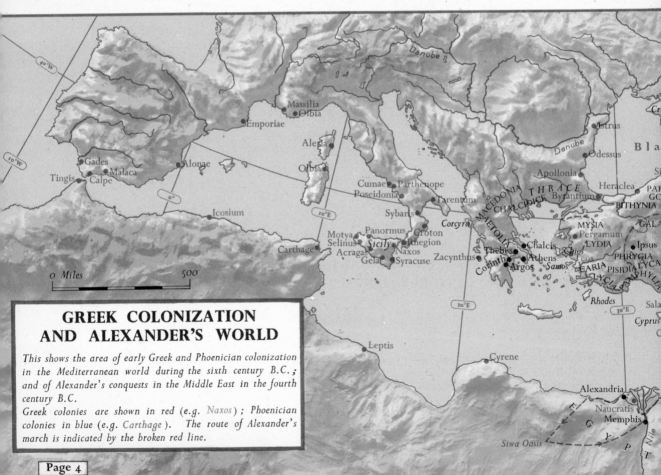

Danube

Massilia

Olbia

Emporiae

Aleria

Olbia

Danube

Istrus

Odessus

Bla

Apollonia

Gades

Malaca

Tingis Calpe

Alone

Heraclea

Byzantium

MACEDONIA

THRACE

CHALCIDICE

BITHYNIA

Icosium

Cumae Parthenope

Poscidonia

Tarentum

MYSIA

Pergamum

LYDIA

Ipsus

PHRYGIA

Carthage

Sybaris

Corcyra

Motya

Panormus

Croton

Rhegion

Selinus *Sicily*

Acragas Naxos

Gela Syracuse

Zacynthus

Thebes

Chalcis

Chios

Teos

CARIA

PISIDIA

PAMPHYLIA

LYCIA

Corinth

Athens

Samos

Argos

Rhodes

Cyprus

Leptis

Cyrene

Alexandria

Naucratis

Memphis

Siwa Oasis

EGYPT

Nile

0 Miles 500

GREEK COLONIZATION AND ALEXANDER'S WORLD

This shows the area of early Greek and Phoenician colonization in the Mediterranean world during the sixth century B.C.; and of Alexander's conquests in the Middle East in the fourth century B.C.

Greek colonies are shown in red (e.g. Naxos); Phoenician colonies in blue (e.g. Carthage). The route of Alexander's march is indicated by the broken red line.

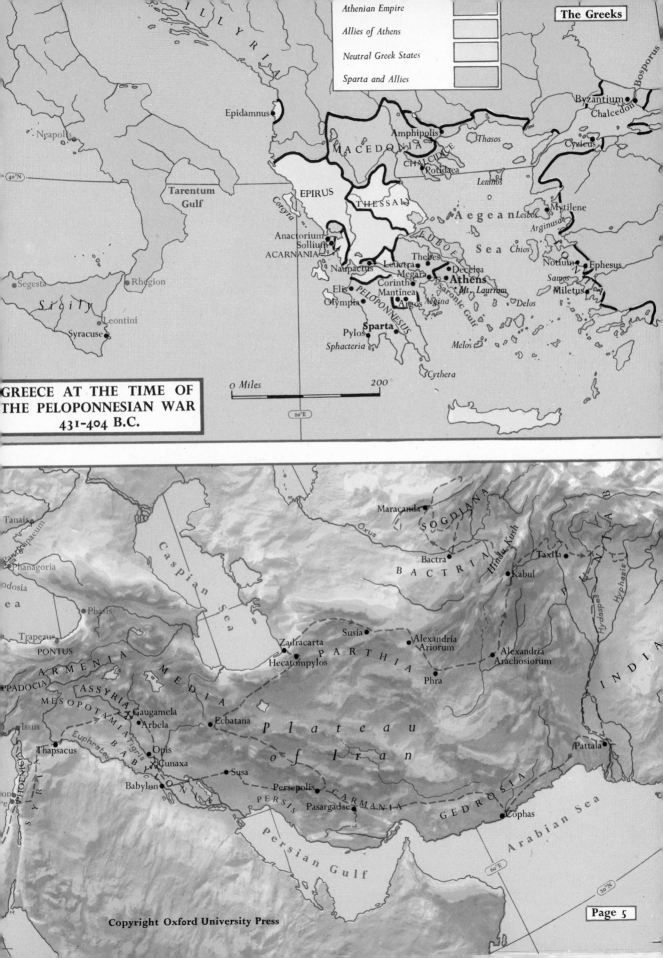

The Greeks

Athenian Empire
Allies of Athens
Neutral Greek States
Sparta and Allies

GREECE AT THE TIME OF
THE PELOPONNESIAN WAR
431-404 B.C.

0 Miles 200

ILLYRIA

Epidamnus

Neapolis

40°N

Tarentum
Gulf

Corcyra

EPIRUS

MACEDONIA

Amphipolis

Thasos

CHALCIDICE

Potidaea

Lemnos

THESSALY

Aegean

Lesbos

Mytilene

Arginusae

Sea

Chios

Anactorium
Sollium
ACARNANIA

Naupactus

EUBOEA

Thebes

Leuctra

Decelea

Notium

Ephesus

Megara

Athens

Samos

Corinth

Mt. Laurium

Miletus

Elis

PELOPONNESUS

Mantinea

Saronic Gulf

Aegina

Delos

Olympia

Argos

Sparta

Pylos

Sphacteria

Melos

Sicily

Segesta

Rhegion

Leontini

Syracuse

Cythera

Byzantium
Chalcedon

Bosporus

Cyzicus

IONIA

20°E

Tanais

Hypacum

Phanagoria

odosia

Sea

Phasis

Trapezus

PONTUS

ARMENIA

PPADOCIA

Issus

ASSYRIA

MESOPOTAMIA

Gaugamela

Arbela

MEDIA

Ecbatana

Caspian

Sea

Zadracarta

Hecatompylos

PARTHIA

Susia

Oxus

Maracanda

SOGDIANA

Bactra

BACTRIA

Hindu Kush

Taxila

Kabul

PUNJAB

Alexandria
Ariorum

Phra

Alexandria
Arachosiorum

INDIA

Hydaspes

Hyphasis

Plateau

of

Iran

SYRIA

PHOENICIA

Thapsacus

Euphrates

Tigris

Opis

BABYLONIA

Cunaxa

Babylon

Susa

Persepolis

Pasargadae

PERSIS

CARMANIA

GEDROSIA

Pattala

Cophas

Persian Gulf

Arabian Sea

60°E

20°N

Page 5

Copyright Oxford University Press

L. Geneva

Lugdunum

A L P S

Danube

PANNON

Ticinus

Mediolanum

Verona

VENETIA

CISALPINE GAUL

Po

ILLY

Nemaușus

LIGURIA

Bononia

Rubicon

Ravenna

Trebia

Massilia

Apennine Mountains

ETRURIA

Adriatic Sea

Corsica

Nursia

Spoletium

Tiber

Rome

LATIUM

Ostia

Appian Way

Casilinum

APULIA

Cannae

40°N

Volturnus

Neapolis

Beneventum

Cumae

CAMPANIA

Brundis

Sardinia

Herculaneum

Pompeii

Tarentum

LUCANIA

Metapontum

Tarentur

Tyrrhenian Sea

Gulf

10°E

BRUTTIUM

Str. of

Messina

Io

Himera

Sicily

Carthage

Catana

Cirta

Syracuse

Zama

0 Miles   150

THE PELOPONNESUS

(Inset map labels:)
LOCRIS
PHOCIS
Chaeronea
BOEOTIA
Leuctra
Thebes
Plataea
Marathon
Gulf of Corinth
ACHAEA
Eleusis
Megara
Athens
Sicyon
Piraeus
ELIS
Corinth
Salamis
ARGOLIS
Olympia
Mycenae
Mantinea
Argos
Tiryns
ARCADIA
ATTICA
MESSENIA
Sparta
Pylos
LACONIA

(Main map labels:)
DACIA
Sirmium
Danube
Balkan Mountains
Black Sea
Hebrus
Adrianopolis
Strymon
THRACE
Byzantium
Chalcedon
BITHYNIA
Bosporus
Heraclea
Nicomedia
Propontis
Ainos
Philippi
Amphipolis
Nicaea
Thasos
Hellespont
Cyzicus
MACEDONIA
Pella
Abydos
Granicus
PHRYGIA
Olynthus
Mt. Athos
Sigeum
Ilium
Mt. Olympus
Potidaea
Lemnos
THESSALY
Pergamum
EPIRUS
Lesbos
Ephesus
PERSIA
Pharsalus
Phocaea
LYDIA
Corcyra
Chios
Smyrna
ACARNANIA
Actium
EUBOEA
Aegean Sea
Samos
Maeander
AETOLIA
Chaleis
Mycale
CARIA
Delphi
Eretria
Miletus
BOEOTIA
Athens
Halicarnassus
Euryme...
Saronic Gulf
Naxos
PELOPONNESUS
Rhodes
an Sea

Miletus was an important port from which the sea has since receded.

20°E
30°E

Cnossus
Crete
Gortyn

ANCIENT GREECE AND ITALY

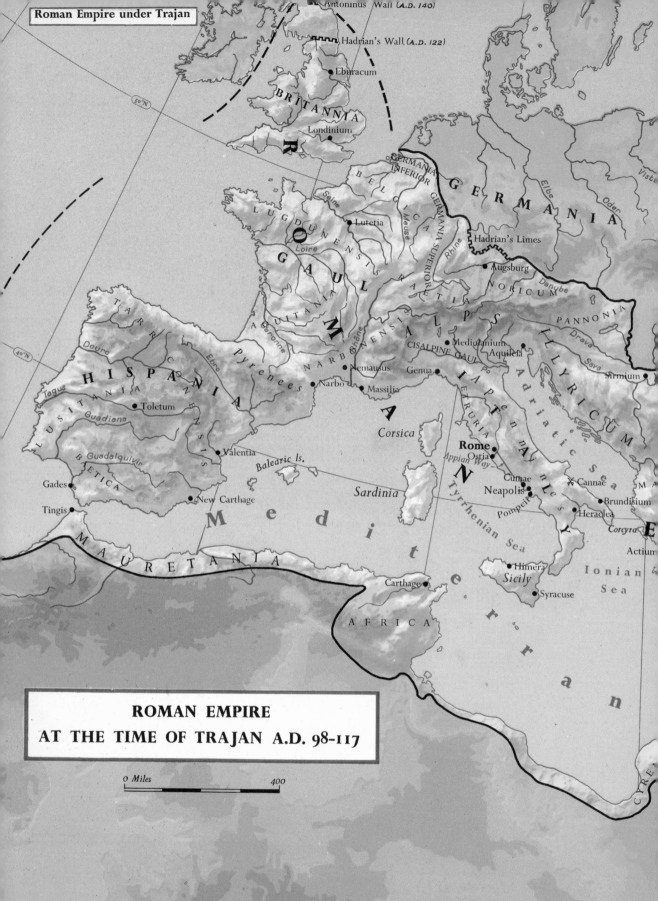

Roman Empire under Trajan

Antoninus Wall (A.D. 140)

Hadrian's Wall (A.D. 122)

Eburacum

BRITANNIA

Londinium

GERMANIA INFERIOR

GERMANIA

BELGICA

GERMANIA SUPERIOR

Lutetia

Hadrian's Limes

Seine

Meuse

Rhine

Augsburg

Elbe

Oder

Vistula

LUGDUNENSIS

GAUL

Loire

RAETIA

NORICUM

Danube

Drave

PANNONIA

Save

A Garonne

AQUITANIA

Rhône

NARBONENSIS

ALPS

Mediolanium

CISALPINE GAUL

Aquileia

Po

ILLYRICUM

Sirmium

TARRACONENSIS

Douro

Pyrenees

Ebro

Nemausus

Genua

APENNINES

Adriatic Sea

HISPANIA

Narbo

Massilia

ETRURIA

LUSITANIA

Tagus

Toletum

Corsica

Rome

Ostia

Appian Way

Cumae

Neapolis

Cannae

Brundisium

Heraclea

Corcyra

Actium

Guadiana

Valentia

Balearic Is.

Sardinia

Tyrrhenian Sea

Pompeii

Guadalquivir

BAETICA

Gades

New Carthage

Tingis

Mediterranean

MAURETANIA

Himera

Sicily

Ionian Sea

Carthage

Syracuse

AFRICA

ROMAN EMPIRE
AT THE TIME OF TRAJAN A.D. 98-117

0 Miles   400

C I A

E S I A

aube

T H R A C E

Adrianople

Philippi Byzantium

M

Athens ASIA

P

Rhodes

Crete

n   S e a

nia

Prut Dniester

Black Sea

Nicomedia BITHYNIA

Pergamum

Sinope

PONTUS

Ancyra

CAPPADOCIA

Phasis

Caspian Sea

A R M E N I A

Euphrates

Tigris

Antioch

SYRIA

Dura Europos

Palmyra

PARTHIAN

EMPIRE

Tyre Damascus

R

Jerusalem PALESTINE

Alexandria

Memphis

EGYPT

Nile

Red Sea

A R A B I A

ROMAN EMPIRE AFTER DIOCLETIAN
Administrative Divisions

Diocletian (A.D. 245-313) divided the empire into four prefectures: Gaul, Italy, Illyricum and the East. Each of these in turn were subdivided into dioceses and pro-consulates. The prefectures are shown on this map by color and the dioceses and pro-consulates by name.

.... Prefecture of Italy

....   ,,   Gaul

....   ,,   the East

....   ,,   Illyricum

Line of administrative division of the Empire, first instituted by Diocletian. This also represents the approximate division between the Greek and Latin halves of the Empire.

0 Miles   400

Map labels: DIOCESE OF BRITAIN — Carlisle, Newcastle, York, Chester, Gloucester. GERMANIA — Tournai, Cologne, Bonn, Trier, Mainz, Strasbourg, Ratisbon, Vienna. DIOCESE OF GAUL — Tours, Bordeaux, Lyons. DIOCESE OF ITALY — Milan, Aquileia, Venice, Bologna, Ravenna, Belgrade, Narbonne, Marseilles, Nicaea. DIOCESE OF SPAIN — Tarragona, Cordova, Seville, Cádiz. DIOCESE OF ROME — Ostia, Rome, Monte Cassino, Spalato, Brindisi. Mediterranean. DIOCESE OF AFRICA — Hippo, Tunis, PROCONSULATE OF AFRICA, Tripoli. Rivers: Loire, Rhône, Ebro, Rhine, Elbe, Oder, Vistula, Danube.

S A R M A T I A

Dnieper

Dniester

A C I A

Volga

C a s p i a n S e a

SE

B l a c k S e a

DIOCESE
OF
THRACE

Danube

• Trebizond

• Adrianople

• Constantinople

DIOCESE

SE

Salonika •

• Nicaea

OF

NIA

DIOCESE

• Larissa

ONTUS

SULATE

D I O C E S E

• Smyrna

OF

ACHAIA

• Ephesus

ASIA

PROCONSULATE ASIA

• Athens

• Tarsus

Euphrates

Tigris

• Antioch

• Rhodes

• Seleucia

• Palmyra

DIOCESE OF THE EAST

30°E

• Damascus

a n

S e a

• Jerusalem

• Alexandria

CESE OF E

Nile

G Y P T

DIOCESE OF THE EAST

• Thebes

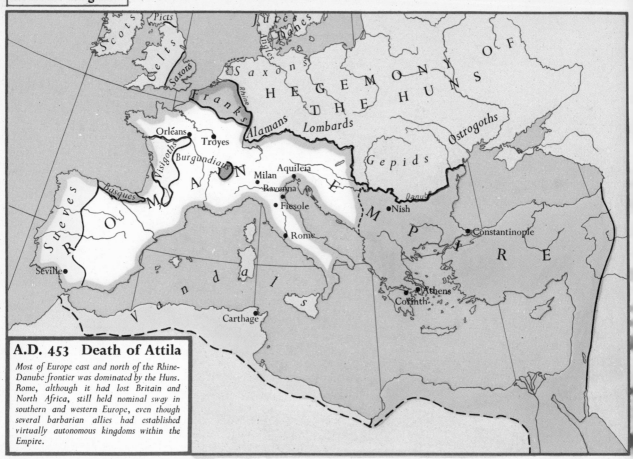

A.D. 453 Death of Attila

Most of Europe east and north of the Rhine-Danube frontier was dominated by the Huns. Rome, although it had lost Britain and North Africa, still held nominal sway in southern and western Europe, even though several barbarian allies had established virtually autonomous kingdoms within the Empire.

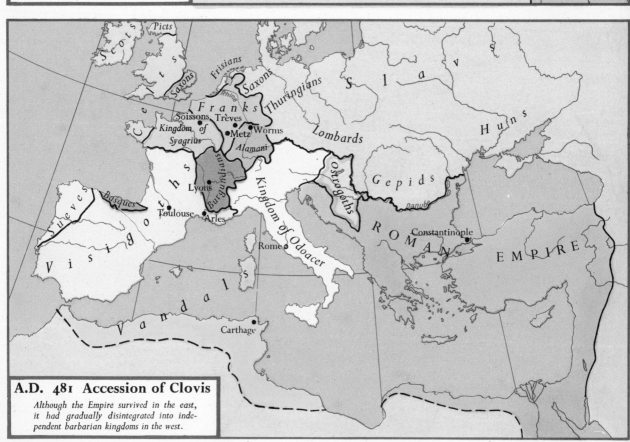

A.D. 481 Accession of Clovis

Although the Empire survived in the east, it had gradually disintegrated into independent barbarian kingdoms in the west.

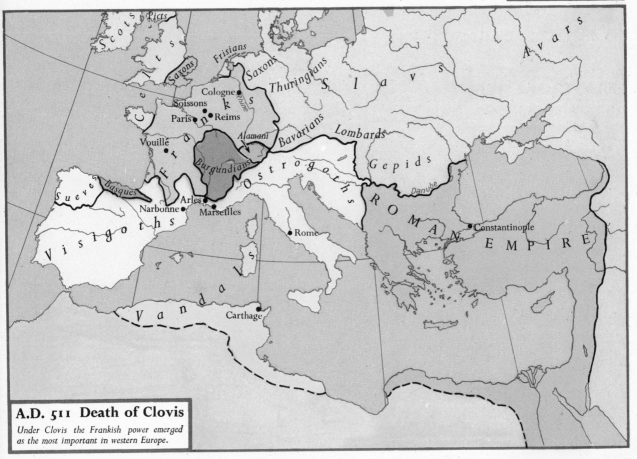

A.D. 511 Death of Clovis

Under Clovis the Frankish power emerged as the most important in western Europe.

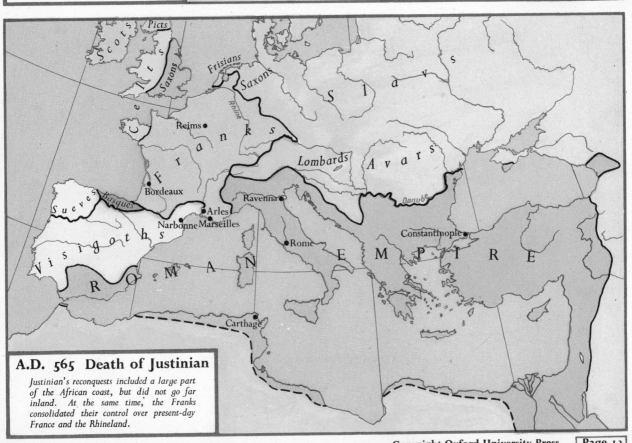

A.D. 565 Death of Justinian

Justinian's reconquests included a large part of the African coast, but did not go far inland. At the same time, the Franks consolidated their control over present-day France and the Rhineland.

Byzantine, Islamic & Frankish Empires

BYZANTINE, ISLAMIC AND FRANKISH EMPIRES
about A.D. 800

0 Miles   450

Frankish Territory

Before Clovis

Acquired by Clovis including Brittany which became his tributary

Acquired by subsequent Merovingians

„   „   Charles Martel & Pepin

„   „   Charlemagne

Tributary to Charlemagne

EXTENSION OF FRANKIS:

NEUSTRIA

AUSTR

AQUITAINE

BURGUNDY

SPANISH MARCH

BY

North Sea

York
ANGLO-SAXONS
Thames
London
Canterbury

Aix-la-Chapelle

Fontenoy
Testry
Soissons   Laon
Paris   Reims
Verdun
Cologne
Fulda

CAROLINGIAN EMPIRE

Strasbourg

Tours
Poitiers

St. Gall

Lyons

Salzburg

KINGDOM OF ASTURIAS

Roncesvalles
Ebro
Saragossa

EMIRATE OF OMMIADS

Barcelona

Cordova

Arles

Pavia   Milan
Bobbio   Venice
Ravenna

TRIBUTARY TO CHARLEMAGNE

Elbe

S L A V S

Kiev
Dnieper

A V A R S

M A G Y A R S

KHANATE OF BULGARIA
Danube

Bla c

Spoleto
Rome
Monte Cassino
Benevento
Naples   DUCHY OF
Amalfi   BENEVENTO

Durazzo

Constantinople
Chalcedon
Nicaea

Corfu

Sardinia

Mediter

BYZANTINE EMPI

Ephesus
Athens   Iconi

Carthage

Sicily

ranean Se

Crete

Cyprus

DOMINION

OF

IDRISIDS

A

B

B

A

S

Alexand
Cairo

20°W   10°W   50°N   40°N   20°E   30°E

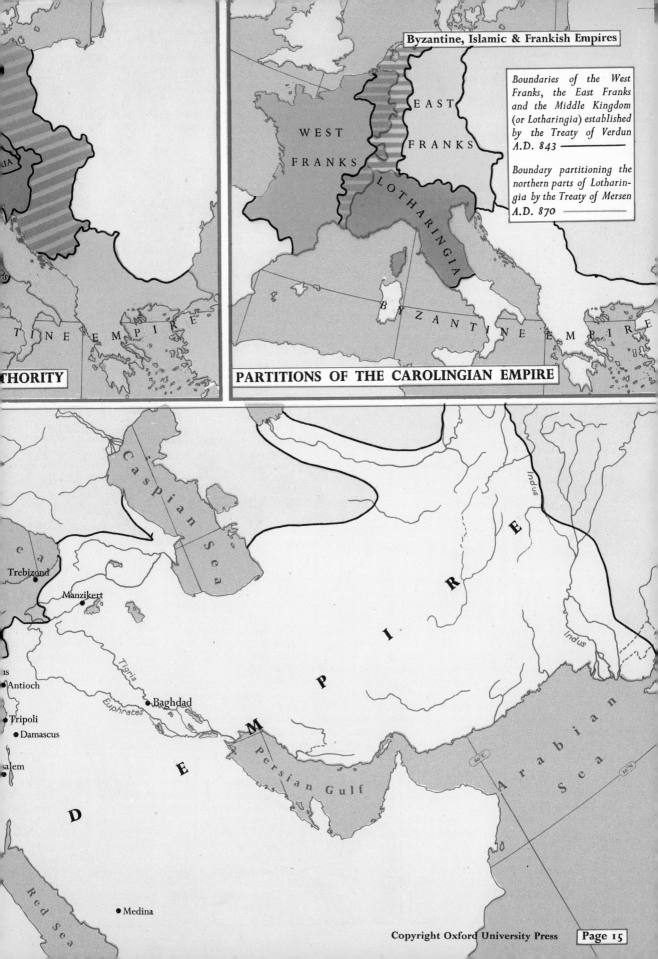

WEST

FRANKS

EAST

FRANKS

LOTHARINGIA

B Y Z A N T I N E   E M P I R E

*Boundaries of the West
Franks, the East Franks
and the Middle Kingdom
(or Lotharingia) established
by the Treaty of Verdun
A.D. 843* ————

*Boundary partitioning the
northern parts of Lotharingia by the Treaty of Mersen
A.D. 870* ————

PARTITIONS OF THE CAROLINGIAN EMPIRE

THORITY

...TINE EMPIRE

Trebizond

Manzikert

Caspian Sea

Indus

Indus

Antioch

Tigris

Euphrates

Baghdad

Tripoli

Damascus

...salem

Persian Gulf

Arabian Sea

Red Sea

Medina

E M P I R E

60°E

20°N

30°N

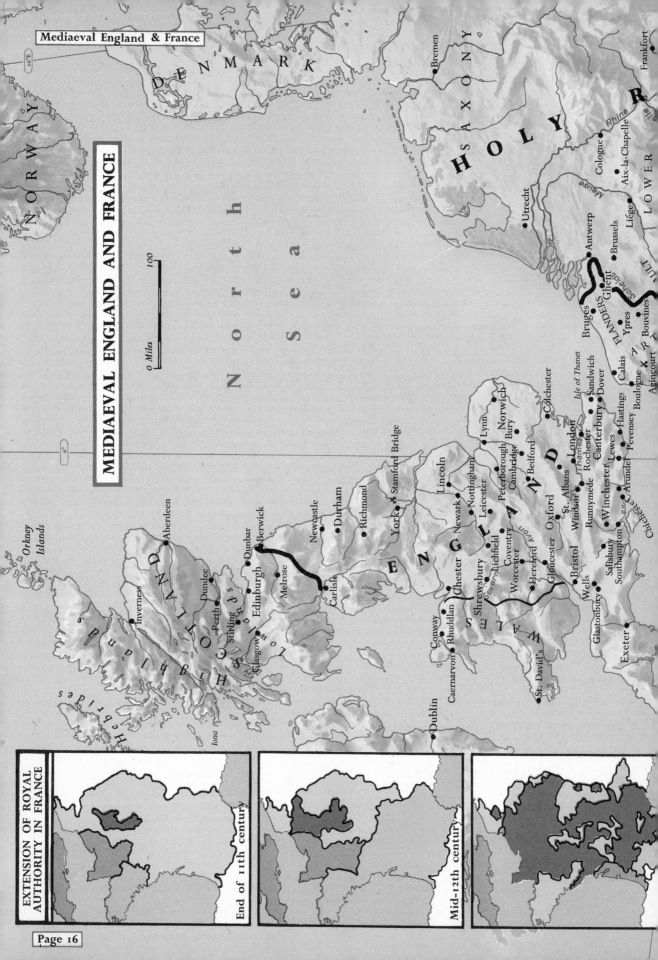

MEDIAEVAL ENGLAND AND FRANCE

NORWAY

DENMARK

SAXONY

HOLY R

LOWER

North Sea

Orkney Islands

Hebrides

Iona

SCOTLAND

HIGHLANDS

Inverness

Aberdeen

Dundee

Perth

Stirling

Glasgow

Edinburgh

Melrose

Dunbar

Berwick

Carlisle

Newcastle

Durham

Richmond

York

Stamford Bridge

Lincoln

Newark

Nottingham

Leicester

Lichfield

Coventry

Chester

Shrewsbury

Rhuddlan

Conway

Caernarvon

WALES

St. David's

Hereford

Worcester

Gloucester

Severn

Avon

Bristol

Wells

Glastonbury

Safisbury

Southampton

Exeter

Oxford

Bedford

Cambridge

Peterborough

Bury

Norwich

Lynn

St. Albans

Windsor

London

Thames

Runnymede

Winchester

Rochester

Canterbury

Lewes

Arundel

Chichester

Hastings

Pevensey

Dover

Sandwich

Isle of Thanet

Colchester

Calais

Boulogne

Agincourt

Bouvines

Ypres

Bruges

Ghent

Antwerp

Brussels

FLANDERS

ARTOIS

Sénéchal

Liège

Aix-la-Chapelle

Cologne

Rhine

Utrecht

Bremen

Frankfort

Meuse

Lowlands

ENGLAND

Dublin

EXTENSION OF ROYAL AUTHORITY IN FRANCE

End of 11th century

Mid-12th century

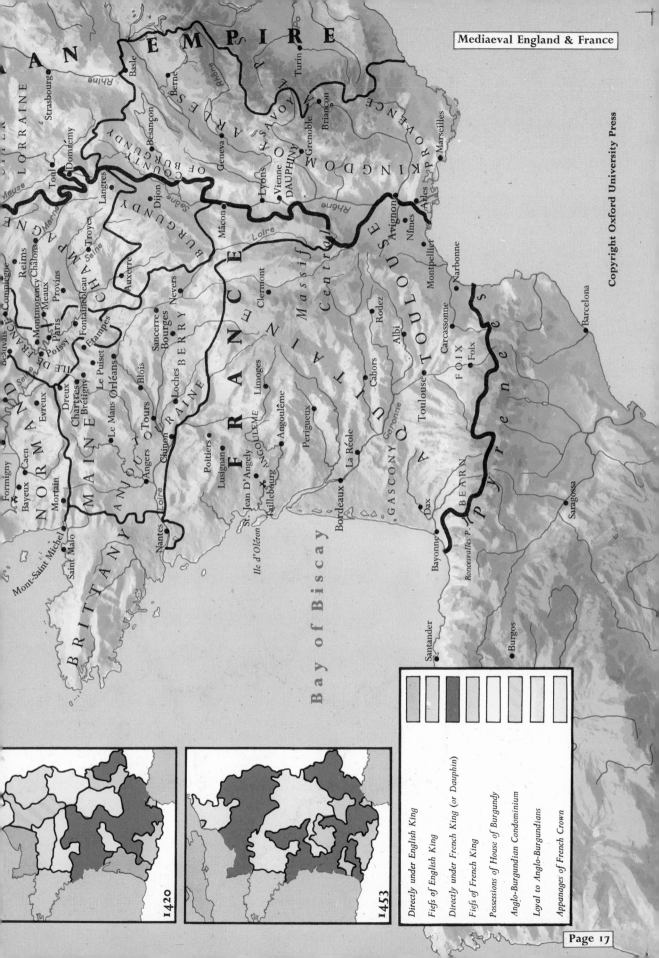

G E R M A N   E M P I R E

Po
Turin
Basle
Berne
Strasbourg
Rhine
Rhône
LORRAINE
I T A L Y
Domrémy
Toul
Besançon
COUNTY OF BURGUNDY
Geneva
SAVOY
Briançon
Grenoble
Marseilles
PROVENCE
Meuse
Marne
CHAMPAGNE
Langres
Dijon
Saône
BURGUNDY
Lyons
Vienne
DAUPHINY
Rhône
KINGDOM
Arles
Avignon
Nîmes
Reims
Châlons
Troyes
Seine
Auxerre
Mâcon
Loire
Narbonne
Barcelona
Montmorency
Meaux
Provins
Beauvais
Compiègne
FRANCE
ÎLE DE FRANCE
Poissy
Paris
Seine
Fontainebleau
Étampes
Sancerre
Bourges
Nevers
BERRY
Clermont
Massif Central
Rodez
Albi
Cahors
TOULOUSE
Montpellier
Carcassonne
FOIX
Foix
Pyrenees
Saragossa
Seine
Dreux
Évreux
Chartres
Brétigny
Le Puiset
Orléans
Blois
Loches
TOURAINE
Limoges
Angoulême
ANGOULÊME
Périgueux
GUIENNE
Garonne
Toulouse
BÉARN
Formigny
Caen
Bayeux
NORMANDY
Mortain
MAINE
Le Mans
ANJOU
Angers
Tours
Chinon
Loire
Poitiers
Lusignan
St. Jean D'Angely
Taillebourg
La Réole
Bordeaux
Dax
Bayonne
Roncesvalles P.
Saint Malo
Mont-Saint-Michel
BRITTANY
Nantes
Île d'Oléron

B a y   o f   B i s c a y

Santander
Burgos

1420

1453

Directly under English King

Fiefs of English King

Directly under French King (or Dauphin)

Fiefs of French King

Possessions of House of Burgundy

Anglo-Burgundian Condominium

Loyal to Anglo-Burgundians

Appanages of French Crown

POMERANIA

PRUSSIA

POLAND

HUNGARY

Cracow

BOHEMIA

MORAVIA

AUSTRIA

Vienna

CARINTHIA

Bornholm

BRANDE'N-BURG

Stettin

Frankfort on Oder

Dresden

Prague

Salzburg

DENMARK

Copenhagen

Magdeburg

Naumburg

Nuremberg

Regensburg

Freising

BAVARIA

Innsbruck

Hamburg

Lübeck

Erfurt

THURINGIA

Bamberg

FRANCONIA

Württemberg

Augsburg

SWABIA

Bremen

Goslar

SAXONY

Frankfort on Main

Mainz

Worms

Speyer

Strasbourg

Lechfeld

Constance

FRIESLAND

Cologne

Aachen

Liége

Trier

Verdun

Toul

UPPER LORRAINE

BURGUNDY

Besançon

Antwerp

Louvain

LOWER LORRAINE

Bruges

Tournai

Bouvines

Douai

Cambrai

FLANDERS

Amiens

CHAMPAGNE

Reims

Troyes

Clairvaux

DUCHY OF BURGUNDY

Cîteaux

Cluny

Vézelay

Paris

Orléans

20°E

10°E

5°E

55°N

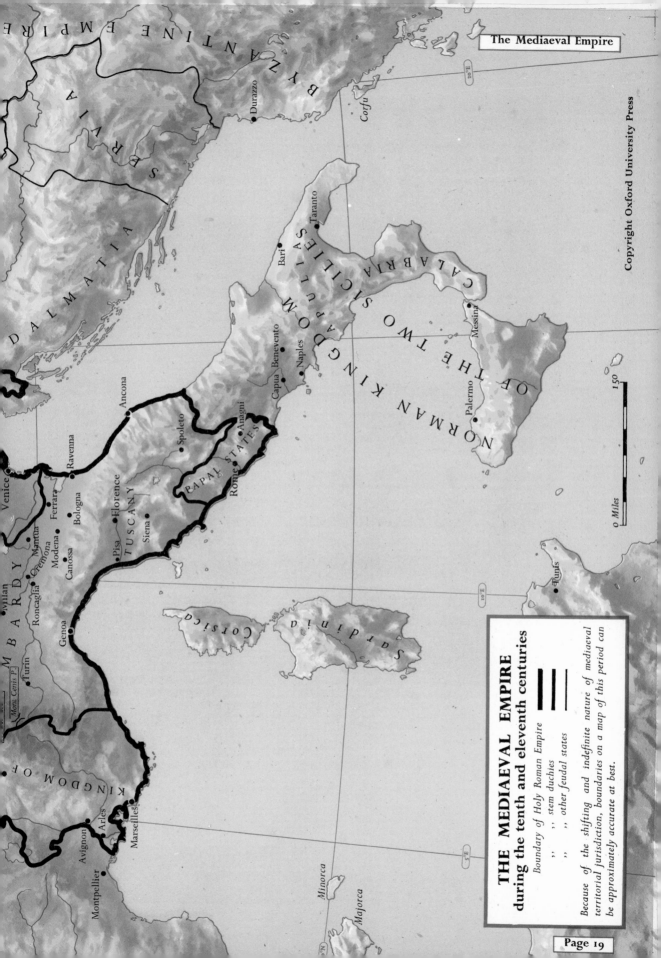

The Mediaeval Empire

Copyright Oxford University Press

BYZANTINE EMPIRE

SERVIA

DALMATIA

Durazzo

Corfu

Taranto

Bari

APULIA

CALABRIA

NORMAN KINGDOM OF THE TWO SICILIES

Messina

Palermo

Benevento

Capua

Naples

Anagni

PAPAL STATES

Rome

Spoleto

Ancona

Ravenna

Venice

Ferrara

Bologna

Modena

Canossa

Cremona

Mantua

Roncaglia

Milan

Turin

Mont Cenis P.

LOMBARDY

Genoa

Florence

Pisa

Siena

TUSCANY

Tunis

CORSICA

Sardinia

Minorca

Majorca

KINGDOM OF

Marseilles

Arles

Avignon

Montpellier

150

0 Miles

THE MEDIAEVAL EMPIRE
during the tenth and eleventh centuries

Boundary of Holy Roman Empire
   ,,   ,,   stem duchies
   ,,   ,,   other feudal states

Because of the shifting and indefinite nature of mediaeval
territorial jurisdiction, boundaries on a map of this period can
be approximately accurate at best.

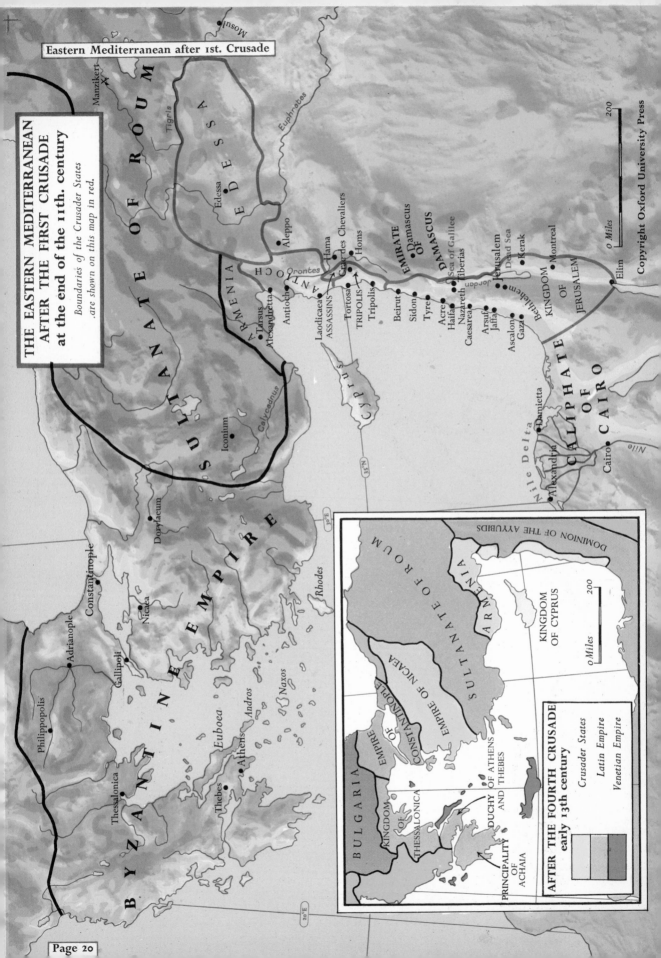

Eastern Mediterranean after 1st. Crusade

THE EASTERN MEDITERRANEAN AFTER THE FIRST CRUSADE at the end of the 11th. century

Boundaries of the Crusader States are shown on this map in red.

SULTANATE OF ROUM

Manzikert ✕

Mosul

Tigris

Euphrates

EDESSA

Edessa

ARMENIA

Aleppo

Tarsus

Alexandretta

Antioch

Laodicaea

ASSASSINS

Orontes

ANTIOCH

Hama

Crac des Chevaliers

Homs

TRIPOLIS

Tortosa

Tripolis

Beirut

Sidon

Tyre

Acre

Haifa

Nazareth

Caesarea

Arsuf

Jaffa

Ascalon

Gaza

EMIRATE OF DAMASCUS

Damascus

Sea of Galilee

Tiberias

Jordan

Bethlehem

Jerusalem

Dead Sea

Kerak

Montreal

KINGDOM OF JERUSALEM

Elim

Colycednus

Iconium

BYZANTINE EMPIRE

Dorylaeum

Constantinople

Nicaea

Adrianople

Gallipoli

Philippopolis

Thessalonica

Euboea

Thebes

Athens

Andros

Naxos

Rhodes

CYPRUS

Nile Delta

Alexandria

Damietta

CALIPHATE OF CAIRO

Cairo

Nile

35°N

30°E

20°E

0 Miles   200

Page 20

AFTER THE FOURTH CRUSADE early 13th century

KINGDOM OF CYPRUS

0 Miles   200

SULTANATE OF ROUM

ARMENIA

EMPIRE OF NICAEA

LATIN EMPIRE OF CONSTANTINOPLE

KINGDOM OF THESSALONICA

BULGARIA

DUCHY OF ATHENS AND THEBES

PRINCIPALITY OF ACHAIA

DOMINION OF THE AYYUBIDS

Crusader States

Latin Empire

Venetian Empire

D Copyright Oxford University Press

ENGLAND AND THE BALTIC
in the later Middle Ages

This is the area of Baltic trade dominated by the Hanseatic League. The Baltic coast from Pomerelia to Estonia and bounded by Poland-Lithuania and Russia represents the area conquered by the Teutonic Knights. Pomerelia and Samogitia were reconquered by the Poles in the fifteenth century.

RUSSIA

Novgorod

FINLAND

Reval
L. Peipus
Dorpat
ESTONIA

LIVONIA

West Dvina

LITHUANIA

Riga
COURLAND
SAMOGITIA
Niemen

PRUSSIA

Königsberg
Memel
Marienberg
Tannenberg

POLAND

Elbing
Danzig
Marienwerder
Kulm
Thorn
Vistula
Marienburg
POMERELIA

Oder

Baltic Sea

Stockholm

Upsala
Dal

Gotland
Wisby

Kalmar

SWEDEN

NORWAY

Glomma
Göta

Oslo

Kolbatz
Monastery

Stettin
Stralsund
Rostock
Wismar
Schwerin
BRANDENBURG

Leipzig

Lund
SCANIA
Malmö

Copenhagen
DENMARK

Kiel
HOLSTEIN
Lübeck
Hamburg
Lüneburg
Elbe
Bremen
Weser

Brunswick

Kattegat

JUTLAND

Skagerrak

Trondheim

Bergen

Stavanger

Faeroe Is.

200

0 Miles

Shetland Is.

Orkney Is.

Aberdeen

SCOTLAND

Berwick
Newcastle

Isle of Man

Hebrides

North Sea

Hull
Lynn
Yarmouth
Boston
ENGLAND
London
Bristol
Southampton
Dover
Bruges
Antwerp
Dordrecht
FLANDERS
Strait of Dover
Zuider Zee

10°E

60°N

10°E

20°E

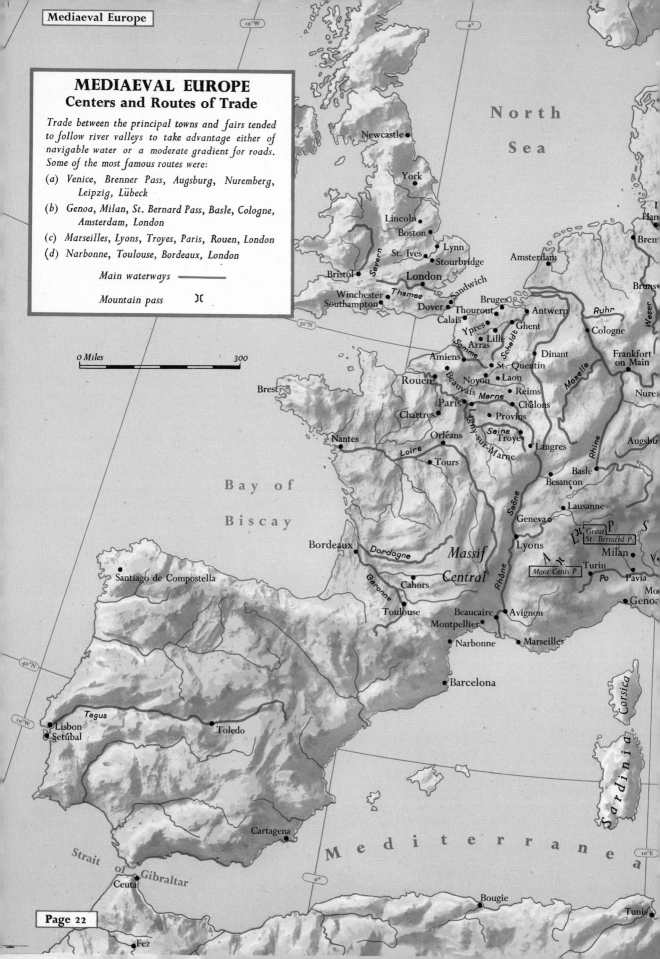

MEDIAEVAL EUROPE
Centers and Routes of Trade

Trade between the principal towns and fairs tended to follow river valleys to take advantage either of navigable water or a moderate gradient for roads. Some of the most famous routes were:

(a) *Venice, Brenner Pass, Augsburg, Nuremberg, Leipzig, Lübeck*

(b) *Genoa, Milan, St. Bernard Pass, Basle, Cologne, Amsterdam, London*

(c) *Marseilles, Lyons, Troyes, Paris, Rouen, London*

(d) *Narbonne, Toulouse, Bordeaux, London*

Main waterways ——————

Mountain pass)(

North Sea

Bay of Biscay

Mediterranean Sea

Newcastle

York

Lincoln
Boston
St. Ives · Lynn
· Stourbridge
Bristol
Winchester
Southampton
London
Thames
Severn
Dover
Sandwich
Calais
Thourout
Bruges
Antwerp
Ypres
Ghent
Lille
Arras
Scheldt
Ruhr
Cologne
Somme
Dinant
Amiens
St. Quentin
Moselle
Frankfort on Main
Rouen
Beauvais
Noyon
Laon
Reims
Paris
Marne
Châlons
Chartres
Lagny-sur-Marne
Provins
Seine
Troyes
Langres
Rhine
Augsbu
Orléans
Loire
Nantes
Tours
Basle
Besançon
Lausanne
Geneva
Saône
Bordeaux
Dordogne
Garonne
Massif Central
Lyons
Geneva
Great St. Bernard P.
Mont Cenis P.
Milan
Rhône
Turin
Po
Pavia
Genoa
Cahors
Toulouse
Beaucaire
Avignon
Montpellier
Narbonne
Marseilles
Santiago de Compostella
Barcelona
Tagus
Lisbon
Setúbal
Toledo
Cartagena
Corsica
Sardinia
Strait of Gibraltar
Ceuta
Bougie
Tunis
Fez
Amsterdam
Bruns
Brest

Wisby

Riga

West Dvina

Libau

Memel

Niemen

Königsberg

Danzig

Baltic Sea

Stettin

Vistula

Bug

Warsaw

Kiev

Spree

Frankfort on Oder

Magdeburg

Dnieper

Oder

Leipzig

Breslau

Cracow

Lemberg

Prague

Dniester

Moldau

Morava

Prut

Munich

Danube

Vienna

Tisza

Buda ● Pest

Kaffa

Brenner P.

Drava

Aquileia

Sava

Belgrade

Venice

Pola

Black Sea

Ferrara

Ravenna

Bologna

Danube

Florence

Ancona

Adriatic Sea

Tiber

Ragusa

Adrianople

Constantinople

Rome

Amalfi

Corfu

Palermo

Messina

Sicily

20°E

Rhodes

30°E

Syracuse

Copyright Oxford University Press

Sea

Crete

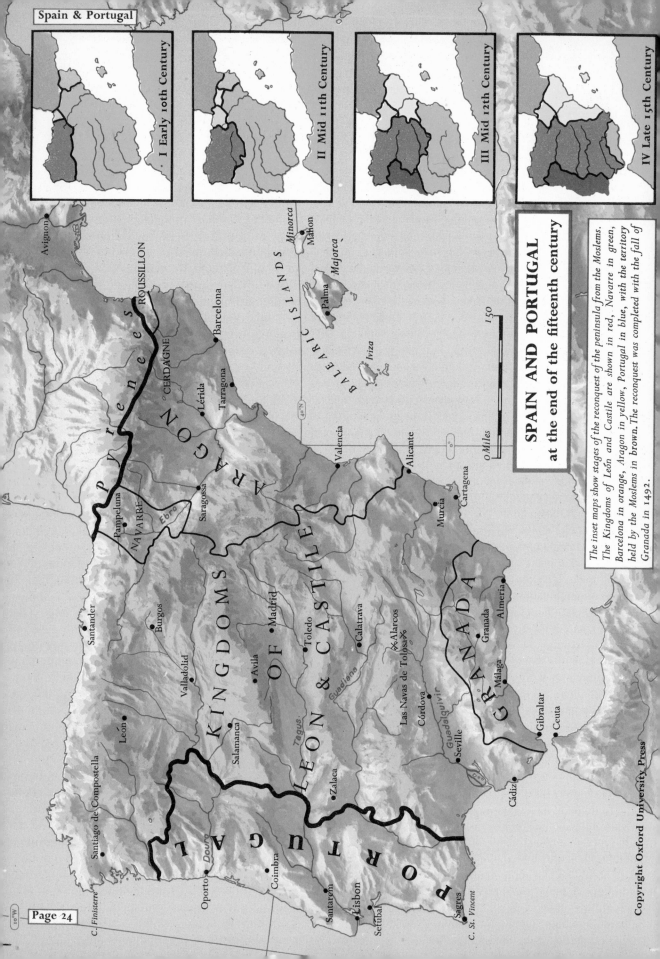

Spain & Portugal

I Early 10th Century

II Mid 11th Century

III Mid 12th Century

IV Late 15th Century

SPAIN AND PORTUGAL
at the end of the fifteenth century

The inset maps show stages of the reconquest of the peninsula from the Moslems. The Kingdoms of León and Castile are shown in red, Navarre in green, Barcelona in orange, Aragon in yellow, Portugal in blue, with the territory held by the Moslems in brown. The reconquest was completed with the fall of Granada in 1492.

Avignon

ROUSSILLON

Pyrenees

CERDAGNE

Barcelona

Lérida

Tarragona

ARAGON

Pampeluna

NAVARRE

Ebro

Saragossa

Santander

Burgos

Valladolid

León

Salamanca

Avila

Madrid

Toledo

Calatrava

KINGDOMS OF LEÓN & CASTILE

Tagus

Guadiana

Alarcos

Las Navas de Tolosa

Valencia

Alicante

Murcia

Cartagena

Santiago de Compostella

C. Finisterre

Oporto

Douro

Coimbra

Santarém

Lisbon

Setúbal

Sagres

C. St. Vincent

PORTUGAL

Zalaca

Córdova

Guadalquivir

Seville

GRANADA

Granada

Málaga

Almería

Gibraltar

Ceuta

Cádiz

BALEARIC ISLANDS

Minorca

Mahon

Majorca

Palma

Iviza

40°N

0 Miles 150

10°W

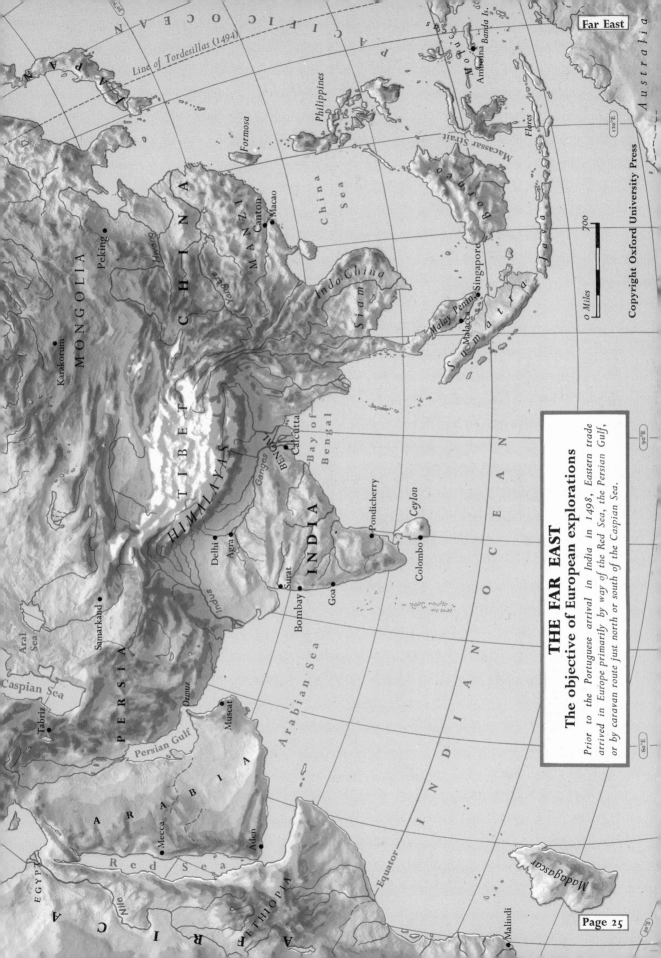

THE FAR EAST
The objective of European explorations

Prior to the Portuguese arrival in India in 1498, Eastern trade arrived in Europe primarily by way of the Red Sea, the Persian Gulf, or by caravan route just north or south of the Caspian Sea.

Copyright Oxford University Press

Line of Tordesillas (1494)

PACIFIC OCEAN

JAPAN

Australia

MONGOLIA

Karakorum

Peking

Hwang

Yangtze

CHINA

MANZI

Canton

Macao

Formosa

Philippines

China Sea

Macassar Strait

Moluccas

Amboina Banda Is.

Flores

TIBET

HIMALAYAS

Indo-China

Siam

Borneo

Java

Sumatra

Malay Penin.

Malacca

Singapore

Aral Sea

Samarkand

PERSIA

Tabriz

Caspian Sea

Ormuz

Muscat

Indus

Delhi

Agra

Surat

Bombay

Goa

INDIA

Ganges

BENGAL

Calcutta

Bay of Bengal

Pondicherry

Ceylon

Colombo

INDIAN OCEAN

Arabian Sea

ARABIA

Mecca

Aden

Red Sea

Nile

EGYPT

ETHIOPIA

AFRICA

Persian Gulf

Madagascar

Malindi

Equator

700

0 Miles

110°E

90°E

60°E

30°S

(20°N)

NORTH

AMERICA

Hudson Bay

Baffin Bay

St. Lawrence

LABRADOR

GREENL

Davis Strait

Cape Farewell

Boston

(1519)
Mexico City
Acapulco

Gulf of
Mexico

Vera Cruz

NOVA
SCOTIA

NEWFOUNDLAND

St. Augustine

GUATEMALA

YUCATAN

Bermuda

Havana

NORTH   ATLANTIC

Cuba
(1492)

San Salvador
(1492)

HONDURAS

EL SALVADOR

NICARAGUA

Jamaica
(1493)

Hispaniola
(1492)

OCEAN

Azores
(1431)

COSTA
RICA

Caribbean Sea

Puerto Rico
(1493)

South Sea

Panama
(1519)

Porto Bello

Cartagena

Darien
(1509)

SPANISH

NEW
GRANADA

MAIN

Bogotá

VENEZUELA

Trinidad
(1498)

Line of Tordesillas (1494)

Tropic of Cancer

Madeira Is.
(1418)

Canary Is.

Cape Bojador
(1434)

RIO
DE
OURO

Quito

BRITISH
GUIANA

DUTCH
GUIANA

FRENCH
GUIANA

Cape Blanco

Lima

Peruvian Andes

Amazon

Cape Verde Is.

Cape Verde
(1446)

Senegal

Gambia

PORTUGUESE
GUINEA

(20°S)

SOUTH

AMERICA

Equator

Valparaíso
Santiago

Asunción
(1537)

Pernambuco

SOUTH   ATLANTI

Rio de Janeiro
(1555)

Santa Catalina

Buenos Aires
(1580)

Rio de la Plata
(1501)

PATAGONIA

Tropic of Capricorn

Strait of Magellan
(1520)

Tierra del
Fuego

Falkland
Is.

(60°S)
Cape Horn
(1616)

(20°W)

A S I A

Arctic Circle
CELAND

Aral
Sea

• Calcutta

INDIA

• Delhi

• Sarai

Caspian Sea

Volga

Black Sea

• Surat
Bombay •
Goa

• Madras

istol •

St. Malo •

Venice •
Genoa •

• Rome

• Constantinople

• Baghdad

Persian Gulf

Ormuz (1515)

Calicut •

to

• Madrid
sbon •
Palos •

Ceuta •

Mediterranean Sea

• Jerusalem

Alexandria •
• Suez
Cairo •

• Mecca

Assuan •

Red Sea

• Aden
(1514)

INDIAN OCEAN

ETHIOPIA

• Timbuktu

AFRICA

Niger

DAHOMEY

Elmina •

Congo

• Malindi (1498)

Zanzibar

Madagascar

Fernando Po
(1472)

São Tomé •
Annobon

Cabinda •
(1482)

• Mozambique
(1498)

60° E

ANGOLA

(1500)

THE GREAT EXPLORATIONS

Delagoa
Bay

The great period of European discovery began when the Portuguese, after gradually exploring the west coast of Africa, rounded the Cape and established the first all-water trade route to the Far East in 1498. As the probability of the Portuguese success became apparent, rivals sought alternative routes. When the Castilians, under Columbus, reached what they took to be the Indies in 1492, the Portuguese king appealed to the Pope. This resulted in the Treaty of Tordesillas which partitioned new lands between the crowns of Castile and Portugal by a line running approximately along 46° longitude west.

OCEAN

Cape of Good Hope
(1488)

Cape Agulhas

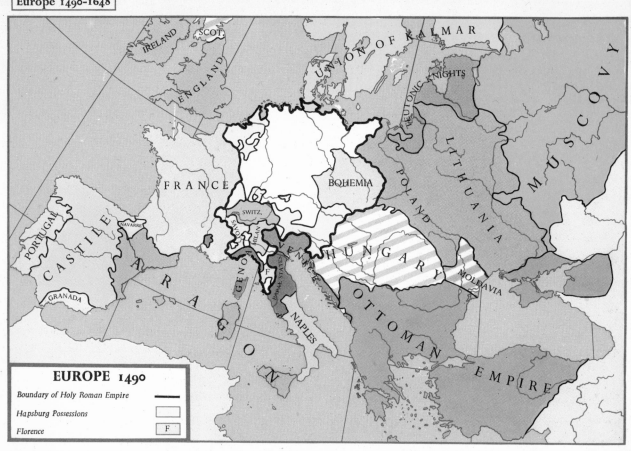

EUROPE 1490

Boundary of Holy Roman Empire ———

Hapsburg Possessions ☐

Florence [F]

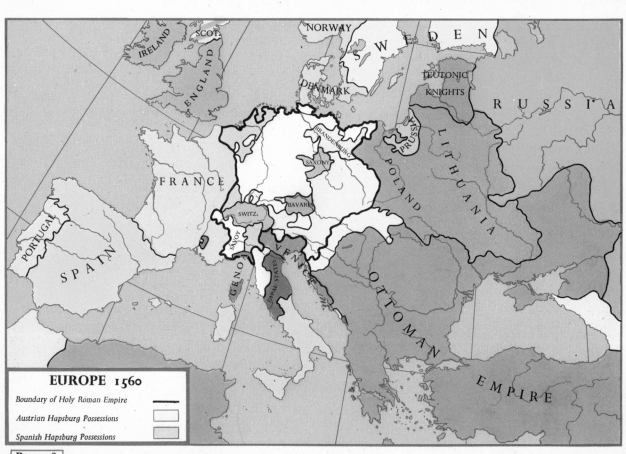

EUROPE 1560

Boundary of Holy Roman Empire ———

Austrian Hapsburg Possessions ☐

Spanish Hapsburg Possessions ☐

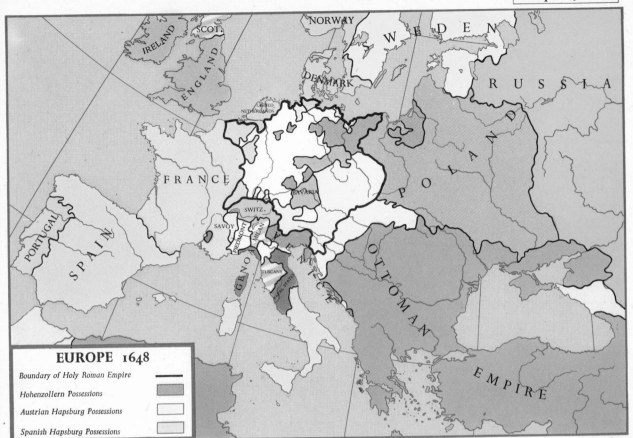

EUROPE 1648

Boundary of Holy Roman Empire

Hohenzollern Possessions

Austrian Hapsburg Possessions

Spanish Hapsburg Possessions

NORWAY

IRELAND   SCOT.

ENGLAND

DENMARK

SWEDEN

RUSSIA

POLAND

FRANCE

BAVARIA

SWITZ.

SAVOY

PIEDMONT   MILAN

GENOA   VENICE

TUSCANY

PAPAL STATE

PORTUGAL

SPAIN

OTTOMAN   EMPIRE

UNITED NETHERLANDS

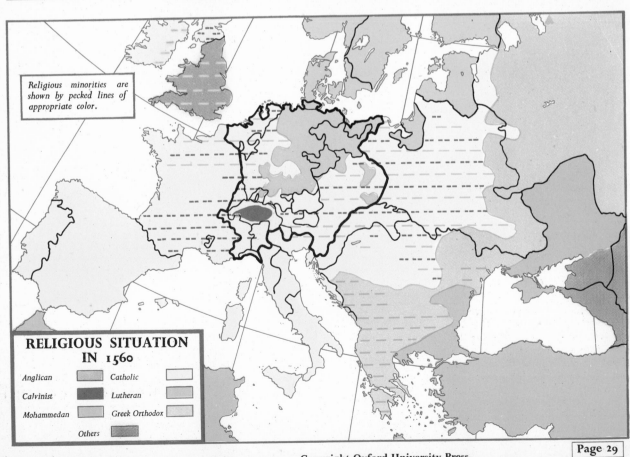

Religious minorities are shown by pecked lines of appropriate color.

RELIGIOUS SITUATION
IN 1560

Anglican

Calvinist

Mohammedan

Others

Catholic

Lutheran

Greek Orthodox

Copyright Oxford University Press

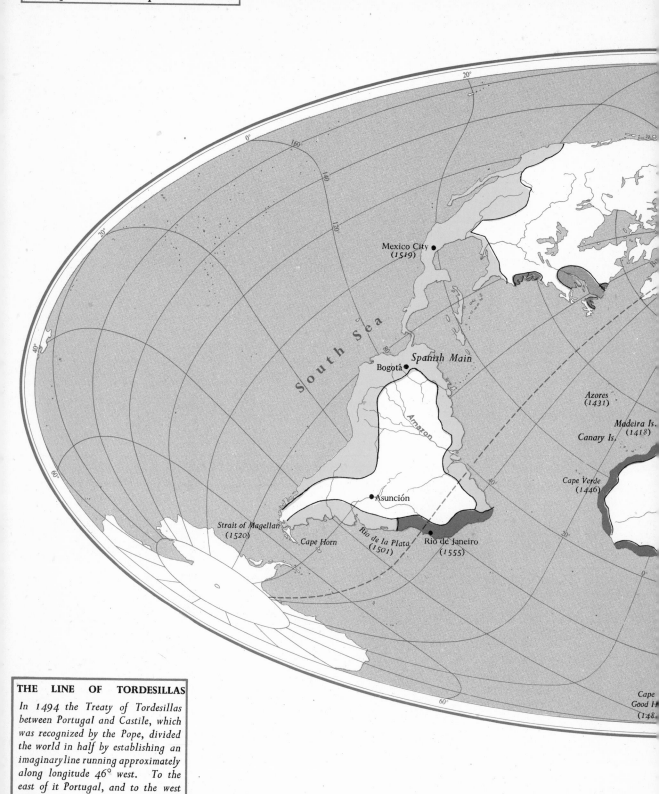

Mexico City
(1519)

South Sea

Spanish Main

Bogotá

Amazon

Azores
(1431)

Madeira Is.
(1418)

Canary Is.

Cape Verde
(1446)

Asunción

Strait of Magellan
(1520)

Cape Horn

Rio de la Plata
(1501)

Rio de Janeiro
(1555)

Cape
Good H
(148.

THE LINE OF TORDESILLAS

In 1494 the Treaty of Tordesillas between Portugal and Castile, which was recognized by the Pope, divided the world in half by establishing an imaginary line running approximately along longitude 46° west. To the east of it Portugal, and to the west Castile, were to have exclusive rights of discovery and conquest. The agreement was broadly, but not exactly, observed.

PRINCIPAL COLONIA

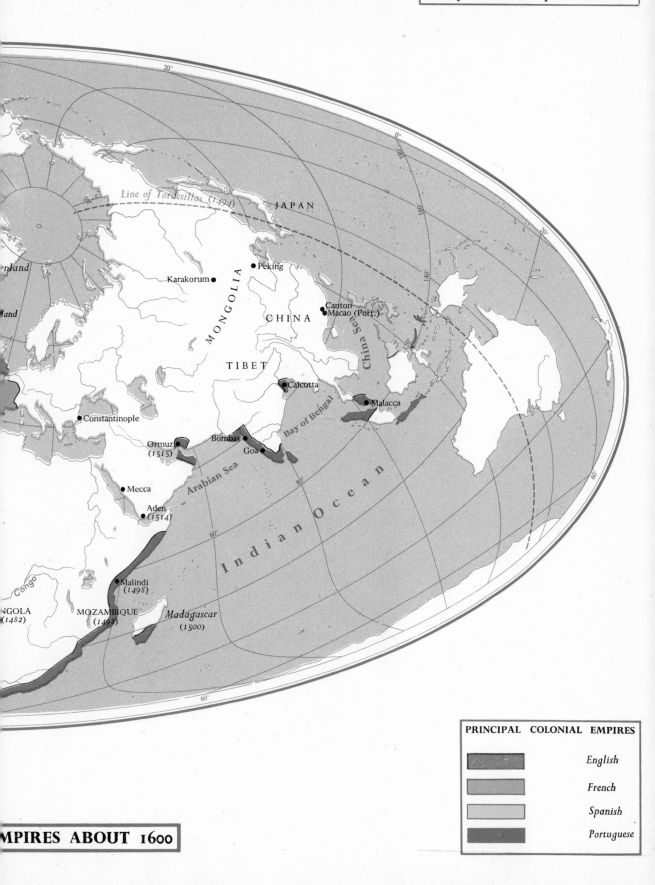

Line of Tordesillas (1494)

JAPAN

nland

land

Karakorum ●

● Peking

MONGOLIA

CHINA

Canton ●
Macao (Port.)

TIBET

China Sea

● Calcutta

● Constantinople

Ormuz ●
(1515)

Bombay ●

Goa ●

Bay of Bengal

Malacca ●

Arabian Sea

● Mecca

Aden ●
(1514)

Indian Ocean

Congo

Malindi ●
(1498)

NGOLA
(1482)

MOZAMBIQUE
(1498)

Madagascar
(1500)

PRINCIPAL COLONIAL EMPIRES

English

French

Spanish

Portuguese

MPIRES ABOUT 1600

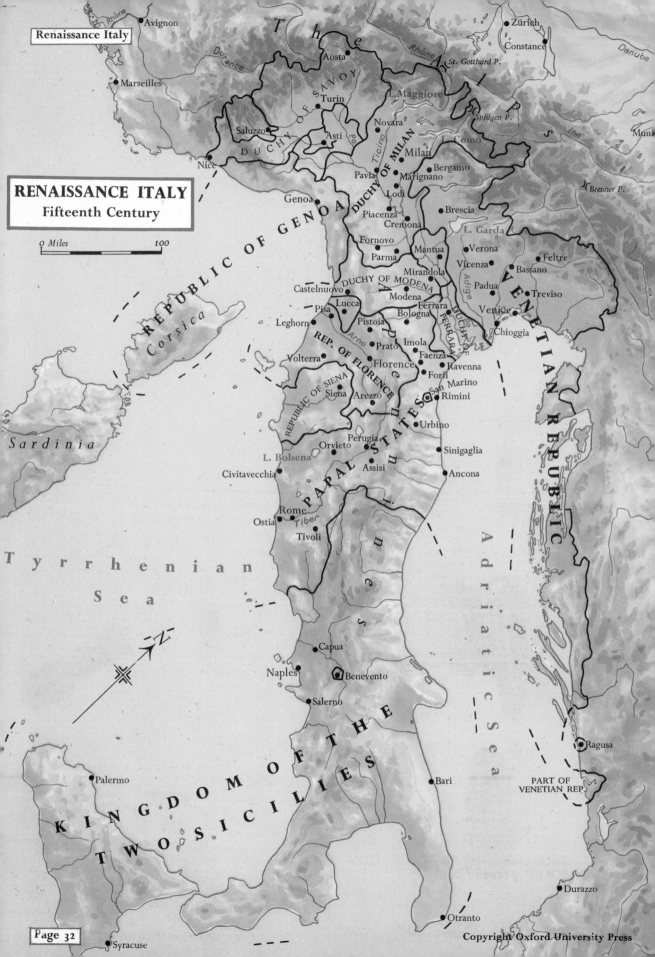

RENAISSANCE ITALY
Fifteenth Century

0 Miles   100

The Alps

Rhône
Durance

Avignon

Marseilles

Nice

Zürich
Constance
Danube

Aosta

DUCHY OF SAVOY

Turin

St. Gotthard P.

L. Maggiore

Splügen P.

Inn

Muni

Brenner P.

Saluzzo

Asti

Novara

Po

Ticino

DUCHY OF MILAN

Milan

L. Como

Pavia

Marignano

Bergamo

Brescia

Lodi

Genoa

Piacenza

Cremona

Mantua

L. Garda

Verona

Vicenza

Feltre

Bassano

REPUBLIC OF GENOA

Fornovo

Parma

Mirandola

DUCHY OF MODENA

Padua

VENETIAN

Treviso

Corsica

Castelnuovo

Modena

Adige

Venice

Pisa

Lucca

Pistoia

Bologna

DUCHY OF FERRARA

Ferrara

Chioggia

Leghorn

Arno

Prato

Imola

Ravenna

REP. OF FLORENCE

Florence

Faenza

Forli

Apennines

Volterra

San Marino

VENETIAN REPUBLIC

REPUBLIC OF SIENA

Siena

Arezzo

Rimini

Urbino

Sardinia

Perugia

Orvieto

Assisi

PAPAL STATES

Sinigaglia

Ancona

L. Bolsena

Civitavecchia

Rome

Tiber

Ostia

Tivoli

Tyrrhenian Sea

Adriatic Sea

Capua

Naples

Benevento

Ragusa

Salerno

KINGDOM OF THE

Palermo

Bari

PART OF
VENETIAN REP.

TWO SICILIES

Durazzo

Otranto

Syracuse

County Abbreviations

Beds	Bedfordshire
Berks	Berkshire
Breck.	Brecknockshire
Bucks	Buckinghamshire
Caer.	Caernarvonshire
Camb.	Cambridgeshire
Cardigan.	Cardiganshire
Carm.	Carmarthenshire
Denbigh.	Denbighshire
Flint.	Flintshire
Glam.	Glamorgan
Gloucester.	Gloucestershire
Here.	Herefordshire
Herts	Hertfordshire
Hunts	Huntingdonshire
Leics	Leicestershire
Mer.	Merionethshire
Mid.	Middlesex
Mon.	Monmouth
Montg.	Montgomeryshire
Northants	Northamptonshire
Notts	Nottinghamshire
Oxon	Oxfordshire
Pem.	Pembrokeshire
Rad.	Radnorshire
Ru.	Rutland
Stafford.	Staffordshire
Warwick.	Warwickshire
W'land	Westmorland
Worcs	Worcestershire

Orkney Islands

Hebrides

Highlands

Inverness

Aberdeen

Dalnaspidal

Lowlands

Dundee
Perth   St. Andrews
Stirling
Glasgow   Dunbar
Edinburgh   Berwick
Ayr   Philiphaugh

NORTHUMBERLAND
Newburn
Newcastle

55°N

Carlisle   Durham
CUMBERLAND   DURHAM
W'LAND
Pennines

Londonderry

ULSTER

Lancaster

YORKSHIRE
Marston Moor   York
Leeds   Selby
Preston   Bradford   Hull

CONNAUGHT

Drogheda

Gainsborough
Lincoln

Dublin

LEINSTER

ANGLESEY
FLINT   CHESHIRE   DERBY-SHIRE
DENBIGH
CAER.
MER.   Shrewsbury   Derby
Nottingham
NOTTS
LINCOLNSHIRE
Norwich

Limerick

MONTG.   SHROP-SHIRE   STAFFORD.   Leicester
CARDIGAN.   RAD.   WORCS   LEICS.   Naseby   NORFOLK
MUNSTER   PEM.   BRECK.   Worcester   WARWICK   NORTHANTS   RU.   HUNTS   CAMB   Cambridge
CARM.   HERE.   SUFFOLK
GLAM.   MON.   GLOUCESTER   Edgehill   BEDS   Ipswich
Pembroke   Gloucester   OXON   Oxford   BUCKS   HERTS   ESSEX   Colchester
BERKS   MID.   London
Bristol   Bath   Brentford   Canterbury
Bridgwater   Wells   Reading   SURREY   KENT
Newbury   Dover
Taunton   SOMERSET   WILTSHIRE   Winchester   SUSSEX
Salisbury   Southampton
DEVONSHIRE   DORSET   HAMPSHIRE   Portsmouth
Exeter   Carisbrooke

CORNWALL   Plymouth
Lostwithiel

0 Miles   100

BRITAIN AT THE TIME OF THE CIVIL WAR
1642—44

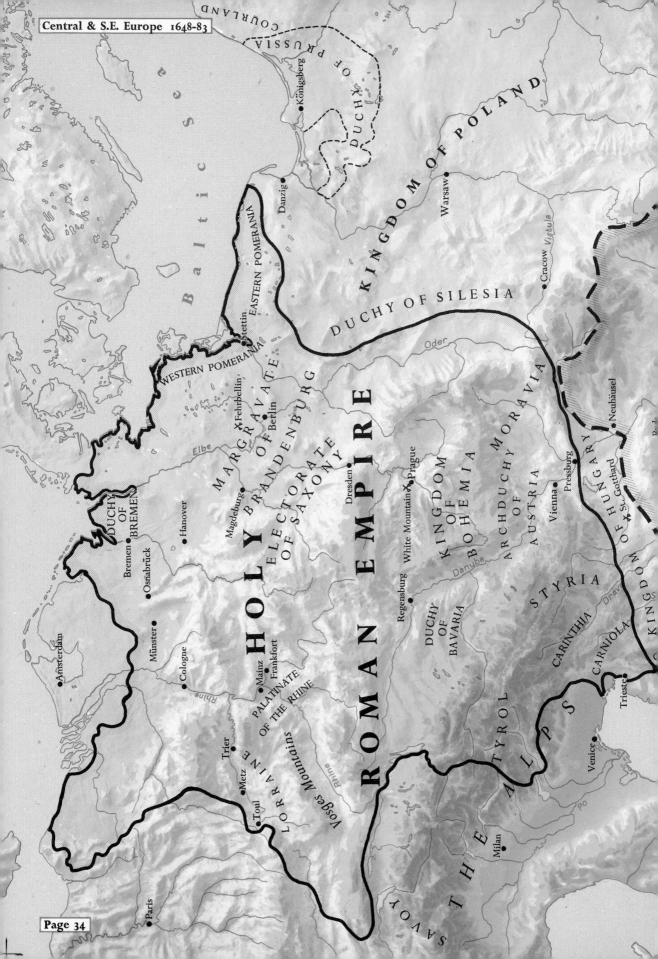

COURLAND

DUCHY OF PRUSSIA

Königsberg

Baltic Sea

Danzig

KINGDOM OF POLAND

Warsaw

EASTERN POMERANIA

DUCHY OF SILESIA

Cracow *Vistula*

Stettin

WESTERN POMERANIA

Oder

Fehrbellin

Berlin

MARGRAVATE OF BRANDENBURG

Neuhäusel

KINGDOM OF HUNGARY

Elbe

Magdeburg

ELECTORATE OF SAXONY

Dresden

ARCHDUCHY OF MORAVIA

Pressburg

St. Gotthard

DUCHY OF BREMEN

Bremen

Hanover

Osnabrück

Münster

Cologne

H O L Y

White Mountain

Prague

KINGDOM OF BOHEMIA

Vienna

AUSTRIA

STYRIA

CARINTHIA

CARNIOLA

R O M A N   E M P I R E

Amsterdam

Mainz

Frankfort

PALATINATE OF THE RHINE

Rhine

Regensburg

Danube

DUCHY OF BAVARIA

Drave

Trieste

Trier

LORRAINE

Metz

Vosges Mountains

Toul

TYROL

T H E   A L P S

Venice

Po

Milan

SAVOY

Paris

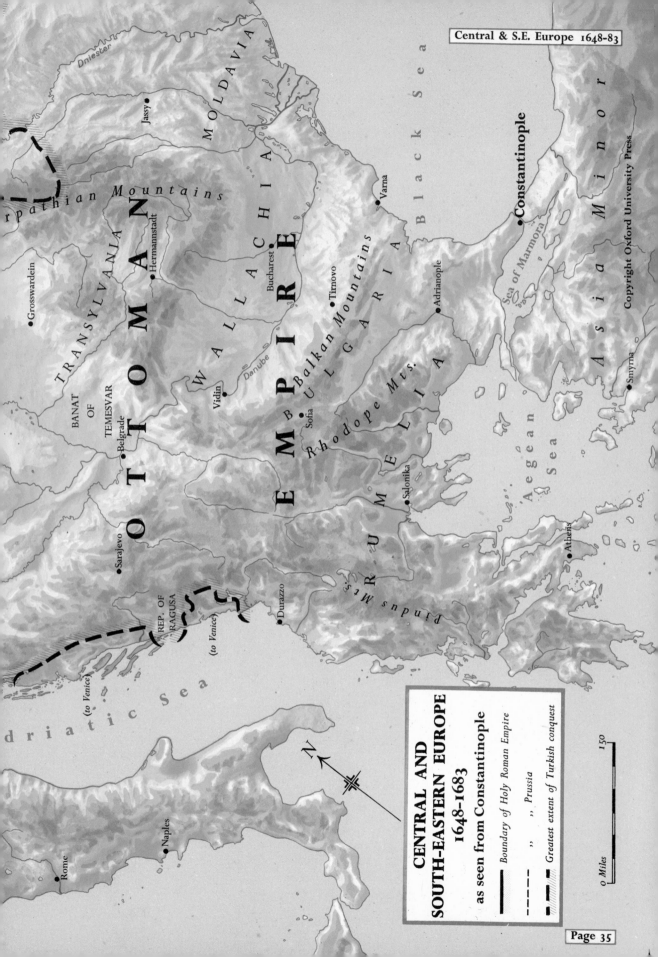

Dniester

MOLDAVIA

Jassy

rpathian Mountains

Carpathian Mountains

Grosswardein

TRANSYLVANIA

Hermannstadt

WALLACHIA

Bucharest

Varna

Black Sea

Constantinople

Asia Minor

Copyright Oxford University Press

BANAT
OF
TEMESVAR

Belgrade

O T T O M A N

Vidin

Danube

E M P I R E

Balkan Mountains

Tirnovo

B U L G A R I A

B

Sofia

Rhodope Mts.

Adrianople

Sea of Marmora

Smyrna

Sarajevo

R U M E L I A

Salonika

Aegean Sea

Athens

REP. OF
RAGUSA

(to Venice)

Durazzo

Pindus Mts.

(to Venice)

driatic Sea

Adriatic Sea

N

Naples

Rome

CENTRAL AND SOUTH-EASTERN EUROPE 1648-1683 as seen from Constantinople

———————— *Boundary of Holy Roman Empire*

– – – – – – ,, ,, *Prussia*

▬ ▬ ▬ *Greatest extent of Turkish conquest*

0 Miles   150

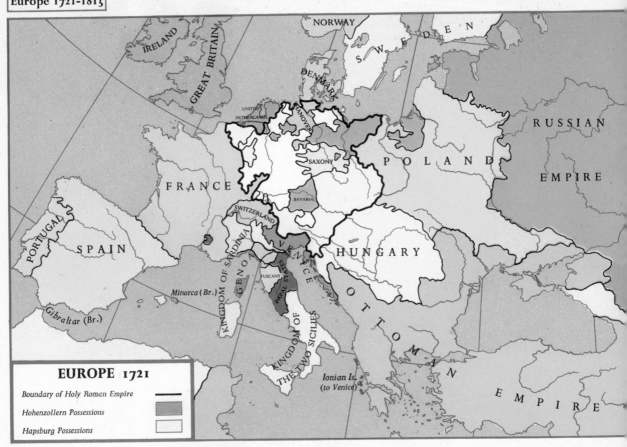

EUROPE 1721

Boundary of Holy Roman Empire

Hohenzollern Possessions

Hapsburg Possessions

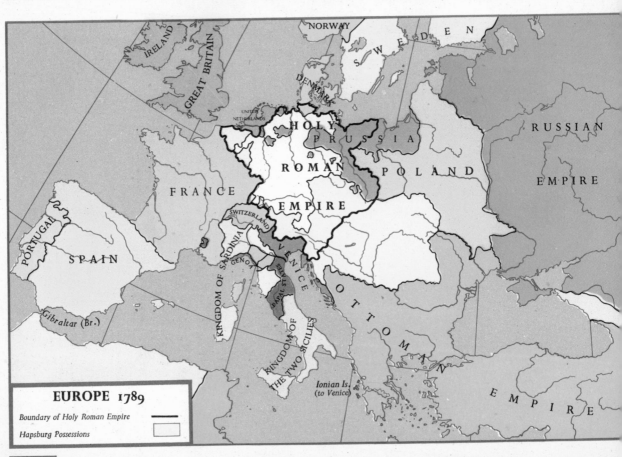

EUROPE 1789

Boundary of Holy Roman Empire

Hapsburg Possessions

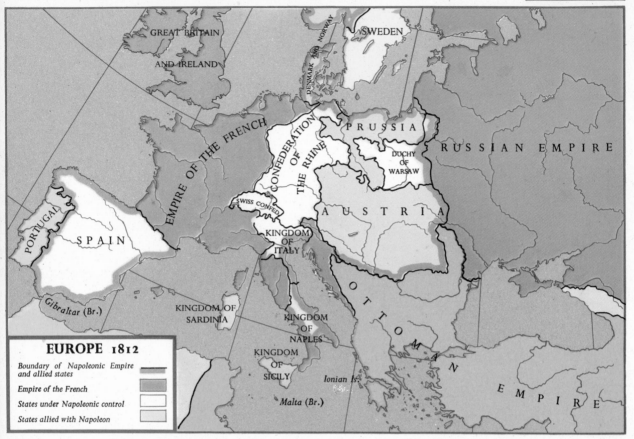

EUROPE 1812

Boundary of Napoleonic Empire
and allied states

Empire of the French

States under Napoleonic control

States allied with Napoleon

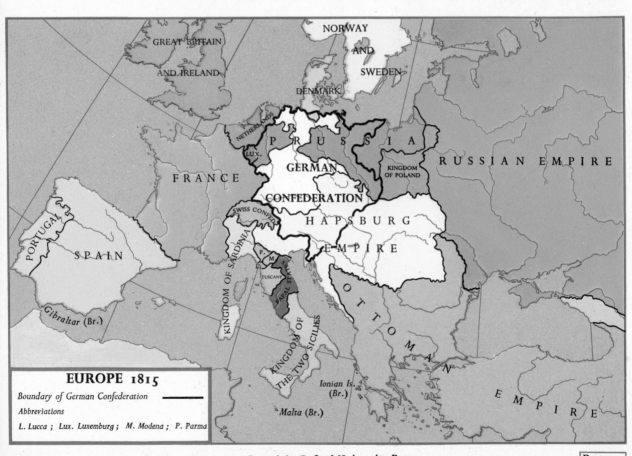

EUROPE 1815

Boundary of German Confederation

Abbreviations

L. Lucca ; Lux. Luxemburg ; M. Modena ; P. Parma

The American Colonies and the North Atlantic

NORTH AMERICA

Mackinac I.

Fort Dearborn

St. Louis

Mississippi

Fort Niagara

Fort Duquesne

Montreal   Stadacona

St. Lawrence

Saratoga

MD.   PA.   N.Y.

N.H.   Mass.

VA.   CONN.   MASS.

Salem

N.J.   Boston

New Amsterdam   Cape Cod

DEL.   R.I.   —Sic!

Philadelphia

Annapolis

NOVA SCOTIA   *Cape Breto*

New Orleans

GA.   S.C.   N.C

Yorktown

Charleston   Wilmington

Chesapeake Bay

Louisb

Gulf of Mexico

Fort Augustine

FLORIDA

CUBA

San Salvador

Bermuda

NORTH ATL

WEST

Jamaica

HAITI

INDIES

Caribbean Sea

Puerto Rico

Lesser Antilles

Curaçao

Antigua

Tropic of Cancer

SOUTH AMERICA

Barbados

0 Miles   600

Trinidad

60°W   50°W   40°W

GREENLAND

LABRADOR

70°N

Cape Farewell

Arctic Circle

ICELAND

FOUNDLAND

FAEROE IS.

Banks

60°N

50°N

Bristol • • London
Plymouth •
• Le Havre
• L'Orient

Bordeaux •

Azores

TIC

40°N

Madrid •
• Lisbon

OCEAN

• Seville

Madeira Is.

THE AMERICAN COLONIES AND THE NORTH ATLANTIC
on the eve of the Revolution
—— *Boundaries of The Thirteen Colonies*

30°W   20°W

SWEDEN

DENMARK

KINGDOM OF HOLLAND

MECKLENBURG

KINGDOM OF PRUSSIA

SAXONY

R U S S I A

E M P I R E

IV

VI

V

C O N F E D E R A T I O N

O F   T H E   R H I N E

III

II

I

E M P I R E   O F   A U S T R I A

O F   T H E

SWISS CONFEDERATION

VALAIS

F R E N C H

KINGDOM OF ITALY

O T T O M A N   E M P I R E

LUCCA

KINGDOM OF ETRURIA

PAPAL STATES

KINGDOM OF NAPLES

40°N

KINGDOM OF SARDINIA

0 Miles   200

KINGDOM OF SICILY

CENTRAL EUROPE AND ITALY 1806

This map shows the principal results of the dissolution of the Holy Roman Empire and the formation of the Confederation of the Rhine

   I *Kingdom of Bavaria*
  II *Kingdom of Württemberg*
 III *Grand Duchy of Baden*
 IV *Grand Duchy of Hesse-Darmstadt*
  V *Duchy of Nassau*
 VI *Grand Duchy of Berg*

             States under French domination

French influence extended over the Confederation of the Rhine, the Swiss Confederation and the Kingdom of Etruria

SWEDEN

DENMARK

HOLSTEIN

MECKLENBURG

OLDENBURG

HANOVER

KINGDOM OF THE NETHERLANDS

KINGDOM OF PRUSSIA

KINGDOM OF PRUSSIA

KINGDOM OF POLAND

R U S S I A

LUX.

PALATINATE

SAXONY

GRAND DUCHY OF BADEN

KINGDOM OF WÜRTTEMBERG

KINGDOM OF BAVARIA

H A P S B U R G   E M P I R E

SWISS CONFEDERATION

F R A N C E

K I N G D O M   O F   S A R D I N I A

LOMBARDY

VENETIA

PARMA

MODENA

LUCCA

TUSCANY

P A P A L   S T A T E S

ITALY

Rutt's

#1

KINGDOM OF THE TWO SICILIES

OTTOMAN   EMPIRE

MONTENEGRO

0 Miles ———————— *200*

CENTRAL EUROPE
AND ITALY 1815

This map shows the principal territorial adjustments agreed to at the Congress of Vienna.

Boundary of German Confederation ▬▬▬▬

CENTRAL AND SOUTH-EASTERN EUROPE AFTER THE CONGRESS OF BERLIN

Central and S.E. Europe

Stockholm

Baltic Sea

Copenhagen
Malmö

DENMARK

Heligoland (Br.)

Dover

NETHERLANDS
Amsterdam
The Hague

BELGIUM
Antwerp
Brussels

FRANCE
Paris

Niemen

Königsberg

PRUSSIA

Danzig

Vistula

Warsaw

RUSSIAN EMPIRE

Bug

Lemberg

GALICIA

Cracow

Posen

Stettin
Oder

Breslau
Oder

Berlin
Frankfort on Oder

Neisse

SLOVAKIA

Morava

MORAVIA
Olmütz
Brünn
Pressburg

Leipzig
Dresden

Prague
Sadowa
Elbe

BOHEMIA

Pilsen

Moldau

Vienna

GERMAN EMPIRE

Hamburg

Bremen
Weser

Cologne
Rhine

Frankfort on Main

Luxemburg
Meuse

Rhine

Munich

Inn

Danube

Linz
Salzburg
Ischl
Gastein

AUSTRIA

Graz
Mur

CARINTHIA

Laibach
CARNIOLA
Fiume
ISTRIA
Trieste

Innsbruck

TYROL

TRENTINO
Trento

Isonzo
Udine
Piave

SWITZERLAND
Zürich
Bern
Rhine
Rhône
Geneva

ITALY
Milan
Po
Adige
Venice
Bologna
Genoa
Florence

Seine
Saône

Page 42

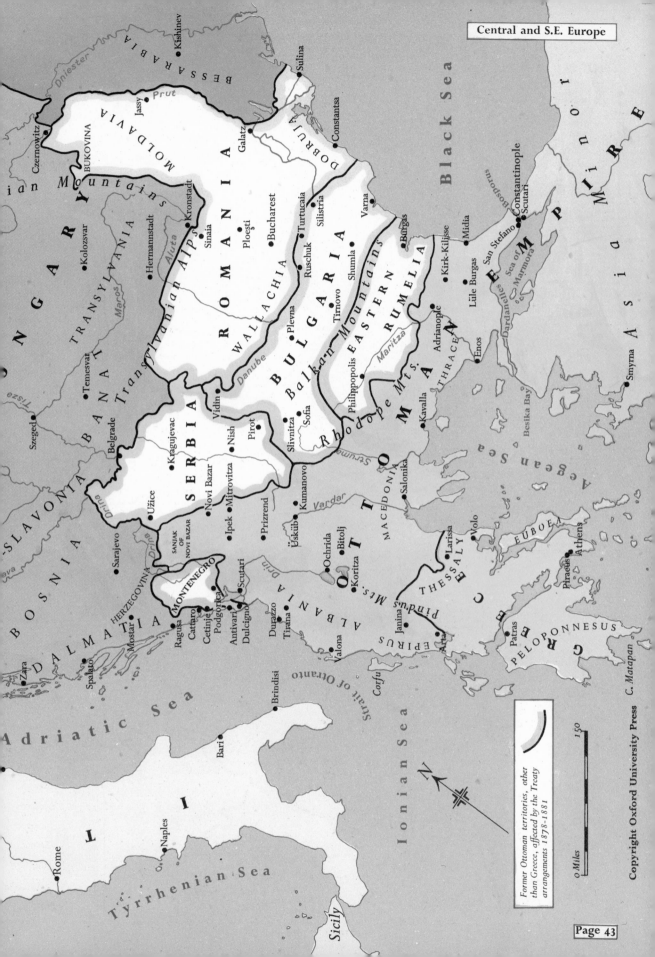

Black Sea

BESSARABIA

Dniester
Prut
Kishinev
Czernowitz
Jassy
BUKOVINA
MOLDAVIA

Sulina

DOBRUJA

Constantsa

an Mountains

Kronstadt
Hermannstadt
Kolozsvar
TRANSYLVANIA
BANAT
Temesvar
Aluta
Sinaia
Ploesti

R O M A N I A

Bucharest
Turtucaia
Silistria
WALLACHIA
Ruschuk
Turnovo
Shumla

Varna
Burgas

Kirk-Kilisse
Midia
San Stefano
Constantinople
Scutari
Bosporus

A S I A

M I N O R

Smyrna

Lüle Burgas

Dardanelles
Sea of Marmora

Danube

VIDIN
Plevna
BULGARIA
Balkan Mountains
EASTERN
RUMELIA

Sofia
Slivnitza
Philippopolis
Maritza
Adrianople

THRACE

Enos

SERBIA
Kragujevac
Nish
Pirot
Belgrade
Szeged
Tisza
Maros

SLAVONIA
BOSNIA
Sarajevo
DALMATIA
Zara
Spalato
HERZEGOVINA
Mostar
Ragusa
Cattaro
Novi Bazar
SANJAK OF NOVI BAZAR
Užice
Drina
Mitrovitza
Ipek
Prizrend
Üsküb
Kumanovo
Vardar
Ochrida
Bitolj
Koritza
MACEDONIA
Salonika

Rhodope Mts.
Strumа
Kavalla

M A C E D O N I A

MONTENEGRO
Podgoritza
Cetinje
Scutari
Antivari
Dulcigno
Durazzo
Tirana
Valona
ALBANIA
Drin
EPIRUS
Janina
Arta
Pindus Mts.
THESSALY
Larissa
Volo

Aegean Sea
EUBOEA

Corfu
Ionian Sea
Brindisi
Bari

Strait of Otranto

Patras
PELOPONNESUS
Piraeus
Athens
G R E E C E

O T T O M A N E M P I R E

Adriatic Sea

Besika Bay

Naples
Rome
I T A L Y
Tyrrhenian Sea
Sicily

N

Former Ottoman territories, other
than Greece, affected by the Treaty
arrangements 1878–1881

0 Miles   150

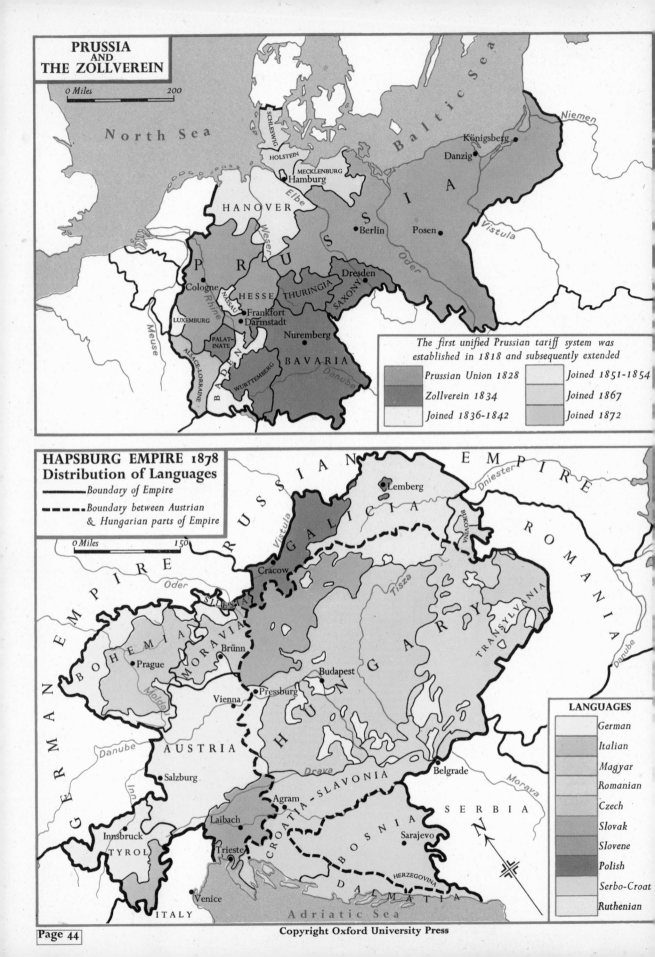

PRUSSIA AND THE ZOLLVEREIN

0 Miles 200

The first unified Prussian tariff system was established in 1818 and subsequently extended

Prussian Union 1828
Zollverein 1834
Joined 1836-1842
Joined 1851-1854
Joined 1867
Joined 1872

North Sea

Baltic Sea

SCHLESWIG
HOLSTEIN
MECKLENBURG
Hamburg
HANOVER
Berlin
Posen
Königsberg
Danzig
P R U S S I A
Cologne
NASSAU
HESSE
THURINGIA
SAXONY
Dresden
Frankfort
Darmstadt
PALAT-INATE
Nuremberg
BADEN
WÜRTTEMBERG
BAVARIA
LUXEMBURG
ALSACE-LORRAINE
Rhine
Meuse
Elbe
Weser
Oder
Vistula
Niemen
Danube

HAPSBURG EMPIRE 1878
Distribution of Languages

—— Boundary of Empire

- - - Boundary between Austrian & Hungarian parts of Empire

0 Miles 150

LANGUAGES

German
Italian
Magyar
Romanian
Czech
Slovak
Slovene
Polish
Serbo-Croat
Ruthenian

G E R M A N   E M P I R E
R U S S I A N   E M P I R E
ROMANIA
GALICIA
Lemberg
Cracow
BUKOVINA
SILESIA
BOHEMIA
Prague
MORAVIA
Brünn
Vienna
Pressburg
Budapest
H U N G A R Y
TRANSYLVANIA
AUSTRIA
Salzburg
Innsbruck
TYROL
Laibach
Trieste
Agram
CROATIA-SLAVONIA
BOSNIA
Sarajevo
Belgrade
S E R B I A
DALMATIA
HERZEGOVINA
Venice
ITALY
Adriatic Sea
Oder
Vistula
Dniester
Tisza
Danube
Drava
Morava
Inn
Moldau

N

SWEDEN

Gulf of Bothnia

FINLAND

White Sea

●Archangel

Pechora

N. Dvina

Lake Onega

Petrozavodsk●

Lake Ladoga

Helsingfors● Vyborg●

G. of Finland

Kronstadt● St. Petersburg●

●Perm

Yekaterinburg

Revel●

ESTONIA

Lake Peipus

●Vologda

●Vyatka

Dorpat● ●Pskov ●Novgorod

Volkhov

Baltic Sea

Riga●

COURLAND

Duna (W. Dvina)

Niemen

EAST RUSSIA

Kovno●

R U S S I A

●Vitebsk

Tver●

Volga

●Kostroma

Yaroslavl●

●Ivanovo Voznesensk

Kama

●Kazan

●Ufa

U r a l   M o u n t a i n s

●Vilna

L I T H U A N I A

●Smolensk

Borodino●

Vladimir●

●Moscow

Nizhni Novgorod●

Vetluga

●Simbirsk

Grodno●

●Minsk

Mogilev●

Kaluga●

Ryazan●

●Samara

●Tula

●Penza

●Orenburg

Warsaw●

●Brest Litovsk

Gomel●

Orel●

Tambov●

P O L A N D

L I T T L E

Chernigov●

Kursk●

Vorenezh●

Saratov●

Uralsk●

Ural

Lemberg●

Zhitomir●

●Kiev

R U S S I A

Dnieper

●Kharkov

Don

GALICIA

Kamenets-Podolsk●

Dniester

Bug

Yekaterinoslav●

Poltava●

Donets

Tsaritsyn●

Volga

A S T R A K H A N

K A Z A K H S T A N

BESSARABIA

Prut

Kishinev●

Odessa●

Kherson●

Rostov● ●Novocherkassk

Taganrog● ●Azov

Astrakhan●

C a s p i a n

TRANSYLVANIA

Sea of Azov

Crimea

Kerch●

Kuban

●Stavropol

ROMANIA

Sevastopol● ●Yalta

Novorossiisk●

Yekaterinodar●

●Vladikavkaz

●Derbent

BULGARIA

B l a c k   S e a

C a u c a s u s   M o u n t a i n s

0 Miles   300

Kutais●

Tiflis● Kura

●Baku

Batum●

T R A N S C A U C A S I A

S e a

Constantinople●

●Kars

●Erivan

Aras

EUROPEAN RUSSIA
in the nineteenth century

Copyright Oxford University Press

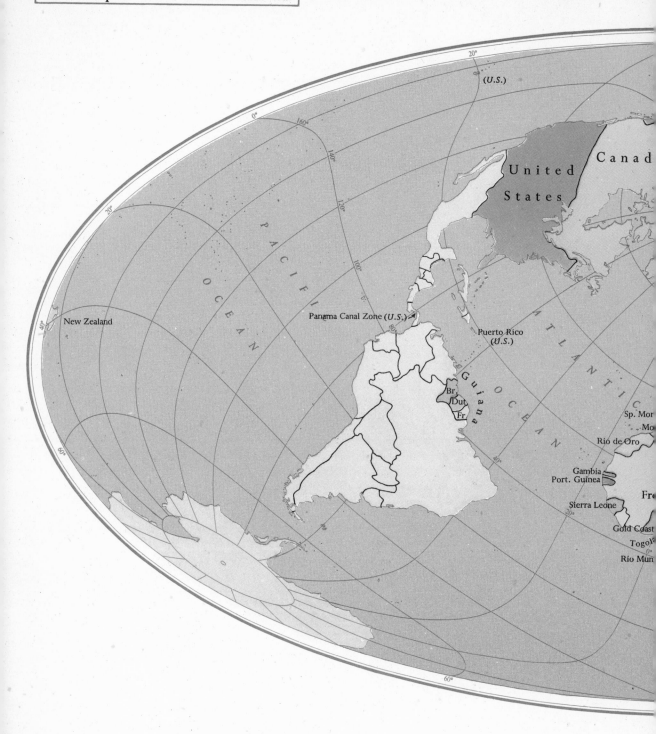

COLONIAL EMPIRES
ON EVE OF
FIRST WORLD WAR

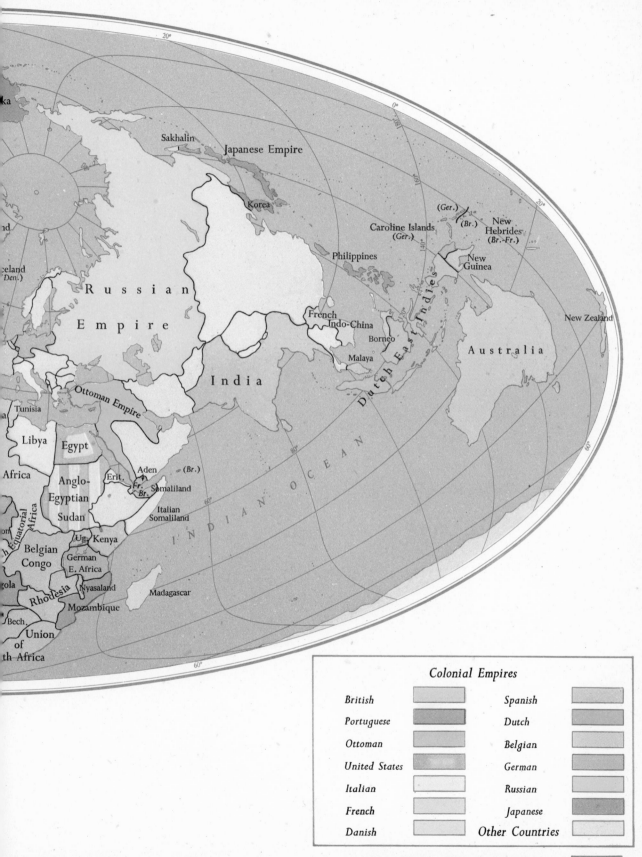

20°

0°

180°

160°

Sakhalin

Japanese Empire

Korea

(Ger.)

(Br.)

New
Hebrides
(Br.-Fr.)

Caroline Islands
(Ger.)

140°

Philippines

New
Guinea

20°

R u s s i a n

E m p i r e

French
Indo-China

Borneo

Dutch East Indies

Australia

120°

New Zealand

60°

ka

nd

celand
Den.)

Malaya

I n d i a

Ottoman Empire

Tunisia

Libya

Egypt

Africa

Anglo-
Egyptian
Sudan

Aden

(Br.)

80°

Erit.
Fr.
Br.

Somaliland

Italian
Somaliland

60°

I N D I A N   O C E A N

60°

on
h Equatorial
Africa

Belgian
Congo

Ug.

Kenya

German
E. Africa

ola

Rhodesia

Nyasaland

Mozambique

Madagascar

Bech.

Union
of
th Africa

60°

Colonial Empires

British		*Spanish*	
Portuguese		*Dutch*	
Ottoman		*Belgian*	
United States		*German*	
Italian		*Russian*	
French		*Japanese*	
Danish		*Other Countries*	

LITHUANIA

SWEDEN

Baltic Sea

DENMARK

Memel

Tilsit

Königsberg

EAST PRUSSIA

Tannenberg

FREE TERRITORY OF DANZIG

Gdynia

Danzig

Niemen

POLAND

Warsaw

Kraków

Łódź

Poznań

Vistula

Bug

CZECHOSLOVAKIA

Olmütz

Brno

Prague

Bratislava

HUNGARY

Budapest

ROMANIA

AUSTRIA

Vienna

Salzburg

Innsbruck

Bolzano

Mura

Drava

Tisza

Danube

Morava

Copenhagen

Malmö

North Sea

GREAT BRITAIN

Kiel

Hamburg

Stettin

Bremen

Wilhelmshaven

Hanover

Brunswick

Magdeburg

Berlin

GERMANY

Leipzig

Halle

Göttingen

Erfurt

Weimar

Jena

Dresden

Chemnitz

Breslau

Carlsbad

Pilsen

Regensburg

Munich

Augsburg

Ulm

Stuttgart

Salzburg

Liechtenstein

Zürich

Basle

SWITZERLAND

Bern

Lausanne

Mulhouse

Strasbourg

Nancy

Metz

Saarbrücken

SAAR

Trier

Mainz

Coblenz

Wiesbaden

Frankfort

Mannheim

Heidelberg

RHINELAND

Bonn

Cologne

Düsseldorf

Essen

Dortmund

Duisburg

Aachen

NETHERLANDS

Amsterdam

The Hague

Rotterdam

Antwerp

BELGIUM

Brussels

Lille

LUXEMBURG

Luxemburg

Reims

Amiens

Paris

FRANCE

Dijon

Oder

Neisse

Elbe

Spree

Weser

Ems

Rhine

Main

Neckar

Danube

Inn

Rhine

Scheldt

Meuse

Marne

Seine

Somme

Loire

Doubs

Aare

Aar

Moselle

Ticino

Elbe

Oder

Vistula

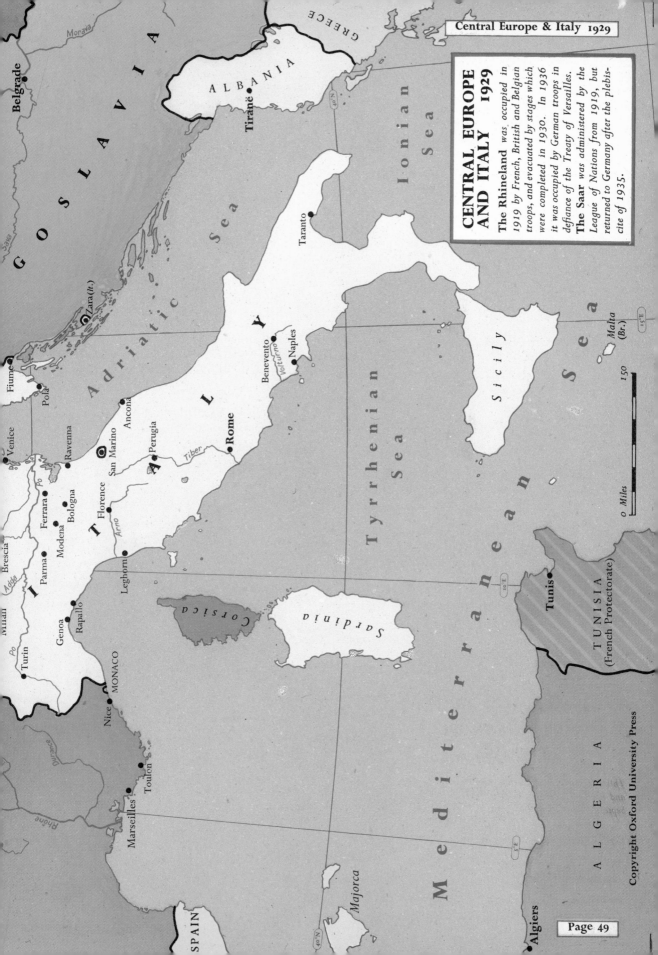

CENTRAL EUROPE AND ITALY 1929

The Rhineland was occupied in 1919 by French, British and Belgian troops, and evacuated by stages which were completed in 1930. In 1936 it was occupied by German troops in defiance of the Treaty of Versailles. The Saar was administered by the League of Nations from 1919, but returned to Germany after the plebiscite of 1935.

GREECE

Morava

Belgrade

ALBANIA

Tiranë

YUGOSLAVIA

Ionian Sea

Taranto

Sava

Adriatic Sea

Fiume

Zara (It.)

Pola

Venice

Ravenna

Ancona

San Marino

Perugia

Rome

Tiber

Benevento

Volturno

Naples

ITALY

Sicily

Malta (Br.)

Brescia

Milan

Adda

Ferrara

Modena

Bologna

Parma

Florence

Arno

Po

Leghorn

Tyrrhenian Sea

Genoa

Rapallo

Turin

Corsica

Sardinia

Tunis

TUNISIA
(French Protectorate)

Monaco

Nice

Mediterranean Sea

ALGERIA

Durance

Marseilles

Toulon

Rhône

SPAIN

Majorca

Algiers

15° E

150

0 Miles

10° E

5° E

45° N

40° N

Copyright Oxford University Press

Page 49

0 Miles   450

Iceland

ATLANTIC OCEAN

North Sea

Skagerrak

Baltic

NORWAY

Narvik
Namsos
Trondheim
Andalsnes
Oslo
Stockholm

SWEDEN

FIN

Helsinki
Hangö
Narv
ESTONIA

Gulf of Finla

Riga
LATVIA

LITH.
Vilna
Velik

Glasgow
Belfast
Edinburgh
Dublin
Liverpool
GREAT BRITAIN
Coventry
Southampton
London
Dover
Portsmouth
Calais
Brest
Cherbourg
Dieppe
Compiègne
Caen
St. Nazaire
Nantes
Paris Reims
Dunkirk

DENMARK
Copenhagen
Wilhelmshaven
Hamburg
Amsterdam Bremen
Rotterdam
Antwerp Arnhem
Brussels
Aachen
Liège
Luxemburg
RUHR

Kiel
Belsen
Peenemünde

Danzig
GER.
(E. Prus.)

POLAND

Warsaw
Łódź
Lublin

Breslau
Auschwitz
Cracow
Lvov

Berlin
Leipzig
Torgau
Remagen
Buchenwalde

GERMANY

FRANCE

Bordeaux
Oradour
Vichy
Hendaye
Lyons

Bern
SWITZ.
Munich
Dachau
Berchtesgaden

Lidice
Prague
CZECHOSLOVAKIA

AUSTRIA
Vienna
Wiener Neustadt
Budapest
HUNGARY

PORTUGAL
Lisbon
Madrid
SPAIN
Pyrenees
Bay of Biscay

Marseilles Nice
Toulon
Turin Milan
Genoa
La Spezia
Pisa Rimini

Trieste

Corsica

ROMANIA
Ploesti
Bucharest

Belgrade
YUGOSLAVIA

BULGARIA
Sofia

Tangier
Gibraltar
SP. MOROCCO
Casablanca
FRENCH MOROCCO
Oran
Algiers
ALGERIA

Sardinia

Rome
Anzio
Cassino
Salerno
Taranto

ITALY

Adriatic Sea

ALBANIA
Tiranë
Skoplje
Koritsa
GREECE
Athens
C. Matapan
Cos
Rhodes

Mediterranean

Bône
Bizerte
Tunis
C. Bon
Kasserine
Syracuse
Sicily
Malta
TUNISIA
Mareth
Tripoli

Crete

WAR IN EUROPE
1939-1945

This map shows the theater of combat between Germany and her allies and Great Britain and her allies from September 1939 to May 1945.

Furthest advance of Axis military power   ·········

Boundary of unoccupied France, June 1940-Nov. 1942   – – –

Pre-war national boundaries   ———

Derna
Benghazi
Tobruk
LIBYA
Mersa-Matruh
El Alam
Ale

War in Europe 1939-1945

THE RHINE

HOLLAND

Arnhem
Nijmegen
Munster • Ems
Wesel
Eindhoven
Venlo
Duisburg Essen Dortmund
Hamm
Krefeld
Düsseldorf Wuppertal
Ruhr Möhne Dam

BELGIUM
Liége
Namur
Eupen
Malmédy
Cologne
Bonn
Aachen
Remagen
Sieg

Ardennes
Bastogne
Eifel
Coblenz
Lahn

Sedan
Trier
Luxemburg
Moselle
Bingen
Mainz
Frankfort
Main
Mannheim

FRANCE
Verdun
Metz
SAAR
Saarbrücken
Meuse
Karlsruhe

0 Miles   50
Nancy
Saverne
Strasbourg
Vosges
Black
Forest

UNION OF
SOVIET
SOCIALIST
REPUBLICS

White
Sea
Murmansk
Archangel
Kalinin
Moscow
Kuibyshev
Smolensk
Tula
Bryansk
Orel
Kursk
Volga
Kharkov
Don
Voroshilovgrad
Stalingrad
Kremenchug
Dnepropetrovsk
Rostov
Volga
Taganrog
Bataisk
Perekop
Krasnodar
Maikop
Novorossiisk
Yalta
Black
Sea
Caucasus Mts.
Grozny
Caspian
Sea
Baku
Batum

Ankara
TURKEY

Kabul
AFGHANISTAN

Tehran

IRAN

Mosul

SYRIA
Habbaniya
Baghdad
LEBANON
Beirut
Damascus
IRAQ
Jerusalem
TRANSJORDAN
Abadan
Basra
PALESTINE
Port Said
Suez Canal
SAUDI ARABIA
Persian Gulf
Suez

War in the Pacific

U. S. S. R.

OUTER
MONGOLIA

CHINA

MANCHUKUO

NEPAL

INDIA

Calcutta

Chungking

Nanking

Vladivostok

KOREA

JAPAN

NO

Attu
Kiska

Aleutia

Lashio
Mandalay
YUNNAN

Changsha

Hiroshima
Nagasaki

Tokyo
Yokohama
Sagami Bay

BURMA

Kweilin

Kyushu

Honshu

Burma Road

Bay of
Bengal

Rangoon

SIAM

Hong Kong
(Br.)

Formosa

Ryukyu Is.

Inland Sea

Okinawa

P

Bonin Is.

Iwo Jima

A

Midway I.

C

I

Isthmus
of Kra

Gulf
of
Siam

Saigon

FRENCH INDO-CHINA

Luzon

Bataan
Corregidor
Mindoro

Manila

Philippine

Marianas Is.

Saipan
Guam

Wake I.

Leyte

Islands

Yap

Eniwetok I.

Kwajalein

Truk I.

Marshall Is.

E

Isthmus

MALAYA

Sumatra

Singapore

BR.
BORNEO

Mindanao

Angaur

Borneo

Celebes

Caroline Islands

O

C

Gilbert
Islands

Tarawa

Equator

NETHERLANDS EAST INDIES

Java Sea

Java

Bali

Hollandia

New

Guinea

Bismarck
Arch.

Rabaul

Savo I.

Nanumea

Java Sea

(Port.)

Timor

Port Moresby

Buna

Solomon Islands

Guadalcanal

Coral

Sea

New Caledonia (Fr.)

Fiji Is.

Port
Darwin

P

INDIAN

OCEAN

20°S

AUSTRALIA

Sydney

Melbourne

NEW

ZEALAND

Wellington

Tropic of Capricorn

Antarctic

80°E   100°E   60°S   120°E

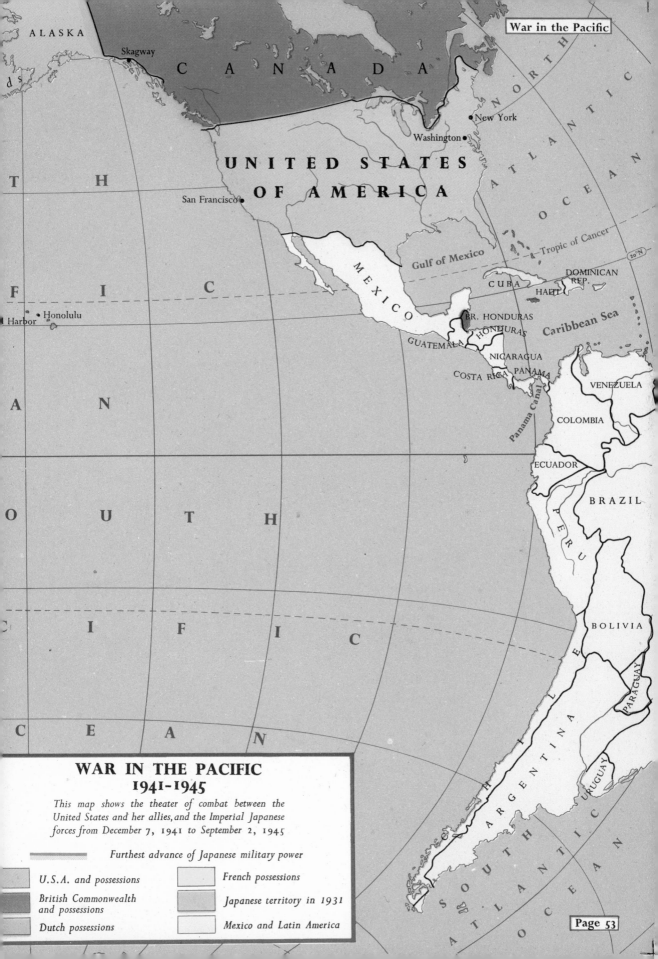

ALASKA

Skagway

C A N A D A

North New York

Washington

UNITED STATES

OF AMERICA

San Francisco

T H

F I C

Honolulu
Harbor

A N

O U T H

C I F I C

C E A N

MEXICO

Gulf of Mexico

Tropic of Cancer

20°N

CUBA

DOMINICAN
REP.

HAITI

BR. HONDURAS

HONDURAS

GUATEMALA

NICARAGUA

COSTA RICA

PANAMA

Panama Canal

Caribbean Sea

VENEZUELA

COLOMBIA

ECUADOR

P E R U

BRAZIL

BOLIVIA

PARAGUAY

A R G E N T I N A

URUGUAY

C H I L E

S O U T H

A T L A N T I C

O C E A N

ATLANTIC OCEAN

NORTH

WAR IN THE PACIFIC
1941-1945

*This map shows the theater of combat between the
United States and her allies, and the Imperial Japanese
forces from December 7, 1941 to September 2, 1945*

——————— *Furthest advance of Japanese military power*

U.S.A. and possessions

British Commonwealth
and possessions

Dutch possessions

French possessions

Japanese territory in 1931

Mexico and Latin America

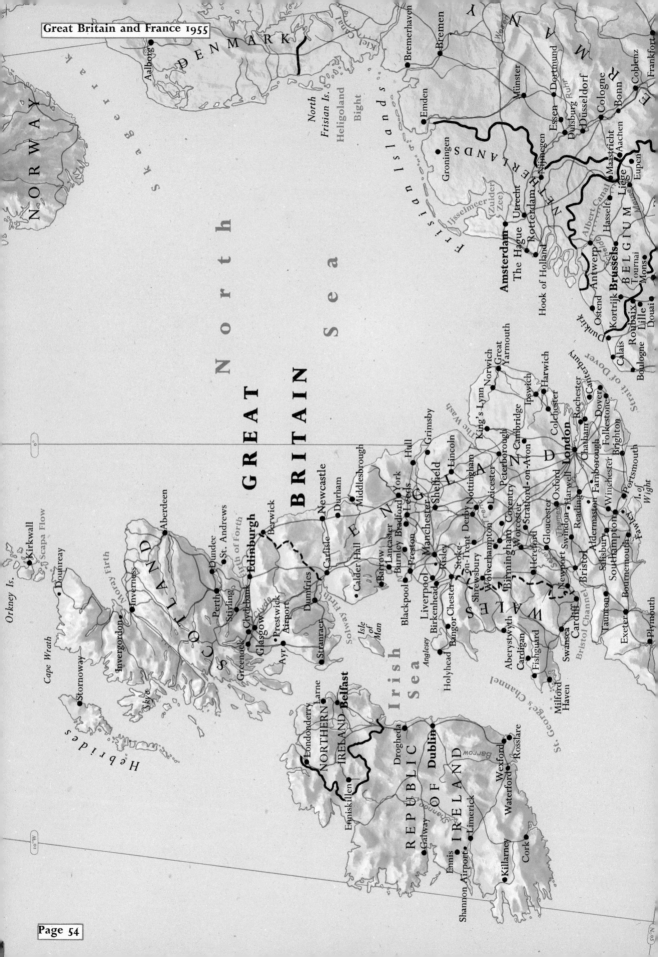

NORWAY

DENMARK

Aalborg

Kiel Canal

Bremerhaven

Bremen

GERMANY

Münster

Dortmund

Ruhr

Essen

Duisburg

Düsseldorf

Cologne

Bonn

Coblenz

Frankfurt

Skagerrak

North Frisian Is.

Heligoland

Heligoland Bight

Emden

Groningen

NETHERLANDS

Zuider Zee

IJsselmeer (Zuider Zee)

Utrecht

Amsterdam

The Hague

Rotterdam

Hook of Holland

Maastricht

Aachen

Eupen

Frisian Islands

Ostend

Antwerp

Brussels

BELGIUM

Tournai

Mons

Dunkirk

Kortrijk

Roubaix

Lille

Douai

Calais

Boulogne

Albert Canal

Hasselt

Liège

North Sea

GREAT BRITAIN

Orkney Is.

Kirkwall

Scapa Flow

Dounreay

Cape Wrath

Stornoway

Hebrides

Skye

Inveraordon

Moray Firth

Inverness

SCOTLAND

Aberdeen

Dundee

St. Andrews

Perth

Stirling

Firth of Forth

Edinburgh

Barwick

Clydebank

Glasgow

Greenock

Prestwick Airport

Ayr

Clyde

Dumfries

Stranraer

Solway Firth

Carlisle

Calder Hall

Isle of Man

Newcastle

Durham

Middlesbrough

York

Leeds

Bradford

Preston

Burnley

Lancaster

Barrow

Blackpool

Liverpool

Birkenhead

Bangor

Chester

Holyhead

Anglesey

ENGLAND

Hull

Grimsby

Lincoln

Sheffield

Manchester

Risley

Stoke-on-Trent

Derby

Nottingham

Leicester

Coventry

Birmingham

Wolverhampton

Shrewsbury

Hereford

WALES

Aberystwyth

Cardigan

Fishguard

Milford Haven

Swansea

Cardiff

Bristol Channel

St. George's Channel

Taunton

Exeter

Plymouth

Bournemouth

Fawley

I. of Wight

Portsmouth

Brighton

Southampton

Winchester

Salisbury

Aldermaston

Farnborough

Reading

Swindon

Harwell

Gloucester

Newport

Worcester

Stratford-on-Avon

Oxford

Thames

London

Reading

Peterborough

Cambridge

Ipswich

Harwich

Colchester

Rochester

Canterbury

Dover

Folkestone

Chatham

Strait of Dover

King's Lynn

Norwich

Great Yarmouth

The Wash

Irish Sea

Larne

Belfast

Londonderry

NORTHERN IRELAND

Enniskillen

Drogheda

Dublin

REPUBLIC OF IRELAND

Galway

Shannon

Ennis

Shannon Airport

Limerick

Killarney

Cork

Waterford

Wexford

Rosslare

Barrow

St. George's Channel

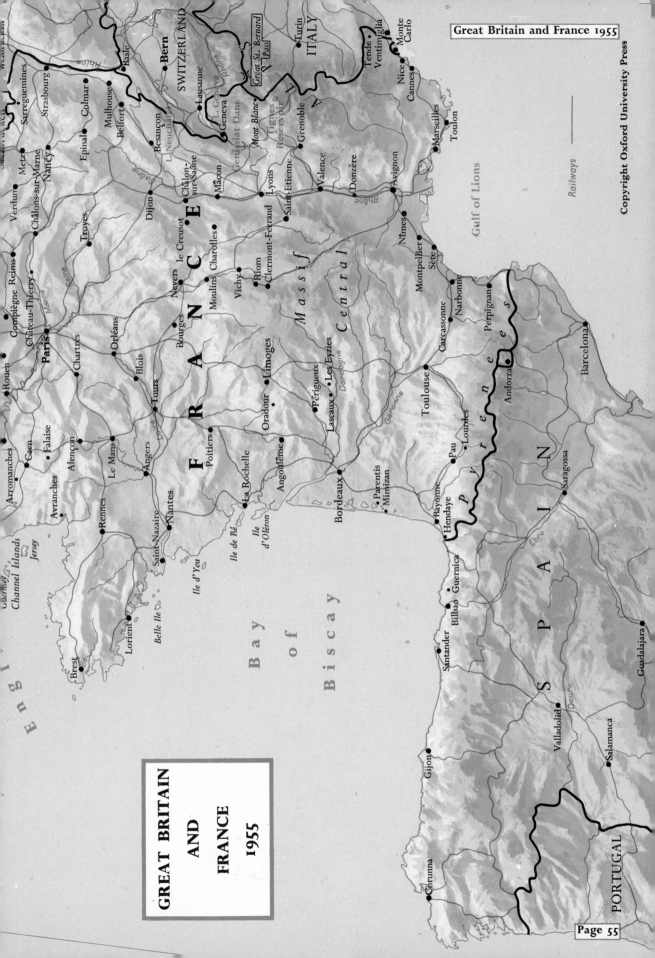

Railways ⸺

GREAT BRITAIN
AND
FRANCE
1955

SWITZERLAND

Great St. Bernard Pass

Turin
ITALY

Tende
Ventimiglia
Nice
Monte Carlo
Cannes

Basle
Bern
Lausanne
L. Geneva
Geneva
Rhône
Mont Blanc
Tignes Reservoir
Grenoble
Neuchâtel
Besançon
L. Neuchâtel
Genissiat Dam

Sarreguemines
Strasbourg
Colmar
Mulhouse
Belfort
Epinal
Metz
Nancy
Verdun
Château-Thierry
Châlons-sur-Marne
Troyes
Dijon
Mâcon
Chalon-sur-Saône
Lyons
Saint-Étienne
Valence
Donzère
Avignon
Nîmes
Marseilles
Toulon

Reims
Compiègne
Paris
Chartres
Orléans
Blois
Tours
Nevers
le Creusot
Bourges
Moulins
Charolles
Vichy
Riom
Clermont-Ferrand

F R A N C E

Rouen

Caen
Falaise
Alençon
Avranches
Le Mans
Angers
Rennes
Saint-Nazaire
Nantes
Arromanches

Guernsey
Channel Islands
Jersey

Brest
Lorient
Belle Ile
Ile d'Yeu

Ile de Ré
Ile d'Oléron
La Rochelle
Poitiers
Limoges
Oradour
Angoulême
Périgueux
Les Eyzies
Lascaux
Dordogne

M a s s i f
C e n t r a l

Montpellier
Sète
Narbonne
Carcassonne
Perpignan

B a y

o f

B i s c a y

Bordeaux
Garonne
Parentis
Mimizan
Toulouse
Bayonne
Hendaye
Lourdes
Pau

Andorra

P y r e n e e s

S P A I N

Gulf of Lions

Barcelona
Saragossa
Ebro
Guernica
Bilbao
Santander
Gijon
Corunna
Valladolid
Douro
Salamanca
Guadalajara

PORTUGAL

E n g l
Western Approaches
Rhine
Seine
Marne
Rhône

U. S. S. R.

IRAN

Tabriz
Tehran
Bandar Abbas

Persian Gulf
Abadan
Khanaqin
Baghdad
IRAQ
Euphrates
Tigris

KUWAIT

SAUDI
ARABIA

Arabian Desert

Medina

Mecca

Jidda

Red Sea

TURKEY

Ankara

SYRIA
JORDAN
LEBANON
ISRAEL
Cyprus

Aqaba

Suez
Port Said
Damietta
Alexandria
Cairo

Nile

GREECE
Athens
Crete

Mediterranean Sea

EGYPT

Aswan

Wadi Halfa
Nubian Desert

Port Sudan

Atbara

Khartoum

Libyan Desert

LIBYA

Benghazi

G. of Sidra
TRIPOLITANIA
Tripoli
Gat

ITALY
Rome

Marseilles
FRANCE

Madrid
SPAIN
PORTUGAL
Lisbon

Gibraltar
Tangier
SP. MOR.
Tetuan
Rabat
Casablanca
Safi
Mogador
Marrakech
Agadir
IFNI (Sp.)

MOROCCO
Atlas Mountains

Oran
Algiers
Constantine
Tunis
Bizerte
Sfax
C. Bon
G. of Gabes
TUNISIA

ALGERIA

Sahara Desert

Timbuktu

MAURITANIA

SPANISH SAHARA

Canary Islands

Madeira Is.

C. Bojador

C. Blanc

Cape Verde Is.

St.-Louis
C. Vert
Dakar
SENEGAL
GAMBIA
PORT. GUINEA
FRENCH GUINEA
Conakry
Freetown
SIERRA LEONE
Monrovia
LIBERIA

FRENCH WEST AFRICA

FRENCH SUDAN

Niamey
Niger

Sokoto
Zinder
Kano
NIGERIA
Ibadan
Lagos
DAHOMEY
TOGO
Accra
GOLD COAST
Kumasi
Takoradi
IVORY COAST
C. Three Points

Bight of Benin
Gulf of Guinea

ADEN PROT.
Aden
YEMEN
Str. of Bab el Mandeb
Gulf of Aden

BRIT. SOM.
Hargeisa
FR. SOM.
Djibouti

SOMALIA

Mogadiscio

ERITREA
Asmara
Adowa
L. Tana
Blue Nile
Addis Ababa
ETHIOPIA
(ABYSSINIA)

SUDAN

Kodok

White Nile

EQUATORIA

UBANGI-SHARI

FRENCH EQUATORIAL AFRICA

L. Chad
Fort Lamy

Benue
Enugu
Calabar
Buea
Douala
CAMEROONS
FRENCH
Fernando Po
Principe
São Tomé
SPANISH GUINEA
Bight of Biafra
Port Harcourt
Annobón
C. Lopez
GABON
Ogoué
Brazzaville
CABINDA

BELGIAN CONGO
Coquilhatville
L. Leopold II
Congo
Ubangi
Uele
Lomami
Kasai
Sankuru
Léopoldville
Matadi
Congo

L. Rudolf

KENYA
Mt. Kenya
Nairobi
Mombasa
Malindi
Kilindini
Zanzibar
Tanga
Kilimanjaro
Mt. Kilimanjaro

UGANDA
L. Kyoga
Entebbe
L. Victoria
Kisumu
L. Albert
L. Edward
L. Kivu
TANGANYIKA
Ujiji
Lake
Farquhar Is.
Ascension I.

Equator
Tropic of Cancer

ATLANTIC

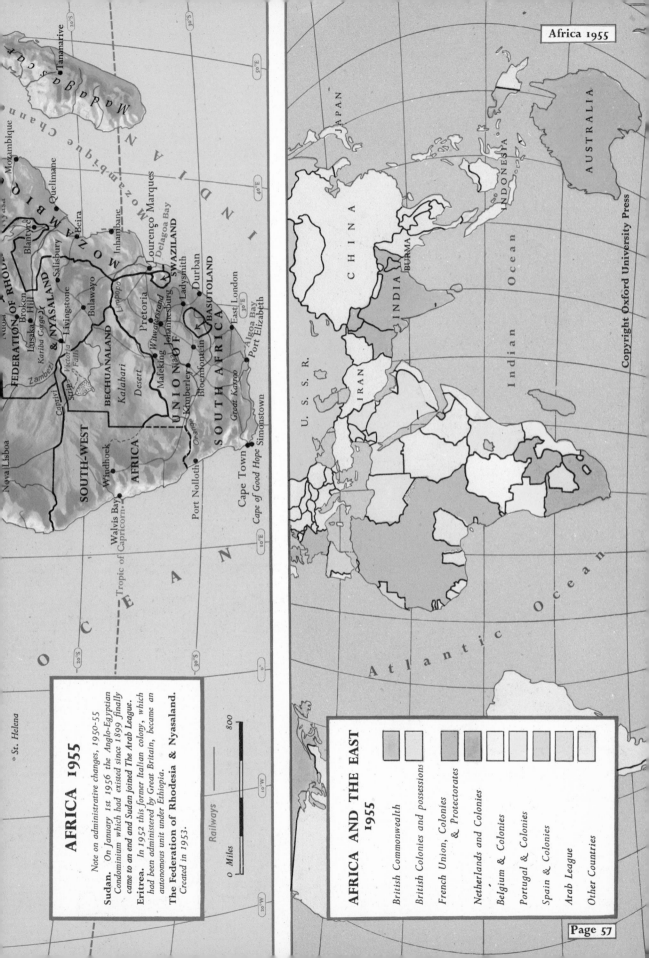

AFRICA 1955

Note on administrative changes, 1950-55
Sudan. On January 1st 1956 the Anglo-Egyptian Condominium which had existed since 1899 finally came to an end and Sudan joined The Arab League.
Eritrea. In 1952 this former Italian colony, which had been administered by Great Britain, became an autonomous unit under Ethiopia.
The Federation of Rhodesia & Nyasaland. Created in 1953.

Railways

0 Miles   800

AFRICA AND THE EAST 1955

British Commonwealth
British Colonies and possessions
French Union, Colonies & Protectorates
Netherlands and Colonies
Belgium & Colonies
Portugal & Colonies
Spain & Colonies
Arab League
Other Countries

Africa 1955

Copyright Oxford University Press

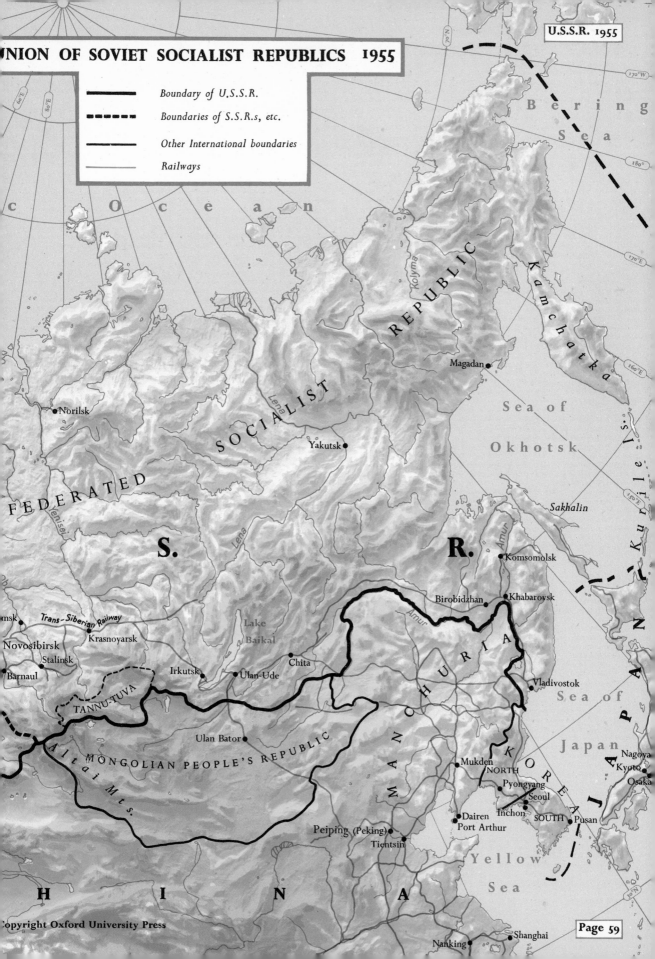

UNION OF SOVIET SOCIALIST REPUBLICS 1955

———	*Boundary of U.S.S.R.*
– – –	*Boundaries of S.S.R.s, etc.*
—·—	*Other International boundaries*
———	*Railways*

Bering Sea

Arctic Ocean

Kamchatka

Kurile Is.

Sea of Okhotsk

SOCIALIST REPUBLIC

FEDERATED

S.

R.

Norilsk

Yakutsk

Magadan

Sakhalin

Komsomolsk

Lena

Kolyma

Yenisei

Trans-Siberian Railway

Krasnoyarsk

Novosibirsk

Stalinsk

Barnaul

Irkutsk

Ulan-Ude

Chita

Lake Baikal

Birobidzhan

Khabarovsk

Vladivostok

Sea of Japan

TANNU-TUVA

Altai Mts.

MONGOLIAN PEOPLE'S REPUBLIC

Ulan Bator

MANCHURIA

KOREA

Japan

Nagoya

Kyoto

Osaka

Mukden

NORTH

Pyongyang

Seoul

Inchon

Dairen

Port Arthur

SOUTH

Pusan

Peiping (Peking)

Tientsin

Yellow Sea

H I N A

Nanking

Shanghai

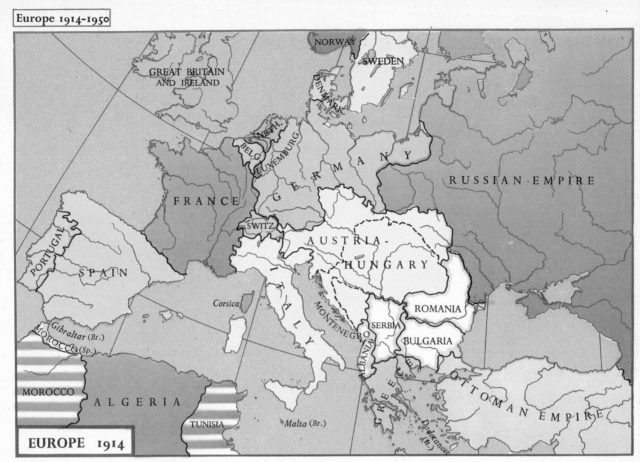

EUROPE 1914

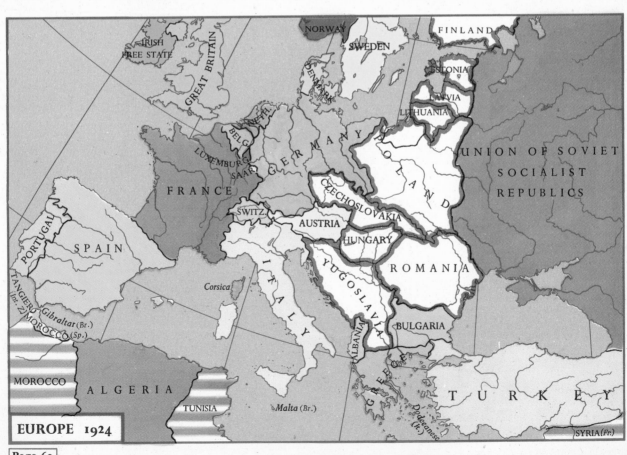

EUROPE 1924

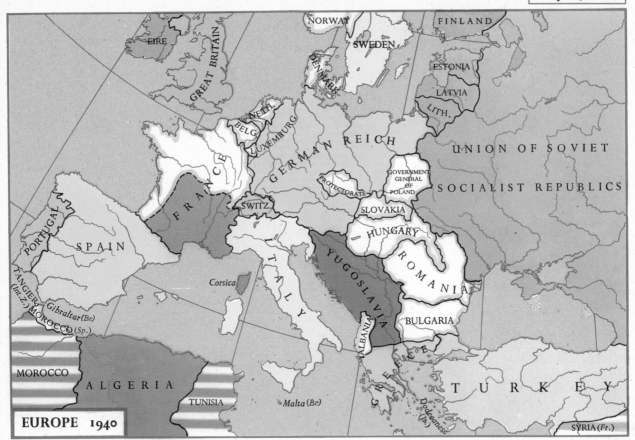

EUROPE 1940

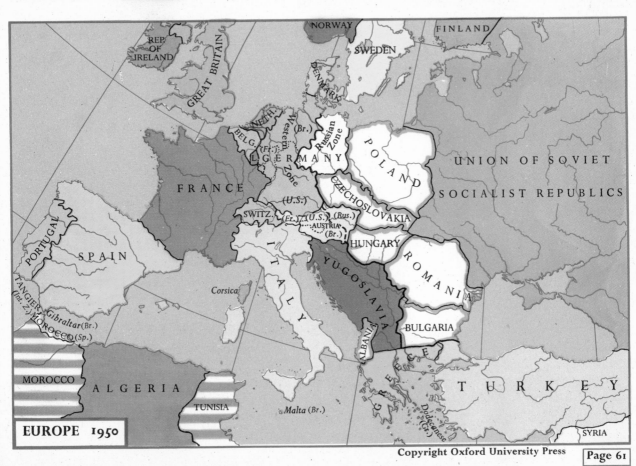

EUROPE 1950

Port Said
LEBANON
SYRIA
Cairo
Suez
ISRAEL
JORDAN
IRAQ
Tabriz
Caspian Sea

Khanaqin
Baghdad
Tehran

EGYPT
Aral Sea
Syr Darya

U. S. S. R.
Lake Balkhash

Nubian
Desert
Medina
KUWAIT
Abadan
Plateau
of Iran
IRAN
Bukhara
Samarkand
Tien
Kashgar
Turkistan
Takla

SUDAN
SAUDI
Port Sudan
Khartoum
Jidda
Mecca
ARABIA
Persian Gulf
Hindu Kush
Kabul
AFGHANISTAN
Khyber Pass
Peshawar
Pamirs
Karakoram
Kunlu

Asmara
L. Tana
Blue Nile
YEMEN
Aden
ADEN PROT.
Gulf of Oman
OMAN
Karachi
Rann of Cutch
BALUCHISTAN
PAKISTAN
Bolan Pass
Lahore
Amritsar
Srinagar
KASHMIR
Himala
Punjab
Simla
Delhi
Indus
Sutlej
Thar
Desert

Addis Ababa
FR. SOM.
Djibouti
Gulf of Aden
Str. of Bab el Mandeb
BRIT. SOMALILAND
Ahmadabad
Kathiawar
Vindhya Ra.
Narbada
IND
Allahabad
Luc
Ben
Jumna

ETHIOPIA
(ABYSSINIA)
ENYA
Nairobi
SOMALIA
Mogadiscio
Socotra
Arabian
Sea
Bombay
Poona
Godavari
Western Ghats
GOA
(Port.)
Hyderabad
Kistna
D
Coast
Malabar Coast
Mysore
Madras
Pondicherry
Coromandel Coast

Mombasa
Equator
Calicut
Nilgiri
Hills
C. Comorin
Ceylon
Colombo

Dar es Salaam

Seychelles

Indian
O

Mozambique
Comoro Is.
Farquhar Is.

Madagascar
20°S

Réunion
Mauritius
Tropic of Capricorn

60°E
70°E
80°E

THE FAR EAST 1955

Note on administrative changes, 1950-55.

Korea. *The boundary between North & South Korea was established as a truce line after the Armistice in 1953.*

Indo-China. *Vietnam, Laos and Cambodia were granted independence within the French Union in 1949, and recognized as fully independent after the French defeat, July 1954, at which time Vietnam was provisionally divided at the 17th parallel between the Communist North and the non-Communist South.*

WORLD POPULATION

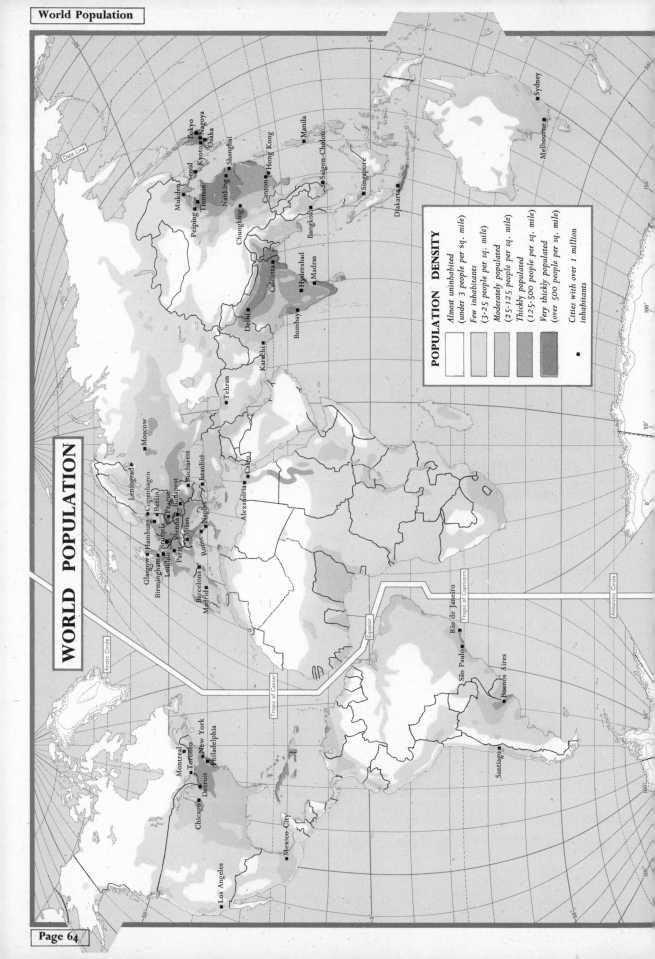

POPULATION DENSITY

Almost uninhabited
(under 3 people per sq. mile)

Few inhabitants
(3-25 per sq. mile)

Moderately populated
(25-125 people per sq. mile)

Thickly populated
(125-500 people per sq. mile)

Very thickly populated
(over 500 people per sq. mile)

■ *Cities with over 1 million*
inhabitants

THE GAZETTEER

The gazetteer is an index of all names, whether of towns, topographical features, or regions, which appear on the maps. Entries are arranged in strict alphabetical order. Where two or more places have the same name, they are listed in order of geographical size or importance. Places which have been known by more than one name are entered under as many names as appear on the various maps, each with the alternates following in parentheses. Other information, for example, the date of discovery or of a battle, is sometimes included immediately after the name.

Geographic designations such as " region ", " island ", " mountain ", " river ", " strait ", " lake ", " sea " or " pass "—unless so familiar as to be unmistakable—are so labeled. In the absence of such indication the names may be assumed to refer to a city, town or port and not an area or physical feature.

Unusual or obscure place names are often followed by the name of the continental area in which they are to be found before more precise clues are given. Area designations, however, even if identical with the names of political units, are not intended to serve as a guide to the existing government, or the government at any particular time, unless dates or clear definitions are noted. Some area names do not lend themselves to precise use, and consequently a general and familiar term, such as Anatolia, Thrace, Macedonia, Mesopotamia, Palestine, India, or Russia, may be used without any implication of precise geographical definition or specific political designation.

Most entries in the gazetteer are followed by a brief geographical description designed to assist the reader to locate the place on the relevant map or maps. No rigorously uniform system of description has been employed but in general the position has been indicated by reference to some important physical feature, well-known region or city.

Usage of nomenclature and orthography is, in so far as practical, that of current historical practice. Occasionally, however, the native form has been employed even though a translation is to be found in much contemporary historical writing.

Each place name is finally followed by the page numbers of maps on which it can be located. Not all maps are necessarily indicated for places which appear with great frequency, but representative pages for early and late periods have been provided.

Abbreviations have been avoided as much as possible. Familiarity with the following list will be of assistance in the use of this gazetteer.

ABBREVIATIONS

AD	Christian Era	L	Lake	SE	Southeast
B	Bay	mt(s)	mountain(s)	SSR	Soviet Socialist Republic
BC	Before Christ	N	North(ern)	Str	Strait
C	Cape	NE	Northeast	SW	Southwest
cen	central	NW	Northwest	St	Saint
Co	County	O	Ocean	territ	territory
E	East(ern)	penin	peninsula	USA	United States of America
Fed	Federation	R	River	USSR	Union of Soviet Socialist
G	Gulf	reg	region		Republics
I(s)	island(s)	S	South(ern)	W	West(ern)

Aachen (Aix-la-Chapelle): W Germany, between Meuse R & Rhine R. *Pp. 18, 48, 50, 51 Inset, 54*

Aalborg: N Denmark. *P. 54*
Aare: R in NW Switzerland. *P. 48*
Abadan: On N coast of Persian G. *Pp. 51, 56*
Abana: R in W Syria. *P. 1*
Abbasid Empire. *Pp. 14, 15*
Abbeville: N France, on Somme R. *P. 54*
Abel: Palestine, N of Sea of Galilee. *P. 1*
Aberdeen: NE Scotland. *Pp. 16, 21, 33, 34*
Aberystwyth: W Wales, on St. George's Channel. *P. 54*
Abydos: Anatolia, on the Hellespont. *P. 7*
Abyssinia *see* Ethiopia
Acapulco: S of Mexico City on Pacific. *P. 26*
Acarnania: W Greece, on Ionian Sea. *Pp. 5a, 7*
Acco *see* Acre
Accra: W Africa, on G of Guinea. *P. 56*
Achaea: N part of Peloponnesus, Greece. *P.7 Inset*
Achaia, Principality of. *P. 20 Inset*
Achaia, Proconsulate of. *P. 11*
Acragas: SW Sicily. *P. 4*
Acre (Acco): W of Sea of Galilee, on Mediterranean Sea. *Pp 1, 2, 20*
Acre, Gulf of: W of Sea of Galilee. *P. 1*
Actium: W Greece, on Ionian Sea. *Pp. 7, 8*
Adda: R in N Italy, from L Como to Po R. *P.49*
Addis Ababa: Cen. Ethiopia (Abyssinia). *Pp. 56, 62*
Aden (*1514*): On SW coast of Arabia. *Pp. 25, 27, 31, 47, 56, 62*
Aden, Gulf of: Between S coast of Arabia & E Africa. *Pp 56, 62*
Aden Protectorate: S Arabia. *Pp. 56, 62*
Adige: R in NE Italy. *Pp. 22, 32, 42, 49*
Adrianople (Edirne) (*battle 378*): Thrace, NW Turkey in Europe. *Pp. 9, 11, 20, 23, 35, 43*
Adrianopolis *see* Adrianople *P. 7*
Adriatic Sea: E of Italy. *Pp. 6, 8, 23, 32, 35, 43, 44, 49, 50*
Aduwa: N Ethiopia, S of Asmara. *P. 56*
Aegean Sea: Arm of Mediterranean Sea. *Pp. 4a, 5a, 7, 35, 43*
Aegina: I, SE of Greece. *Pp. 4a, 5a*
Aegina, Gulf of *see* Saronic Gulf
Aenus *see* Ainos
Aeolis: Reg, NW Anatolia. *P. 4a*
Aetolia: Reg, cen. Greece. *Pp. 4, 7*
Afghanistan: W cen. Asia. *Pp. 51, 62*
Africa. *Pp. 8, 27, 56, 57*
Africa, Diocese of. *P. 10*
Africa, Proconsulate of. *P. 10*
Agadir: On SW coast of Morocco. *P. 56*
Agincourt (*battle 1415*): France, N of Somme R. *P. 16*
Agra: N India, on Jumna R. *P. 25*
Agram (Zagreb): on upper Sava R. *Pp. 42, 44*
Agulhas, Cape: S Africa, SE of Cape of Good Hope. *P. 27*
Ahmadabad (Ahmedabad): W India. *P. 62*
Ai: Palestine, NW of Dead Sea. *P. 1*
Ainos (Aenus, Enez, Enos): S Thrace, near mouth of Hebrus R. *P. 7*
Aix-la-Chapelle (Aachen): W Germany, between Meuse R & Rhine R. *Pp.14, 16*
Akkad: Reg. near Babylon in valley of Tigris R & Euphrates R. *P. 3*
Akmolinsk: NW of L Balkhash. *P. 58*
Alalia *see* Aleria
Alamani, The. *Pp. 12, 13*
Alamans, The. *P. 12*
Alarcos (*battle 1195*): S Spain. *P. 24*
Alaska: NW portion of N America. *Pp. 47, 53*
Albania: W Balkan penin. on Adriatic Sea. *Pp. 43, 49, 50, 58, 60, 61*
Albert Canal: NE Belgium, from Liége to Antwerp. *P. 54*
Albert, Lake: Between Uganda & Belgian Congo. *P. 56*
Albertville: Belgian Congo, W of L Tanganyika. *P. 56*
Albi: S France, NE of Toulouse. *P. 17*
Aldermaston: S cen. England. *P. 54*
Alençon: SW of Paris, on tributary of Loire R. *P. 55*
Aleppo: N Syria. *P. 20*
Aleria (Alalia): E Corsica. *P.4*
Aleutian Is.: Extending 1,200 miles W from S Alaska. *P. 52*
Alexandretta: NW Syria on Mediterranean Sea. *P. 20*
Alexandria: W Nile delta. *Pp. 4, 9, 11, 14, 20, 27, 50, 56, 64*
Alexandria Arachosiorum (Kandahar): On Alexander's route, SW of Hindu Kush. *P.5*
Alexandria Ariorum (Artacoana): On Alexander's route, between Caspian Sea & Hindu Kush. *P. 5*

Algeria: Reg, N Africa. *P. 47, 49, 50, 56, 60, 61*
Algiers: N Africa. *Pp. 49, 50, 56*
Algoa Bay: SE Africa. *P. 57*
Alicante: On SE coast of Spain. *P. 24*
Allahabad: NW cen. India on Ganges R. *P. 62*
Al-Madina *see* Medina
Almeria: On S coast of Spain, E of Gibraltar. *P. 24*
Alonae: On E coast of Spain. *P. 4*
Alpine passes: *see various maps of South cen. Europe*
Alps: Mountain system of S Europe. *Pp. 6, 8, 14, 17, 22, 32, 34, 42, 55*
Alsace-Lorraine: Territ. ceded to Germany in 1871. *P. 44*
Altai Mts: Mongolia. *P. 59*
Aluta: Tributary of lower Danube R. *P. 43*
Amalfi: On SW coast of Italy. *Pp. 14, 23*
Amazon: R in S America, flowing E from Andes Mts to Atlantic. *Pp. 26, 30*
Amboina: I of Moluccas, off SE Asia. *P. 25*
Ambracian Gulf: W coast of Greece. *P. 4a*
Amiens: N France, on Somme R. *Pp. 18, 22, 48, 54*
Amman (Rabbath-ammon): Jordan. *P. 58*
Ammon: Reg. E of Canaan, NE of Dead Sea. *P. 1 Inset, 2*
Amoy (Szeming): SE China. *P. 63*
Amphipolis: E Macedonia. *Pp. 5a, 7*
Amritsar: E Punjab, India. *P. 62*
Amsterdam: W Netherlands. *Pp. 22, 34, 42, 48, 50, 54, 58*
Amu Darya: R in cen. & W Asia. *P. 62*
Amur: R in Manchuria & USSR, flowing into Sea of Okhotsk. *P. 59*
Anactorium: W Greece. *P. 5a*
Anagni: Cen. Italy, E of Rome. *P. 19*
Anatolia: W penin. of Asia, between Black Sea & Mediterranean Sea. *See Front Endpaper.*
Ancona: On E coast of cen. Italy. *Pp. 19, 23, 32, 43, 49*
Ancyra *see* Ankara
Andalsnes: SW Norway. *P. 50*
Andaman Is: India, two groups of islands in the B of Bengal. *P. 63*
Andorra: On S slope of Pyrenees, between France & Spain. *P. 55*
Andros: I, E of Athens. *P. 20*
Angaur: S Palau Is, Pacific. *P. 52*
Angers: W France, on tributary of Loire R. *Pp. 17, 55*
Angles, The. *P. 12*
Anglesey: I & Co, NW England. *Pp. 33, 54*
Anglo-Egyptian Sudan: NE Africa, S of Egypt. *P. 47*
Anglo-Saxons, The. *P. 14*
Angola: SW Africa. *Pp. 27, 31, 47, 57*
Angoulême: Reg. & city, W France. *Pp. 17, 55*
Anjou: Reg. NW France, N of Loire R. *P. 17*
Ankara (Ancyra): W cen. Turkey in Asia. *Pp. 51, 58*
Annan: SW China, on Burma Road. *P. 63*
Annapolis: Nova Scotia. *P. 38*
Annobón: I in G of Guinea, SW of São Tomé. *Pp. 27, 56*
Antigua: I in Lesser Antilles, N of S America. *P. 38*
Anti-Lebanon Range: Syria. *P. 2*
Antilles, Lesser: Island chain, N of S America. *P. 38*
Antioch: Reg. in ancient Syria. *P. 20*
Antioch: Syria. *Pp. 9, 11, 15, 20*
Antivari (Bar): On NE coast of Adriatic Sea. *P. 43*
Antoninus' Wall: Roman wall in Scotland. *P. 8*
Antwerp: N Belgium, at mouth of Scheldt R. *Pp. 16, 18, 21, 22, 42, 48, 50, 54*
Anzio: Italy, S of Rome. *P. 50*
Aosta: NW Italy on tributary of Po R. *P. 32*
Apennines: Mts, cen. Italy. *Pp. 6, 8, 32*
Apollonia (Sozopol): E Thrace, on coast of Black Sea. *Pp. 4, 9*
Appian Way: Roman Road, SE from Rome. *Pp. 6, 8*
Apulia: Reg, SE Italy. *P. 19*
Aqaba: SW Jordan. *P. 56*
Aqaba, Gulf of: NE extension Red Sea. *Pp. 1, 2*
Aquileia: Extreme N end of Adriatic Sea. *Pp. 8, 10, 12, 23*
Aquitaine: Reg, SW France. *Pp. 14 Inset, 17*
Aquitania: Reg, SW Gaul. *P. 8*
Arabah: Reg, S from Dead Sea to G of Aqaba. *P. 2*
Arabia: Reg, SW Asia. *Pp. 9, 25*
Arabian Desert. *Pp. 1, 2, 56*
Arabian Sea: Indian O, between India & Arabia. *Pp. 5, 15, 25, 31, 62*

Aragon: Reg, NE Spain. *Pp. 24, 28*
Aral Sea: SW Russia. *Pp. 25, 27, 58, 62*
Aram: Reg, NE of Palestine. *Pp. 1 Inset, 2*
Aras: Tributary of Kura R, in Transcaucasia. *P. 45*
Arbela: E of Tigris R. *P. 5*
Arcadia: Cen. Peloponnesus, Greece. *P. 7 Inset*
Archangel: N Russia, on SE coast of White Sea. *Pp. 51, 58*
Arctic Ocean: N of the Arctic Circle. *P. 58*
Ardennes: Mts in SE Belgium. *P. 51 Inset*
Arezzo: N cen. Italy, SE of Florence. *P. 32*
Argentina. *P. 53*
Arginusae: Is, E Aegean Sea. *P. 5a*
Argolis: Reg, E Peloponnesus, Greece. *P. 7 Inset*
Argos: NE Peloponnesus, Greece. *P. 7 Inset*
Arles: SE France, on Rhône R. *Pp. 12, 13, 14, 17, 19*
Arles, Kingdom of. *Pp. 17, 19*
Armenia: Reg, W Asia, SE of Black Sea. *Pp. 5, 9, 20*
Armenian SSR: USSR, SE of Black Sea. *P. 58*
Arnhem: E Netherlands, on Rhine R. *Pp. 50, 51 Inset*
Arno: R in cen. Italy. *Pp. 22, 32, 49*
Arnon: R flowing into Dead Sea. *Pp. 1, 2*
Arras: N France, NE of mouth of Somme R. *Pp. 22, 54*
Arromanches: NW France, on N coast of Normandy. *P. 55*
Arsuf: Palestine, on coast N of Jaffa. *P. 20*
Arta: NW Greece. *P. 43*
Artacoana *see* Alexandria Ariorum
Artemisium: N Euboea, on Aegean Sea. *P. 4a*
Artois: Reg, N France, between Somme R & Scheldt R. *P. 16*
Arundel: S England. *P. 16*
Arvad (Arwad): On coast of Syria, W of Orontes R. *P. 1*
Ascalon (Ashkelon): On coast of Palestine. *P. 20*
Ashdod (Azotus): Palestine, S of Joppa. *P. 1*
Ashkelon (Ascalon): On coast of Palestine. *P. 1*
Ashkhabad: USSR, SE of Caspian Sea. *P. 58*
Ashtaroth: E of Sea of Galilee. *P. 1*
Asia. *P. 9*
Asia, Diocese of. *P. 11*
Asia, Proconsulate of. *P. 11*
Asia Minor: W penin. of Asia. *Pp. 35, 43*
Asmara: NE Africa, near Red Sea. *Pp. 56, 62*
Assam: Asia, reg. NE of Burma. *P. 63*
Assassins: N Syria, near Antioch. *P. 20*
Asshur (Assur): On Tigris R. *P. 3*
Assisi: Cen. Italy. *P. 32*
Assur *see* Asshur
Assuan: Egypt, on Nile R. *P. 27*
Assyria: E of Tigris R. *Pp. 3, 5*
Assyrian Empire. *P. 3*
Asti: NW Italy, on tributary of Po R. *P. 32*
Astin Tagh: Mts in cen. Asia, N Tibet, S Sinkiang. *P. 63*
Astrakhan: Reg. & city, S Russia. *P. 45*
Asturias, Kingdom of: NW Spain. *P. 14*
Asunción: Paraguay. *Pp. 26, 30*
Aswan: SE Egypt, on Nile R. *P. 56*
Atbara: On Nile R, S of Nubian Desert. *P. 56*
Athenian Empire: E cen. Greece & Euboea. *P. 5a*
Athens: Greece, near Saronic G. *Pp. 4, 5a, 7, 9, 11, 12, 14, 20, 35, 43, 50, 56, 58*
Athens, Allies of. *P. 5a*
Athens, Duchy of Thebes and: Reg, E Greece. *P. 20 Inset*
Athos, Mt: NE Greece. *Pp. 4a, 7*
Atlantic Ocean. *Pp. 26, 38, 39, 46, 56, 57*
Atlas Mts: NW & N Africa. *P. 56*
Attica: Reg, E Greece. *P. 7 Inset*
Attu: I, W end of Aleutian Is, SW Alaska. *P. 52*
Augsburg: Germany, S of upper Danube R. *Pp. 8, 18, 48*
Auschwitz (Oświęcim): S Poland. *P. 50*
Australia. *Pp. 47, 52, 57 Inset*
Austrasia: Reg. of Merovingian Franks. *P. 14 Inset*
Austria: Cen. Europe. *Pp. 18, 37, 44, 48, 50, 58, 60, 61*
Austria, Archduchy of. *P. 34*
Austria, Empire of. *P. 40*
Austria-Hungary. *Pp. 42, 60*
Auxerre: France, NW Burgundy. *P. 17*
Avaris: On Mediterranean coast of Egypt. *P. 2*
Avars, The. *Pp. 13, 14*
Avignon: SE France, on Rhône R. *Pp. 17, 19, 22, 24, 32, 55*
Avila: Cen. Spain. *P. 24*
Avon: R in cen. England. *Pp. 16, 33*
Avranches: France, on W coast of Normandy. *P. 55*
Ayr: on W coast of Scotland. *Pp. 33, 54*
Ayyubids, Dominion of the. *P. 20 Inset*

Azerbaijan SSR: Reg. in USSR, E Transcaucasia. *P. 58*

Azores: Is, N Atlantic, off Portugal. *Pp. 26, 30, 39*

Azotus *see* Ashdod

Azov: Russia, SW Rostov. *P. 45*

Azov, Sea of: NE of Crimea. *P. 45*

Bab el Mandeb: Strait between SW Arabia & Africa, uniting Red Sea & G of Aden. *Pp. 56, 62*

Babylon: On Euphrates R. *Pp. 3, 5*

Babylonia: Reg. SW Asia, lower Euphrates R. *Pp. 3, 5*

Bactra: SW Asia, S of Oxus R. *P. 5*

Bactria: Reg. SW Asia, near Oxus R. *P. 5*

Baden: Reg. in Austria, SW of Vienna. *P. 44*

Baden, Grand Duchy of: S Germany. *Pp. 40, 41*

Baetica: Reg, S Spain. *P. 8*

Baffin Bay: N Atlantic, W of Greenland. *Pp. 26, 30*

Baghdad: Iraq, on Tigris R. *Pp. 15, 27, 51, 56, 58, 62*

Baikal, Lake: USSR, S Siberia. *P. 59*

Baku: On W coast of Caspian Sea. *Pp. 45, 51, 58*

Balaton, Lake: Between Danube R & Drava R. *P. 42*

Balearic Is.: W Mediterranean. *Pp. 8, 24*

Bali: I off SE Asia, E of Java. *P. 52*

Balikh: R flowing S into Euphrates R. *P. 2*

Balkan Mts: S of lower Danube R. *Pp. 7, 35, 43*

Balkhash, Lake: S. USSR, in Kazakh SSR. *Pp. 58, 62*

Baltic Sea: N Europe. *Pp. 21, 23, 34, 42, 44, 45, 48, 50, 58*

Baluchistan: Reg, Pakistan. *P. 62*

Bamberg: E Franconia, on Main R. *P. 18*

Banat: Reg, S cen. Hungary. *P. 43*

Banat of Temesvar: E of Tisza R, above confluence with Danube R. *P. 35*

Banda Is: S cen. Moluccas. *P. 25*

Bandar Abbas: S Iran, on Persian G. *P. 56*

Bangkok: S Thailand (Siam). *Pp. 63, 64*

Bangor: On NW coast of Wales. *P. 54*

Bangweulu, Lake: Africa, N Rhodesia. *P. 57*

Bar *see* Antivari

Barbados: I, Lesser Antilles, West Indies. *P. 38*

Barcelona: On E coast of Spain. *Pp. 14, 17, 22, 24, 55, 64*

Barents Sea: N of Norway & USSR. *P. 58*

Bari: SE Italy, on Adriatic Sea. *Pp. 19, 32, 43*

Barnaul: USSR, on upper Ob R. *P. 59*

Barrow: On NW coast of England. *P. 54*

Barrow: R in SE Ireland. *P. 54*

Basle (Basel): W Switzerland on Rhine R. *Pp. 17, 22, 48, 55*

Basques, The. *Pp. 12, 13*

Basra: On Euphrates R, near head of Persian G. *P. 51*

Bassano: NE Italy, NW of Venice. *P. 32*

Bastogne: SE Belgium, Ardennes Mts. *P. 51 Inset*

Basutoland: Reg, S Africa. *P. 57*

Bataan: Philippine Is, penin. W Luzon. *P. 52*

Bataisk: Russia, near mouth of Don R. *P. 51*

Bath: SW England. *P. 33*

Batum: Russia, on SE coast of Black Sea. *Pp. 45, 51*

Batumi: USSR, on SE coast of Black Sea. *P. 58*

Bavaria: Reg. S Germany. *Pp. 14 Inset, 18, 28, 29, 36, 44*

Bavaria, Duchy of. *P. 34*

Bavaria, Kingdom of. *Pp. 40, 41*

Bavarians, The. *P. 13*

Bayeux: N Normandy. *P. 17*

Bayonne: On SW coast of France. *Pp. 17, 55*

Béarn: Reg, SW France. *P. 17*

Beaucaire: S France, on Rhône R. *P. 22*

Beauvais: N France, between Somme R & Seine R. *Pp. 17, 22, 55*

Bechuanaland: Reg, S Africa. *Pp. 47, 57*

Bedford: Cen. England. *P. 16*

Bedfordshire: Co in cen. England. *P. 33*

Beersheba (Bires Saba): S Palestine. *Pp. 1, 2*

Beira: On E coast of Mozambique. *P. 57*

Beirut: On E Mediterranean coast. *Pp. 20, 51, 58*

Belfast: On coast of N Ireland. *Pp. 50, 54*

Belfort: NE France, between Saône R & Rhine R. *P. 55*

Belgica: Reg, NE Gallia (Gaul). *P. 8*

Belgium: NW Europe. *Pp. 42, 48, 54, 58, 60, 61*

Belgrade: On confluence of Danube R & Sava R. *Pp. 10, 23, 35, 43, 44, 49, 50, 58*

Belle Ile: I in Bay of Biscay. *P. 55*

Belorussian SSR: W. USSR. *P. 58*

Belsen: NW Germany, W of Elbe R. *P. 50*

Benares: N India, on Ganges R. *P. 62*

Benevento: S Italy, NE of Naples. *Pp. 14, 19, 32, 49*

Benevento, Duchy of. *P. 14*

Beneventum: S Italy, near Neapolis (Naples). *P. 6*

Bengal: Reg, NE India. *Pp. 25, 63*

Bengal, Bay of: Indian O. *Pp. 25, 31, 52, 63*

Benghazi: On coast of N Africa. *Pp. 50, 56*

Benguela: Africa, on coast of Angola. *P. 57*

Beni Hasan: Egypt, on Nile R. *P. 2*

Benin, Bight of: W Africa, N section of G of Guinea. *P. 56*

Benue: R in Nigeria. *P. 56*

Berchtesgaden: S Germany, near Austrian border. *P. 50*

Berg, Grand Duchy of: Germany, on Rhine R, E of Cologne. *P. 40*

Bergama *see* Pergamum

Bergamo: N Italy, NE of Milan. *P. 32*

Bergen: On SW coast of Norway. *P. 21*

Bering Sea: N of Pacific. *P. 59*

Berkshire: Co, S England. *P. 33*

Berlin: Germany, on Spree R, between Elbe R & Oder R. *Pp. 34, 42, 44, 48, 50, 58, 64*

Bermuda: Is in W Atlantic. *Pp. 26, 38*

Bern: Switzerland, SW of Zürich. *Pp. 17, 42, 48, 50, 55, 58*

Berry: Reg, cen. France. *P. 17*

Berwick: N England, close to Scottish border. *Pp. 16, 21, 33, 54*

Besançon: E France, on tributary of Saône R. *Pp. 17, 18, 22, 55*

Besika Bay: Dardanelles, on Aegean Sea. *P. 43*

Bessarabia: Reg, SE Europe, between Dniester R & Prut R. *Pp. 43, 45*

Bethel: Palestine, near Jerusalem. *P. 1*

Bethlehem: Palestine, SW of Jerusalem. *Pp. 1, 20*

Beth-shemesh: Palestine, W of Jerusalem. *P. 1*

Bhutan: Reg, NE India. *P. 63*

Biafra, Bight of: W Africa, E section of G of Guinea. *P. 56*

Białystok: NE Poland. *P. 58*

Bilbao: N Spain. *P. 55*

Bingen: W Germany, on Rhine R. *P. 51 Inset*

Bires Saba *see* Beersheba

Birkenhead: On NW coast of England near Welsh border. *P. 54*

Birmingham: Cen. England. *Pp. 54, 64*

Birobidzhan: SE. USSR, N & W of Amur R. *P. 59*

Biscay, Bay of: Atlantic O, on W coast of France & N Coast of Spain. *Pp. 17, 22, 50, 55*

Bismarck Archipelago: Is, in W Pacific, NE of New Guinea. *P. 52*

Bithynia: Reg, in NW Anatolia. *Pp. 4, 7, 9*

Bitolj (Monastir): Between Pindus Mts & Vardar R. *P. 43*

Bizerte: N Africa, on coast of Tunisia. *Pp. 50, 56*

Black Forest: Germany, E of Rhine R. *P. 51 Inset*

Blackpool: On NW coast of England. *P. 54*

Black Sea (Euxine Sea). *Pp. 4, 7, 9, 11, 14, 23, 27, 35, 45, 51, 58*

Blanc, Cape: NW coast of Africa. *P. 56*

Blanco, Cape: W coast of Africa. *P. 26*

Blantyre: Fed. of Rhodesia & Nyasaland, S of Nyasa. *P. 57*

Bloemfontein: Cen. S Africa. *P. 57*

Blois: N cen. France, on tributary of Loire R. *Pp. 17, 55*

Blue Nile: Sudan, tributary of Nile R. *Pp. 56, 62*

Bobbio: N Italy, NE of Genoa. *P. 14*

Bodrum *see* Halicarnassus

Boeotia: Reg, in Greece, NW of Athens. *Pp. 4a, 7, 7 Inset*

Bogotá: NW. S America. *Pp. 26, 30*

Bohemia: Reg. cen. Europe. *Pp. 18, 28, 42, 44*

Bohemia, Kingdom of. *P. 34*

Bojador, Cape: NW Africa. *Pp. 26, 56*

Bokhara *see* Bukhara

Bolan Pass: N Baluchistan. *P. 62*

Bolivia. *P. 53*

Bologna (Bononia): N Italy. *Pp. 10, 19, 23, 32, 42, 49*

Bolsena, Lake: Italy, W of Tiber R. *P. 32*

Bolzano: N Italy, NW of Venice. *P. 48*

Bombay: On W coast of India. *Pp. 25, 27, 31, 62, 64*

Bon, Cape: N Africa, coast of Tunisia. *Pp. 50, 56*

Bône: On coast of Algeria. *P. 50*

Bonin Islands: W Pacific O, near Japan. *P. 52*

Bonn: W Germany, on Rhine R. *Pp. 10, 48, 51 Inset, 54, 58*

Bononia (Bologna): N Italy. *P. 6*

Bordeaux: France, on lower Garonne R. *Pp. 10, 13, 17, 22, 39, 50, 55*

Borneo: I in S China Sea. *Pp. 25, 47, 52, 63*

Borneo, North: portion of Borneo I. *P. 63*

Bornholm: I. E of Denmark. *P. 18*

Borodino: Cen. Russia, W of Moscow. *P. 45*

Bosnia: Reg. hinterland of NE Adriatic coast. *Pp. 43, 44*

Bosporus: Narrow strait between Europe & Asia, connecting Sea of Marmora with Black Sea. *Pp. 4a, 5a, 7, 43*

Boston: E England. *Pp. 21, 22, 26*

Boston: USA, harbor in E Massachusetts. *P. 38*

Bothnia, Gulf of: N Baltic Sea, between Sweden & Finland. *P. 45*

Bougie: N Africa. *P. 22*

Boulogne: N France, on English Channel. *Pp 16, 54*

Bourges: Cen. France. *Pp. 17, 55*

Bournemouth: on S coast of England. *P. 54*

Bouvines (*battle 1214*): NE France. *Pp. 16, 18*

Bozrah (El Buseira): SW Syria. *Pp. 1, 2*

Bradford: N cen. England. *Pp. 33, 54*

Brahmaputra: R in NE India. *P. 63*

Brandenburg: NE cen. Germany. *Pp. 18, 21, 28*

Brandenburg, Margravate of. *P. 18*

Bratislava (Pressburg): S cen. Czechoslovakia. *P. 48*

Braunschweig *see* Brunswick

Brazil. *P. 53*

Brazzaville: W Africa, on Congo R. *P. 56*

Brecknockshire: Co in Wales. *P. 33*

Bremen: N Germany, on Weser R. *Pp. 16, 18, 21, 22, 34, 42, 48, 50, 54*

Bremen, Duchy of. *P. 34*

Bremerhaven: On N coast of Germany. *P. 54*

Brenner: Pass over the Alps. *Pp. 23, 32*

Brentford (*battle 1642*): W of London. *P. 33*

Brescia: N Italy, E of Milan. *Pp. 32, 49*

Breslau (Wrocław): SE Germany, on Oder R. *Pp. 23, 42, 48, 50*

Brest: NW France, on Atlantic. *Pp. 22, 50, 55*

Brest Litovsk: W Russia, on Bug R. *Pp. 45, 58*

Brétigny: N cen. France. *P. 17*

Bridgwater: SW England. *P. 33*

Brighton: On S coast of England. *P. 54*

Brindisi (Brundisium): Italy, on S coast of Adriatic Sea. *Pp. 10, 43*

Bristol: SW England. *Pp. 16, 21, 22, 27, 33, 39, 54*

Bristol Channel: Arm of Atlantic O, between S Wales & SW England. *P. 54*

Britain *see* Great Britain

Britain, Diocese of. *P. 10*

Britannia: Roman Britain. *P. 8*

Brittany: Reg. of NW France. *P. 17*

Brno (Brünn): Cen. Czechoslovakia. *P. 48*

Broken Hill: Fed. of Rhodesia & Nyasaland. *P. 57*

Bruges: NW Belgium. *Pp. 16, 18, 21, 22*

Brundisium (Brindisi): Italy, on S coast of Adriatic Sea. *P. 6, 8*

Brunei: Reg. in Borneo. *P. 63*

Brünn (Brno): N of Vienna. *Pp. 42, 44*

Brunswick (Braunschweig): Cen. Germany, on Weser R. *Pp. 21, 22, 34*

Brussels: Cen. Belgium. *Pp. 16, 42, 48, 50, 54, 58, 64*

Bruttium (Calabria): Reg. in S Italy. *P. 6*

Bryansk: Cen. Russia, SW of Moscow. *P. 51*

Bucharest: SE Romania. *Pp. 35, 43, 50, 58, 64*

Buchenwald: Cen. Germany, W of upper Elbe R. *P. 50*

Buckinghamshire: Co, S cen. England. *P. 33*

Buda: Cen. Hungary, on Danube R. *Pp. 23, 34*

Budapest: Hungary, on Danube R. *Pp. 42, 44, 48, 50, 58, 64*

Buea: Africa, SE Nigeria. *P. 56*

Buenos Aires: Argentina. *Pp. 26, 64*

Bug: R in Russia, flowing into Black Sea. *Pp. 9, 23, 42, 45, 48, 58*

Bukhara (Bokhara): USSR, in Uzbek SSR, E of Caspian Sea. *Pp. 58, 62*

Bukovina: Reg, E cen. Europe. *Pp. 43, 44*

Bulawayo: Fed. of Rhodesia & Nyasaland. *P. 57*

Bulgaria: SE Europe. *Pp. 20 Inset, 35, 43, 45, 50, 58, 60, 61*

Bulgaria, Khanate of. *P. 14*

Buna: On NE coast of New Guinea. *P. 52*

Burgas: S of Balkan Mts, on coast of Black Sea. *P. 43*

Burgos: Spain, S of upper Ebro R. *Pp. 17, 55*

Burgundians, The. *Pp. 12, 13*

Burgundy: Reg. in E France. *Pp. 14 Inset, 17, 18*

Burgundy, County of. *P. 17*

Burgundy, Duchy of. *P. 17*

Burma: SE Asia. *Pp. 52, 57 Inset, 63*

Burma Road: Motor highway from Lashio to Chungking. *Pp. 52, 63*

Burnley: NW England. *P. 54*

Bury: E. England. *P. 16*
Byblos (Jubayl): W of Lebanon Mts. *Pp. 1, 2*
Byzantine Empire. *Pp. 14, 15, 19, 20*
Byzantium (Istanbul, Constantinople): On Bosporus. *Pp. 4, 5a, 7, 9*

Cabinda: W Africa, N of Congo R. *Pp. 27, 56*
Cabul: Palestine, SE of Acre. *P. 1*
Cádiz (Gades): On SW coast of Spain. *Pp. 10, 24*
Caen: NW France. *Pp. 17, 50, 55*
Caernarvon: NW Wales. *P. 16*
Caernarvonshire: Co, NW Wales. *P. 33*
Caesarea: On coast of Kingdom of Jerusalem. *P. 20*
Cahors: S cen. France. *Pp. 17, 22*
Cairo: Egypt, on Nile R. *Pp. 14, 20, 27, 51, 56, 62, 64*
Cairo, Caliphate of. *P. 20*
Calabar: Africa, E of Niger R. *P. 56*
Calabria (Bruttium): Reg. of S Italy. *P. 19*
Calais: On N coast of France. *Pp. 16, 22, 50, 54*
Calatrava: Cen. Spain. *P. 24*
Calcutta: India, SW Bengal. *Pp. 25, 27, 31, 52, 63, 64*
Calder Hall: NW England, E of I of Man. *P. 54*
Calicut: India, on Malabar Coast. *Pp. 27, 63*
Calpe: Coast of S Spain. *P. 4*
Calycadnus: R in Anatolia. *P. 20*
Cambodia: Reg, SE Indo-China. *P. 63*
Cambrai: N France, on Scheldt R. *P. 17*
Cambridge: E England. *Pp. 16, 33, 54*
Cambridgeshire: Co, E England. *P. 33*
Cameroons: Reg, W Africa, on G of Guinea. *P. 47*
Cameroon Mt: W Africa. *P. 56*
Campania: Reg, S Italy. *P. 6*
Canaan: Reg. between Jordan R & Mediterranean Sea. *P. 2*
Canada: N America. *Pp. 46, 53*
Canary Is: Atlantic O, NW of Africa. *Pp. 26, 30, 56*
Cannae (*battle 216 B.C.*): SE Italy. *Pp. 6, 8*
Cannes: On SE coast of France. *P. 55*
Canossa: N Italy. *P. 19*
Canterbury: SE England. *Pp. 14, 16, 33, 54*
Canton: SE China. *Pp. 25, 31, 63, 64*
Cape Breton I: E Canada. *P. 38*
Capes are listed under their names
Cape Town: On SW coast of S Africa. *P. 57*
Cape Verde Is: In Atlantic O, W of Africa. *Pp. 26, 56*
Cappadocia: Reg. of E Anatolia. *Pp. 5, 9*
Caprivi Strip: NE corner of SW Africa. *P. 57*
Capua (Casilinum): S Italy, N of Naples. *Pp. 19, 32*
Carcassonne: S France. *Pp. 17, 55*
Carchemish: Syria, on Euphrates R. *P. 2*
Cardiff: On SE coast of Wales. *P. 54*
Cardigan: On W coast of Wales. *P. 54*
Cardiganshire: Co, W Wales. *P. 33*
Caria: Reg, SW Anatolia, on Aegean Sea. *Pp. 4, 7*
Caribbean Sea: Arm of Atlantic O, NW of S America. *Pp. 26, 38, 53*
Carinthia: Reg. in Austria. *Pp. 18, 34, 42*
Carisbrooke: I of Wight, S England *P. 33*
Carlisle: NW England. *Pp. 10, 16, 33*
Carlsbad (Karlovy Vary): Czechoslovakia, N of Prague. *P. 48*
Carmania: Reg, S of Plateau of Iran. *P. 5*
Carmarthenshire: Co, S Wales. *P. 33*
Carmel, Mt: Palestine, SE of G of Acre. *P. 1*
Carniola: Reg, NE of Adriatic Sea. *Pp. 34, 42*
Caroline Is: Archipelago in W Pacific, SE of Philippine Is. *Pp. 47, 52*
Carolingian Empire: W cen. Europe. *P. 14*
Carpathian Mts: E cen. Europe. *Pp. 35, 43*
Cartagena (New Carthage): On S coast of Spain. *Pp. 22, 24, 26*
Carthage (Tunis): N Africa, W of Sicily. *Pp. 4, 6, 8, 12, 13, 14*
Casablanca: NW Africa, on W coast of Morocco. *Pp. 50, 56*
Casilinum (Capua): S Italy, N of Neapolis (Naples). *P. 6*
Caspian Sea: E of Black Sea. *Pp. 3, 5, 9, 11, 15, 25, 27, 45, 51, 58*

Cassino: Cen. Italy, SE of Rome. *P. 50*
Castelnuovo: NW Italy, SE of Genoa. *P. 32*
Castile: Reg, cen. Spain. *P. 28*
Castile, Kingdom of Léon and. *P. 24*
Castra Regina (Ratisbon) *see* Regensburg
Catana (Catania): E Sicily. *P. 6*
Cattaro: On NE coast of Adriatic Sea. *P. 43*
Caucasus Mts: Between Black Sea & Caspian Sea. *Pp. 45, 51, 58*
Cauvery: R in India, S of Madras. *P. 62*
Celebes: Is. E of Borneo, S of Philippine Is. *Pp. 52, 63*
Celebes Sea: W Pacific, S of Philippine Is. *P. 63*
Celts, The. *Pp. 12, 13, 14*
Cerdagne: Reg, NE Spain. *P. 24*
Cetinje: Montenegro, on coast of Adriatic Sea. *P. 43*
Ceuta: NW Morocco, on Strait of Gibraltar. *Pp. 22, 24, 27, 30*
Ceylon: I in Indian O, S of India. *Pp. 25, 62*
Chad, Lake: NW cen. Africa. *P. 56*
Chaeronea: E cen. Greece, SE of Mt Parnassus. *P. 7 Inset*
Chalcedon: Anatolia, across Bosporus from Byzantium (Constantinople). *Pp. 5a, 7, 14*
Chalcidice: Penin. of E Macedonia, NE Greece. *Pp. 4, 5a*
Chalcis (Negropont): Greece, on W coast of Euboea. *Pp. 4, 7*
Châlons-sur-Marne: NE France. *Pp. 17, 22, 55*
Chalon-sur-Saône: E France. *P. 55*
Champagne: Reg, NE France. *Pp. 17, 18*
Chandernagor: India, W Bengal, N of Calcutta. *P. 63*
Changchun (Hsinking): S cen. Manchuria. *P. 63*
Changsha: SE cen. China. *P. 52*
Chang Tang *see* Tibetan Plateau
Channel Is: In English Channel. *P. 55*
Charleston: USA, South Carolina, on Atlantic. *P. 38*
Charolles: E cen. France, between Loire R & Saône R. *P. 55*
Chartres: N cen. France, SE of Paris. *Pp. 17, 22, 55*
Chartreuse, La Grande: In Kingdom of Arles. *P. 19*
Château-Thierry: N France, on Marne R. *P. 55*
Chatham: On SE coast of England, near mouth of Thames R. *P. 54*
Chelyabinsk: Cen. USSR, SE of Ural Mts. *P. 58*
Chemnitz: E cen. Germany, between Saale R & Elbe R. *P. 48*
Chengchow *see* Chenghsien
Chenghsien (Chengchow): E cen. China, on Hwang R. *P. 63*
Cherbourg: On NW coast of France. *Pp. 50, 55*
Chernigov: Cen. Russia, NE of Kiev. *P. 45*
Chersonese *see* Gallipoli
Chesapeake Bay: USA, inlet of Atlantic, between Virginia & Maryland. *P. 38*
Cheshire: Co, NW England. *P. 33*
Chester: NW England. *Pp. 10, 16, 54*
Chichester: Near S coast of England. *P. 16*
Chile. *P. 53*
China. *Pp. 25, 31, 52, 57 Inset, 59, 63*
China, Great Wall of: NE China. *P. 63*
China Sea: Part of Pacific, E & SE of China. *Pp. 25, 31, 52*
Chinnereth, Sea of *see* Galilee, Sea of
Chinon: NW cen. France, in lower valley of Loire R. *P. 17*
Chioggia: NE Italy, S of Venice. *P. 32*
Chios: I in the Aegean Sea. *Pp. 4, 5a, 7*
Chita: USSR, E of L Balkhash. *P. 59*
Chittagong: E Pakistan, near mouth of Ganges R. *P. 63*
Chkalov (Orenburg): USSR, in SW Ural Mts. *P. 58*
Chungking: S China, on Yangtze R. *Pp. 52, 63, 64*
Cilicia: Reg, SE Anatolia, along Mediterranean coast. *Pp. 2, 4*
Cirta: N Africa, W of Carthage. *P. 6*
Cisalpine Gaul. *Pp. 6, 8*
Citeaux: In Duchy of Burgundy. *P. 18*
Citium: On SE coast of Cyprus. *P. 4*
Civitavecchia: On coast of cen. Italy, N of Tiber R. *P. 32*
Clairvaux: NE France, in Duchy of Burgundy. *P. 18*
Clermont: France, in Massif Central. *Pp. 17, 18*
Clermont-Ferrand: France, in Massif Central. *P. 55*
Cluny: E France, in Duchy of Burgundy. *P. 18*
Clyde: R in S Scotland. *Pp. 33, 54*
Clydebank: SW Scotland, on Clyde R. *P. 54*
Cnossus: Near N coast of Crete. *P. 7*

Coblenz: W Germany, on Rhine R. *Pp. 48, 51 Inset, 54*
Cod, Cape: NE coast of USA. *P. 38*
Coimbra: Cen. Portugal. *P. 24*
Colchester: SE England, N of mouth of Thames R. *Pp. 16, 33, 54*
Colmar: E France, between upper Moselle R & Rhine R. *P. 55*
Cologne (Köln): W Germany, on Rhine R. *Pp. 10, 13, 14, 16, 18, 22, 34, 42, 44, 48, 51 Inset, 54*
Colombia. *P. 53*
Colombo: Ceylon. *Pp. 25, 62*
Como: N Italy, N of Milan. *P. 49*
Como, Lake: N Italy. *P. 32*
Comorin, Cape: S extremity of India. *P. 62*
Comoro Is: Indian O, NW of Madagascar. *Pp. 57, 62*
Compiègne: N France, on Oise R. *Pp. 17, 50, 55*
Conakry: W Africa, on coast of French Guinea. *P. 56*
Congo: R in W cen. Africa, flowing into S Atlantic. *Pp. 27, 31, 56*
Connaught: Reg, W Ireland. *P. 33*
Constance (Konstanz): S Germany, on L Constance. *Pp. 18, 32*
Constantine: NE Africa. *P. 56*
Constantinople (Istanbul, Byzantium): On Bosporus. *Pp. 11, 12, 13, 14, 20, 23, 27, 31, 35, 43, 45*
Constantsa: SE Romania, on Black Sea. *P. 43*
Conway: On N coast of Wales. *P. 16*
Copenhagen: E Denmark. *Pp. 18, 21, 42, 48, 50, 58, 64*
Cophas: On Alexander's route along coast of Arabian Sea. *P. 5*
Coquilhatville: Cen. Africa, NW Belgian Congo. *P. 56*
Coral Sea: NE of Australia. *P. 52*
Corcyra *see* Corfu
Cordova (Corduba): S Spain on Guadalquivir R. *Pp. 10, 14, 24*
Corfu (Corcyra): I in N Ionian Sea. *Pp. 14, 19, 23, 43*
Corinth: E cen. Greece. *Pp. 4, 5a, 7 Inset, 12*
Corinth, Gulf of: Inlet of Ionian Sea, W cen. Greece. *P. 7 Inset*
Corinth, Isthmus of: E cen. Greece, between Peloponnesus & Attica. *P. 4a*
Cork: On SW coast of Ireland. *P. 54*
Cornwall: Co, in extreme SW England. *P. 33*
Coromandel Coast: SE India. *P. 62*
Corregidor: I in Philippine Is. *P. 52*
Corsica: I in W Mediterranean Sea. *Pp. 6, 8, 19, 32, 49, 50, 61*
Corunna: On NW coast of Spain. *P. 55*
Cos: I in Mediterranean Sea, SW of Anatolia. *P. 50*
Costa Rica: S cen. America. *Pp. 26, 53*
Coucy: NE France, in valley of Oise R. *P. 17*
Courland: Reg, SE Baltic coast. *Pp. 21, 34, 45*
Courtrai *see* Kortrijk
Coventry: Cen. England. *Pp. 16, 50, 54*
Crac des Chevaliers: Crusader castle, in Tripolis. *P. 20*
Cracow (Kraków): S Poland, on Vistula R. *Pp. 18, 23, 34, 42, 44, 50*
Crécy (*battle 1346*): N France, in valley of Oise R. *P. 17*
Cremona: N Italy, on Po R. *Pp. 19, 32*
Crete: I in E Mediterranean Sea, SE of Greece. *Pp. 7, 9, 14, 23, 50, 56*
Crimea: Penin, S Russia, extending into Black Sea. *Pp. 4, 45, 58*
Croatia: SE Europe, reg, between Sava R & Adriatic Sea. *P. 34*
Croatia-Slavonia: Reg. of Austria-Hungary. *Pp. 43, 44*
Croton: On SE coast of Italy. *P. 4*
Crusader States. *P. 20 Inset*
Cuba: I in West Indies, S of Florida. *Pp. 26, 53*
Cumae: Italy, on coast W of Neapolis (Naples). *Pp. 4, 6, 8*
Cumberland: Co, NW England. *P. 33*
Cunaxa (*battle 401 B.C.*): Babylonia, E of Euphrates R. *P. 5*
Curaçao: I in Caribbean Sea. *P. 38*
Cyprus: I in E Mediterranean Sea. *Pp. 2, 4, 14, 20, 51, 56*
Cyprus, Kingdom of. *P. 20 Inset*
Cyrenaica: Reg, N Africa. *P. 9*
Cyrene: On NE coast of Africa. *Pp. 4, 9*
Cythera: I in Mediterranean Sea, near Peloponnesus. *P. 5a*
Cyzicus: Anatolia, on S shore of Sea of Marmora (Propontis). *P. 5a*
Czechoslovakia: E cen. Europe. *Pp. 48, 50, 58, 60, 61*
Czernowitz: N of Carpathian Mts, on Prut R. *P. 43*

Dachau: S Germany, near Munich.   *P. 50*
Dacia: Reg, N of lower Danube R.   *Pp. 7, 9, 11*
Dacia, Diocese of.   *P. 10*
Dahomey: Reg, W Africa, N of G of Guinea.   *Pp. 27, 56*
Dairen: China, on S coast of Liaotung Penin.   *Pp. 59, 63*
Dakar: W Africa, S of Cape Vert.   *P. 56*
Dal: R in S cen. Sweden.   *P. 21*
Dalmatia: Reg, E of Adriatic Sea.   *Pp. 19, 43, 44*
Dalnaspidal (*battle 1654*): Cen. highlands, Scotland.   *P. 33*
Damascus (Esh Shâm): Syria.   *Pp. 1, 2, 9, 11, 15, 20, 51, 58*
Damascus, Emirate of.   *P. 20*
Damietta: N Egypt, on Nile Delta.   *Pp. 20, 56*
Dan: N of Sea of Galilee.   *P. 1*
Danes, The.   *P. 12*
Danube: R in cen. & SE Europe.   *Pp. 4, 7, 9, 11, 14, 23, 32, 35, 42, 43, 44, 48*
Danzig: N Poland, on G of Danzig, W of mouth of Vistula R.   *Pp. 21, 23, 34, 42, 44, 48, 50*
Danzig, Free Territory of.   *P. 48*
Dardanelles (Hellespont): Strait between Europe & Asia (Anatolia).   *Pp. 43, 50*
Dar es Salaam: On E coast of Africa.   *Pp. 56, 62*
Darien (*1509*): On N coast of Central America.   *P. 26*
Darmstadt: Hesse, E of Rhine R.   *P. 44*
Dauphiny: Reg, E of Rhône R.   *P. 17*
Davis Strait: W of Greenland.   *P. 26*
Dax: In extreme SW France.   *P. 17*
Dead Sea: Palestine.   *Pp. 1, 2, 20*
Debreczen: Austria-Hungary, E of Tisza R.   *P. 43*
Deccan: Reg, cen. India.   *P. 62*
Decelea: Greece, N of Athens.   *P. 5a*
Delagoa Bay: Africa, on SE coast of Mozambique.   *Pp. 27, 56*
Delhi: NW cen. India, on Jumna R.   *Pp. 25, 27, 62, 64*
Delos: I in S Aegean Sea.   *Pp. 4a, 5a*
Delphi: Cen. Greece, above G of Corinth.   *Pp. 4a, 7, 9*
Denbigh: Co, N Wales.   *P. 33*
Denmark: NW Europe.   *Pp. 16, 18, 21, 28, 29, 36, 37, 40, 41, 48, 50, 54, 58, 60, 61*
Derbent: Caucasus, on W coast of Caspian Sea.   *P. 45*
Derby: Cen. England, in valley of Trent R.   *Pp. 33, 54*
Derbyshire: Co, cen. England.   *P. 33*
Derna: N Africa, NE Libya.   *P. 50*
Detroit: USA.   *P. 64*
Devonshire: Co, SW England.   *P. 33*
Dibon (Dhiban): E of Dead Sea, N of Arnon R.   *Pp. 1, 2*
Dieppe: N France, on English Channel.   *Pp. 17, 50, 55*
Dijon: E France, in valley of Saône R.   *Pp. 17, 48, 55*
Dinant: S Belgium on Meuse R.   *Pp. 22, 54*
Diocese of the East.   *P. 11*
Djakarta: On Java I.   *Pp. 63, 64*
Djibouti: On E coast of Africa.   *Pp. 56, 62*
Dnepropetrovsk (Yekaterinoslav): E cen. Ukraine, USSR, on Dnieper R.   *Pp. 51, 58*
Dnieper: R in E Europe, W & SW Russia, flowing into Black Sea.   *Pp. 11, 14, 23, 45, 58*
Dniester: R in SE Europe, flowing into Black Sea.   *Pp. 9, 11, 23, 35, 43, 44, 45, 50, 58*
Dobruja: Reg, SE Romania.   *P. 43*
Dodecanese: Is, SE Aegean Sea.   *Pp. 60, 61*
Dominican Republic.   *P. 53*
Domrémy: NE France, on Meuse R.   *P. 17*
Don: R in SE Russia, flowing S into Sea of Azov.   *Pp. 45, 51, 58*
Donets: R in Russia, flowing into Don R.   *P. 45*
Donzère: S France, on lower Rhône R.   *P. 55*
Dor (Tantura): on coast of Palestine.   *P. 1*
Dordogne: R in SW France.   *Pp. 22, 55*
Dordrecht: NW of Antwerp.   *P. 21*
Dorpat (Tartu): Estonia, W of L Peipus.   *Pp. 21, 45*
Dorset: Co, S England.   *P. 33*
Dortmund: W Germany, in valley of Ruhr R.   *Pp. 48, 51 Inset, 54*
Dorylaeum: W Anatolia.   *P. 20*
Douai: N France, in valley of Scheldt R.   *Pp. 18, 54*
Douala: W Africa, on Bight of Biafra.   *P. 56*
Doubs: R in E France, tributary of Saône R.   *P. 48*
Dounreay: In extreme N of Scotland.   *P. 54*
Douro: R in W Spain & N cen. Portugal.   *Pp. 8, 24, 55*
Dover: SE England, on Strait of Dover.   *Pp. 16, 21, 22, 33, 50, 54*
Dover, Strait of: between England & France.   *Pp. 21, 54*

Drava: Tributary of Danube R.   *Pp. 8, 23, 34, 42, 44, 48*
Dresden: E Germany, on Elbe R.   *Pp. 18, 34, 42, 44, 48*
Dreux: N cen. France, SW of Paris.   *P. 17*
Drin: R in Albania.   *P. 43*
Drina: Tributary of Sava R.   *P. 43*
Drogheda: NE Ireland.   *Pp. 33, 54*
Dublin: On E coast of Ireland.   *Pp. 16, 33, 50, 54*
Dubrovnik *see* Ragusa
Duisburg: W Germany, on Rhine R.   *Pp. 48, 51 Inset, 54*
Dulcigno: On E cen. coast of Adriatic Sea, N of Durazzo.   *P. 43*
Dumfries: Scotland, on Solway Firth.   *P. 54*
Düna (W Dvina): R in W Russia.   *P. 45*
Dunbar: On SE coast of Scotland.   *Pp. 16, 33*
Dundee: E Scotland.   *Pp. 16, 33, 54*
Dunkirk: N France, on Strait of Dover.   *Pp. 50, 54*
Dura-Europos: On Euphrates R.   *P. 9*
Durance: R in SE France.   *Pp. 32, 49*
Durazzo (Durrës): On E cen. coast of Adriatic Sea.   *Pp. 14, 19, 32, 35, 43*
Durban: On E coast of S Africa.   *P. 57*
Durham: N England.   *Pp. 16, 33, 54*
Durham: Co, N England.   *P. 33*
Durrës *see* Durazzo
Durrës in Illyria *see* Epidamnus
Düsseldorf: W Germany, on Rhine R.   *Pp. 48, 51 Inset, 54*
Dutch East Indies: Malacca (*1641*) & Is from Sumatra to New Guinea.   *P. 47*
Dvina, North: R in NW Russia, flowing into White Sea.   *P. 45*
Dvina, West (Düna): R in W Russia, flowing into Baltic Sea.   *Pp. 21, 23, 45, 58*
Dzau Dzhikau *see* Vladikavkaz

East London: On coast of S Africa.   *P. 57*
East Pakistan: E of India.   *P. 63*
East Prussia: Reg, NE Germany, S of Baltic Sea.   *Pp. 45, 48, 50*
Eboracum *see* Eburacum
Ebro: R in NE Spain.   *Pp. 8, 10, 14, 24, 55*
Eburacum (York): Brittania.   *P. 8*
Ecbatana: W of Plateau of Iran.   *P. 5*
Ecuador.   *P. 53*
Edessa: Reg. & city, E of upper Euphrates R.   *P. 20*
Edgehill (*battle 1642*): S Warwickshire, cen. England.   *P. 33*
Edinburgh: SE Scotland, on S shore of Firth of Forth.   *Pp. 16, 33, 50, 54*
Edirne *see* Adrianople
Edom: Reg. S of Dead Sea.   *P. 1 Inset*
Edward, Lake: E cen. Africa, between NE Belgian Congo & SW Uganda.   *P. 56*
Egypt: In valley & delta of Nile R.   *Pp. 2, 4, 9, 25, 47, 50, 56, 62*
Egypt, Diocese of.   *P. 11*
Eifel: Mts NW of Moselle R.   *P. 51 Inset*
Eindhoven: W of Maas R.   *P. 51 Inset*
Eire *see* Ireland
Ekaterinburg *see* Yekaterinburg (Sverdlovsk)
Ekaterinodar *see* Yekaterinodar (Krasnodar)
Ekaterinoslav *see* Yekaterinoslav (Dnepropetrovsk)
Ekron: Palestine, W of Jerusalem.   *P. 1*
El Alamein: NW Egypt.   *P. 50*
Elam: Reg. E of lower Tigris R.   *P. 3*
Elbe: R in N Germany.   *Pp. 8, 10, 14, 21, 23, 34, 42, 44, 48, 50*
Elbing: At mouth of Vistula R.   *P. 21*
El Buseira *see* Bozrah
Eleusis: Greece, NW of Athens.   *P. 7 Inset.*
Elim: At head of G of Aqaba, S of Kingdom of Jerusalem.   *P. 20*
Elis: Reg, SW Peloponnesus.   *P. 7 Inset*
Elis: NW Peloponnesus.   *P. 5a*
Elisabethville: Africa, SE Belgian Congo.   *P. 57*
El Khalil *see* Hebron
Elmina: On coast of Africa, W of Niger R.   *P. 27*
El Salvador: Central America.   *P. 26*
Emden: On NW coast of Germany.   *P. 54*
Emporiae: Extreme NE of Spain.   *P. 4*
Ems: R in NW Germany.   *P. 48*
Enez *see* Ainos, Enos
England *see a'so Great Britain*   *Pp. 16, 21, 28, 29, 33, 54*
English Channel: Between England & N. France.   *P. 55*

Eniwetok: I in W Pacific, NW Marshall Is.   *P. 52*
En Nasira *see* Nazareth
Ennis: W cen. Ireland.   *P. 54*
Enniskillen: SW Northern Ireland.   *P. 54*
Enos (Enez, Aenus, Ainos): On E coast Adriatic Sea, at mouth of Maritza R.   *P. 43*
Entebbe: Uganda, on shore of L Victoria.   *P. 56*
Enugu: S Nigeria.   *P. 56*
Ephesus: W Anatolia, on coast of Aegean Sea.   *Pp. 4a, 5a, 7, 11, 14*
Epidamnus: Adriatic Sea, on Illyrian coast.   *P. 5a*
Epinal: NE France, on Moselle R.   *P. 55*
Epirus: Reg, NW Greece.   *Pp. 5a, 7, 43*
Equatoria: Reg, S Sudan.   *P. 56*
Eretria: Greece, on coast of Euboea.   *Pp. 4a, 7*
Erfurt: Germany, Thuringia, between Weser R & Saale R.   *Pp. 18, 48*
Eritrea: Reg, NE Africa, on Red Sea.   *Pp. 47, 56*
Erivan: Transcaucasia.   *P. 45*
Esh Shâm *see* Damascus
Essen: Germany, in valley of Ruhr R.   *Pp. 48, 51 Inset, 54*
Essex: Co, SE England.   *P. 33*
Es Sur *see* Tyre
Estonia: Reg, N Europe, on Baltic Sea.   *Pp. 21, 45, 50, 60, 61*
Estonian SSR. USSR, on Baltic Sea.   *P. 58*
Etampes: N France, S of Paris.   *P. 17*
Ethiopia (Abyssinia): NE Africa, W of Red Sea.   *Pp. 25, 27, 56, 62*
Etruria: Reg, cen. Italy.   *Pp. 6, 8*
Etruria, Kingdom of.   *P. 40*
Euboea (Negropont): I portion of Greece, in Aegean Sea.   *Pp. 4a, 5a, 7, 20, 43*
Eupen: E Belgium.   *Pp. 51 Inset, 54*
Euphrates: R in SW Asia.   *Pp. 3, 5, 9, 11, 15, 20, 56, 62*
Eurymedon: R in S Anatolia.   *P. 7*
Euxine Sea *see* Black Sea
Evreux: SE Normandy.   *P. 17*
Exeter: SW England.   *Pp. 16, 33, 54*
Ezion-geber: At head of G of Aqaba.   *Pp. 1, 2*
Faenza: N Italy.   *P. 32*
Faeroe Is: Between Shetland Is & Iceland.   *Pp. 21, 39*
Falaise: NW France in Normandy.   *P. 55*
Falkland Is: E of Strait of Magellan.   *P. 26*
Falmouth: On extreme SW coast of England.   *P. 16*
Farewell, Cape: S extremity of Greenland.   *Pp. 26, 39*
Farnborough: S England, SW of London.   *P. 54*
Farquhar Is: N of Madagascar.   *Pp. 56, 62*
Fashoda *see* Kodok
Fawley: On S coast of England, N of I of Wight.   *P. 54*
Fehrbellin (*battle 1675*): Germany, E of Elbe R.   *P. 34*
Feltre: NE Italy.   *P. 32*
Fernando Po (*1472*): I in G of Guinea.   *Pp. 27, 56*
Ferrara: N Italy, near Po R.   *Pp. 19, 23, 32, 49*
Ferrara, Duchy of.   *P. 32*
Fès (Fez): Africa, N cen. Morocco.   *P. 56*
Fez (Fès): Africa, N cen. Morocco.   *P. 22*
Fiesole: N Italy.   *P. 12*
Fiji Is: W Pacific.   *P. 52*
Finisterre, Cape: Extreme NW Spain.   *P. 8*
Finland: Reg. & penin. in Baltic Sea.   *Pp. 21, 45, 50, 58, 60, 61*
Finland, Gulf of: S of Finland.   *Pp. 45, 50, 58*
Fishguard: SW coast of Wales, on St. George's Channel.   *P. 54*
Fiume (Rijeka): At head of Adriatic Sea.   *Pp. 42, 49*
Flanders: Reg, NW Europe.   *Pp. 16, 18, 21*
Flintshire: Co, NE coast Wales.   *P. 33*
Florence: Cen. Italy, on Arno R.   *Pp. 19, 23, 28, 32, 42, 49*
Flores: I in chain E of Java.   *P. 25*
Foix: Reg. & city, France, N of Pyrenees.   *P. 17*
Folkestone: SE coast of England, on Strait of Dover.   *P. 54*
Fontainebleau: SE of Paris.   *P. 17*
Fontenoy (*battle 841*): NE of Paris.   *P. 14*
Foochow *see* Minhow
Forli: N Italy, E of Florence.   *P. 32*
Formigny (*battle 1450*): NW Normandy.   *P. 17*
Formosa (Taiwan): I in China Sea, SE of China.   *Pp. 25, 52, 63*
Fornovo: On tributary of Po R.   *P. 32*
Fort Augustine: Florida.   *P. 38*
Fort Dearborn: On S shore of L Michigan.   *P. 38*
Fort Duquesne: On site of Pittsburgh, Pennsylvania, USA.   *P. 38*
Fort Lamy: N cen. Africa, SE of L Chad.   *P. 56*
Forth, Firth of: E Scotland, estuary on North Sea.   *P. 54*
Fort Niagara: On shore of L Ontario.   *P. 38*

France. *Pp. 17, 28, 29, 36, 37, 42, 48, 50, 55, 58, 60, 61*

France (occupied zone): During World War II. *Pp 50, 61*

France (unoccupied): During World War II. *Pp. 50, 61*

Franconia: Reg, S cen. Germany. *P. 18*

Frankfort on Main: Cen. Germany, on Main R. *Pp. 16, 18, 22, 34, 42, 44, 48, 54*

Frankfort on Oder: NE Germany, on Oder R. *Pp. 18, 23, 42*

Franks, The. *Pp. 12, 13*

Freetown: Sierra Leone, Africa. *P. 56*

Freising: Bavaria. *P. 18*

Friesland: Between Rhine R & Weser R. *P. 18*

Frisian Is: Chain of Is in North Sea, off the Netherlands coast. *P. 54*

Frisians, The. *Pp. 12, 13*

Frunze: USSR, S of L Balkhash. *P. 58*

Fukien: Reg, on coast of E China. *P. 63*

Fulda: W cen. Germany, NE Carolingian Empire. *P. 14*

Fünfkirchen (Pécs): Near confluence of Drava R & Danube R. *P. 43*

Fushih *see* **Yenan**

Gabes, Gulf of: Off Tunisia. *P. 56*

Gabon: Reg, SW Africa, at equator. *P. 56*

Gades (Cádiz): On SW coast of Spain. *Pp. 4, 8*

Gainsborough (*battle 1643*): Near Lincoln, E England. *P. 33*

Galatia: Reg, cen. Anatolia. *P. 4*

Galatz: E Romania, on Danube R. *P. 43*

Galicia: Reg, NW Spain. *Pp. 42, 45*

Galilee, Sea of (Sea of Chinnereth): N Palestine. *Pp. 1, 2, 20*

Gallipoli Peninsula (Chersonese): At W entrance to Sea of Marmora. *P. 20*

Galway: On W coast of Ireland. *P. 54*

Gambia: Reg, W Africa. *Pp. 46, 56*

Gambia: R in W Africa. *Pp. 26, 56*

Ganges: R in NE India. *Pp. 25, 63*

Garda, Lake: N of Po R. *P. 32*

Garonne: R in SW France, flowing into Bay of Biscay. *Pp. 8, 17, 22, 55*

Gascony: Reg, SW France. *P. 17*

Gastein: Austria, N of upper Drava R. *P. 42*

Gat (Ghat): In Sahara, SW Libya. *P. 56*

Gath: Palestine, W of Dead Sea. *P. 1*

Gaugamela (*battle 331 B.C.*): Upper valley of Tigris R. *P. 5*

Gaul: Roman France. *P. 8*

Gaul, Diocese of. *P. 10*

Gaza: W of Dead Sea, near coast of Mediterranean Sea. *Pp. 1, 20*

Gdynia: Poland, near mouth of Vistula R. *P. 48*

Gedrosia: Reg, on Arabian Sea. *P. 5*

Gela: S Sicily. *P. 4*

Geneva: SW Switzerland, on L Geneva. *Pp. 17, 22, 42, 48, 55*

Geneva, Lake (Lake Leman): SW Switzerland & E France. *Pp. 6, 55*

Genissiat Dam: Rhône R, SW of L Geneva. *P. 55*

Genoa (Genua, Genova): On NW coast of Italy. *Pp. 19, 22, 27, 28, 29, 32, 36, 42, 49*

Genoa, Republic of. *P. 32*

Genua (Genoa): On NW coast of Italy. *P. 8*

Georgian SSR: USSR, E of Black Sea. *P. 58*

Gepids, The. *Pp. 12, 13*

German Confederation. *P. 37*

Germania: Reg, cen. Europe. *Pp. 8, 10*

Germania Inferior: Reg, lower valley of Rhine R. *P. 8*

Germania Superior: Reg, upper valley of Rhine R. *P. 8*

Germany. *Pp. 48, 50, 54, 58, 60, 61*

Gezer: Palestine, NW of Jerusalem. *P. 1*

Ghat *see* **Gat**

Ghent: Flanders, on Scheldt R. *Pp. 16, 22*

Gibraltar: S Spain, Strait of Gibraltar. *Pp. 24, 36, 37, 50, 60, 61*

Gibraltar, Strait of: Connects Mediterranean Sea & Atlantic, between Spain & Africa. *P. 22*

Gijon: NW Spain, on Bay of Biscay. *P. 55*

Gilbert Is: Archipelago in W cen. Pacific. *P. 52*

Gilead: Reg, E of Jordan R, between Sea of Galilee & Dead Sea. *P. 2*

Glamorganshire: Co, S Wales. *P. 33*

Glasgow: S cen. Scotland, on Clyde R. *Pp. 16, 33, 50, 54, 64*

Glastonbury: SW England, near Bristol Channel. *P. 16*

Glomma (Glom): R in SE Norway. *P. 21*

Gloucester: SW cen. England, on Severn R. *Pp. 10, 16, 33, 54*

Gloucestershire: Co, SW England, near Bristol Channel. *P. 33*

Goa: Reg, on W coast of India. *P. 62*

Goa: W India. *Pp. 25, 27, 31*

Gobi Desert: Cen. Asia, mostly in Mongolia. *P. 63*

Godavari: R in cen. India. *P. 62*

Gold Coast: Reg, W Africa, on G of Guinea. *Pp. 46, 56*

Gomel: Russia, in valley of Dnieper R. *Pp. 45, 51*

Gomorrah *see* **Sodom & Gomorrah**

Good Hope, Cape of (*1488*): SW extremity of Africa. *Pp. 27, 31, 57*

Gorky (Gorki, Nizhni Novgorod): Russia, on upper Volga R. *P. 58*

Gortyn: Cen. Crete. *P. 7*

Goshen: Reg, E of Nile Delta. *P. 2*

Goslar: Saxony, between Weser R & Elbe R. *P. 18*

Gota: R in SW Sweden. *P. 21*

Gotland I: SE coast of Sweden, in Baltic Sea. *P. 21*

Göttingen: Prussia, between Weser R & Saale R. *P. 48*

Granada: Reg, S Spain. *Pp. 24, 28*

Granada: S Spain. *P. 24*

Grand Banks: Off Newfoundland. *P. 39*

Grand Canal: NE China. *P. 63*

Granicus: R in NW Anatolia, flowing into the Propontis. *P. 7*

Graz: Austria, on Mur R, SW of Vienna. *P. 42*

Great Britain. *Pp. 33, 36, 37, 50, 54, 58, 60, 61*

Great Karroo Desert: S Africa. *P. 57*

Great Yarmouth: On extreme E coast of England. *P. 54*

Greece. *Pp. 4a, 5a, 7, 43, 50, 58, 60, 61*

Greenland: NE of N America. *P. 39*

Greenock: On W coast of Scotland, on Clyde R. *P. 54*

Grenoble: Between Rhône R & Alps. *Pp. 17, 55*

Grimsby: On E coast of England, N of The Wash. *P. 54*

Grodno: Russia, in valley of Niemen R. *P. 45*

Groningen: N Netherlands. *P. 54*

Grosswardein: Between Tisza R & Carpathian Mts. *P. 35*

Grozny: Russia, N of Caucasus Mts. *Pp. 51, 58*

Grunwald *see* **Tannenberg**

Guadalajara: Cen. Spain. *P. 55*

Guadalcanal: SE Solomon Is, W Pacific. *P. 52*

Guadalquivir: R in SW Spain. *Pp. 8, 24*

Guadiana: R flowing from Spain through S Portugal to Atlantic. *Pp. 8, 24*

Guam: I in W Pacific, E of Philippine Is. *P. 52*

Guatemala: Central America. *Pp. 26, 53*

Guernica: NE coast of Spain, near B of Biscay. *P. 55*

Guernsey: One of Channel Is. *P. 55*

Guiana: Reg, N coast of S America. *Pp. 26, 46, 56*

Guinea: Reg, W Africa. *Pp. 26, 46, 56*

Guinea, Gulf of: W cen. coast of Africa. *P. 56*

Guryev: At mouth of Ural R, on Caspian Sea. *P. 58*

Habana *see* **Havana**

Habbaniya: Iraq, on Euphrates R. *P. 51*

Hadrian's Limes: Between upper Rhine R & upper Danube R. *P. 8*

Hadrian's Wall: Between England & Scotland. *P. 8*

Hague, The: On SW coast of Netherlands. *Pp. 42, 48, 54*

Haifa: N Palestine, on Mediterranean Sea. *P. 20*

Hainan: I in S China Sea, off S coast of China. *P. 63*

Hainault: Reg, E of upper Scheldt R. *P. 16*

Haiti: I in West Indies. *Pp. 38, 53*

Halicarnassus (Bodrum): W coast of Anatolia. *Pp. 4a, 7*

Halle: Germany, on Saale R. *P. 48*

Hama (Hamath): W Syria, on Orontes R. *P. 20*

Hamath (Hama): W Syria, on Orontes R. *P. 1, 2*

Hamburg: NW Germany, on Elbe R. *Pp. 18, 21, 22, 42, 44, 48, 50, 64*

Hamm: On Lippe R, in Ruhr valley. *P. 51 Inset*

Hampshire: Co, S England. *P. 33*

Han: Tributary of Yangtze R, cen. China. *P. 63*

Hangö: SW extremity of Finland, on Baltic Sea. *P. 50*

Hankow: Cen. China, on Yangtze R. *P. 63*

Hanoi: Indo-China, on Red R. *P. 63*

Hanover: Reg. & city, N Germany. *Pp. 34, 36, 41, 44*

Hapsburg Empire. *Pp. 37, 41*

Haran: On tributary of upper Euphrates R. *P. 2*

Harfleur: France, at estuary of Seine R. *P. 17*

Hargeisa: NE Africa, near G of Aden. *P. 56*

Harwell: S cen. England, W of London. *P. 54*

Harwich: On SE coast of England, NE of London. *P. 54*

Hasselt: NE Belgium, on Albert Canal. *P. 54*

Hastings: S England, on English Channel. *P. 16*

Havana (Habana): On NW coast of Cuba. *P. 26*

Hazor: N of Sea of Galilee. *P. 1*

Hebrides: Is W of Scotland, in N Atlantic. *Pp. 16, 21, 33, 54*

Hebron (El Khalil): W of Dead Sea. *P. 1*

Hebrus (Maritza): R in SE Europe, flowing into N Aegean Sea. *P. 7*

Hecatompylos (Hecatompylus): On Alexander's route, SE of Caspian Sea. *P. 5*

Heidelberg: W cen. Germany, on Neckar R. *P. 48*

Heligoland: I in North Sea, off W coast of Germany. (Schleswig-Holstein) *P. 42*

Heligoland Bight: Arm of North Sea, extending S & E of Heligoland. *P. 54*

Hellespont (Dardanelles): Strait between Europe & Anatolia. *P. 7*

Helsingfors (Helsinki): S Finland, on G of Finland. *P. 45*

Helsinki (Helsingfors): S Finland, on G of Finland. *Pp. 50, 58*

Hendaye: SW France, on Spanish border. *Pp 50, 55*

Heraclea: On S Italian coast. *P. 8*

Heraclea: On Black Sea coast of Anatolia. *Pp. 4, 7*

Hercegovina *see* **Herzegovina**

Herculaneum (Resina): Italy, on coast of Tyrrhenian Sea. *P. 6*

Hereford: W England. *Pp. 16, 54*

Herefordshire: Co, W England. *P. 33*

Hermannstadt: On tributary of Danube R, W of Carpathian Mts. *Pp. 35, 43*

Hermon, Mt: Palestine, E of upper Jordan R. *Pp. 1, 2*

Hertfordshire: Co, SE England, N of London. *P. 33*

Herzegovina: Reg. inland of S Dalmatia. *Pp. 43, 44*

Heshbon (Hesbon): E of Jerusalem, beyond Jordan R. *Pp. 1, 2*

Hesse: Reg, cen. Germany, N of Frankfort on Main. *P. 44*

Hesse-Darmstadt, Grand Duchy of. *P. 40*

Hierosolyma *see* **Jerusalem**

Highlands: Mts in N Scotland. *Pp. 16, 33*

Himalaya Mts: Range along border between India & Tibet. *Pp. 25, 62*

Himera: N coast of Sicily. *Pp. 6, 8*

Hindu Kush Mts: Westerly group of cen. Asian mountain mass. *Pp. 5, 62*

Hippo: W of Tunis. *P. 10*

Hiroshima: SE Japan. *Pp. 52, 63*

Hirson: NE France, on upper Oise R. *P. 54*

Hispania (Spain). *P. 8*

Hispaniola (*1492*): I in cen. West Indies, in Caribbean Sea. *P. 26*

Hittites, The. *P. 2*

Holland *see* **Netherlands**

Holland, Kingdom of. *P. 40*

Hollandia: NE part of New Guinea in East Indies. *P. 52*

Holstein: Reg, Germany, S of Denmark penin. *Pp. 21, 41, 44*

Holyhead: W of Anglesey coast, on Irish Sea. *P. 54*

Holy Roman Empire. *Pp. 17, 18, 34, 36*

Homs: W Syria, on Orontes R. *P. 20*

Honduras: Central America. *Pp. 26, 53*

Hong Kong: On SE coast of China. *Pp. 52, 63, 64*

Honolulu: On Oahu I, mid-Pacific. *P. 53*

Honshu: Main I of group comprising Japan. *Pp. 52, 63*

Hook of Holland: N of mouth of Maas R. *P. 54*

Horn, Cape (*1616*): S extremity of S America. *Pp. 26, 30*

Hsinking *see* **Changchun**

Hudson Bay: N of Eastern Canada, opening to NE on Atlantic. *P. 26*

Huleh, Lake (Waters of Miram): N of Sea of Galilee. *Pp. 1, 2.*

Hull: On E coast of England. *Pp. 21, 33, 54*

Hungary. *Pp. 18, 28, 36, 44, 48, 50, 58, 60, 61*

Hungary, Kingdom of. *P. 34*

Huns, The. *P. 12*

Huntingdonshire: Co, SE England. *P. 33*

Hurrions: Reg. N of upper Tigris R. *P. 3*

Hwang: R in N cen. & E China. *Pp. 25, 63*

Hydaspes: Tributary of Indus R, NW India. *P. 5*

Hyderabad: S cen. India. *Pp. 62, 64*

Hyphasis: Tributary of Indus R, NW India. *P. 5*

Ibadan: Nigeria, NE of Lagos. *P. 56*
Iberian Penin: SW Europe. *See Front Endpaper*
Iceland: E of Greenland. *Pp. 27, 31, 36, 47*
Iconium: S cen. Anatolia. *Pp. 14, 20*
Idrisids, Dominion of. *P. 14*
Ifni: Reg, NW coast of Africa. *P. 56*
Ijsselmeer (Zuider Zee): Netherlands. *P. 54*
Ile de France: Reg, N cen. France, valleys of Oise R & cen. Seine R. *P. 17*
Ili: R in Russian Asia, flowing W into L Balkhash. *P. 62*
Ilium (Troy): Near W coast of Anatolia. *P. 7*
Illyria: Reg, E coast of Adriatic Sea. *Pp. 5, 6*
Illyricum: Reg, NE of Adriatic Sea. *P. 8*
Imola: N Italy, SE of Bologna. *P. 32*
Inchon: W Korea. *P. 59*
India. *Pp. 5, 25, 27, 47, 52,62*
Indian Desert *see* Thar Desert
Indian Ocean. *Pp. 25, 27, 31, 47, 52, 62*
Indo-China: SE Asia *Pp. 25,63*
Indonesia: Chain of Is, SE of Asia. *P. 63*
Indus: R in NW India. *Pp. 15, 25, 62*
Inhambane: SE Africa. *P. 57*
Inland Sea: Japan, between Honshu & Shikoku. *P. 52*
Inn: R flowing from Switzerland, through Austria & Germany, to Danube R. *Pp. 23, 32, 42, 44*
Inner Mongolia: Reg, E Asia. *P. 63*
Innsbruck: W Austria, on Inn R. *Pp. 18, 42, 44, 48.*
Invergordon: NE Scotland near Moray Firth. *P. 54*
Inverness: NE Scotland on Moray Firth. *Pp. 16, 33, 54*
Ionia: Reg, on Aegean Sea, along W coast of Anatolia. *Pp. 4a, 5a, 7*
Ionian Is: In Ionian Sea, off W coast of Greece. *Pp. 36, 37*
Ionian Sea: Part of Mediterranean Sea, between Italy & Greece. *Pp. 7, 8, 43*
Ipek (*battle 301*): N of Drin R. *P. 43*
Ipsus (*battle 301*): W cen. Anatolia. *P. 4*
Ipswich: Near SE coast of England. *Pp. 33, 54*
Iran (Persia). *Pp. 51, 56, 58, 62*
Iran, Plateau of: W Asia, NE of Persian G. *Pp. 5, 62*
Iraq (Mesopotamia): Lower valleys of Tigris R & Euphrates R. *Pp. 51, 56, 58, 62*
Ireland (Eire). *Pp. 28, 29, 36, 54,61*
Irish Free State. *P. 60*
Irkutsk: Near SE shore of L Baikal. *P. 59*
Irrawaddy: R in cen. Burma. *P. 63*
Ischl: Between upper Danube R & Drava R. *P. 42*
Isère: Tributary of Rhône R. *P. 49*
Isonzo: R flowing into N Adriatic Sea. *P. 42*
Israel: Reg, Palestine. *Pp. 1 Inset, 56, 58, 62*
Issus: S Anatolia, at NE extremity of Mediterranean Sea. *P. 5*
Istanbul (Byzantium, Constantinople): At Bosporus, between Black Sea & Sea of Marmora. *Pp. 50, 58, 64.*
Istria: Reg. & penin, N Adriatic Sea. *P. 42*
Istrus: On Black Sea, S of mouth of Danube R. *P. 4*
Italy. *Pp. 8, 19, 32, 43, 44, 49, 50, 58, 60, 61*
Italy, Diocese of. *P. 10*
Italy, Kingdom of. *Pp. 37, 40*
Ivanovo Voznesensk: Russia in Europe, S of Volga R, NE of Moscow. *P. 45*
Iviza: Westernmost I of Balearic Is. *P. 24*
Ivory Coast: W Africa. *P. 56*
Iwo Jima: I, S of Japan. *P. 52*
Izmir *see* Smyrna
Izmit *see* Nicomedia

Jabbok: Eastern tributary of Jordan R. *Pp. 1, 2*
Jabesh-gilead: Palestine, E of Jordan R, S of Sea of Galilee. *P. 1*
Jaffa (Joppa): Palestine, on Mediterranean Sea. *P. 20*
Jamaica (*1493*): I in West Indies. *Pp. 26, 38*
Janina: Between Pindus Mts & Ionian Sea. *P. 43*
Japan. *Pp. 25, 31, 52, 59, 63*
Japan, Sea of: Between Japan, Korea & USSR. *Pp. 59, 63*
Japanese Empire. *P. 47*
Jassy: W of Prut R, E of Carpathian Mts. *Pp. 35, 43*
Java: I, NW of Australia. *Pp. 25, 52, 63*
Java Sea: Between Java & Borneo. *P. 52*
Jena: S cen. Germany, on Saale R. *P. 48*
Jericho: Palestine, N of Dead Sea. *Pp. 1, 2*

Jersey: One of Channel Is. *P. 55*
Jerusalem (Hierosolyma): Palestine, W of N end of Dead Sea. *Pp. 1, 2, 9, 11, 15, 20, 27, 51, 58*
Jerusalem, Kingdom of. *P. 20*
Jidda: W Arabia, on Red Sea. *Pp. 56, 62*
Johannesburg: S Africa, N of Vaal R. *P. 57*
Joppa (Jaffa): Palestine, on Mediterranean Sea. *P. 1*
Jordan: Reg, E of Jordan R. *Pp. 56, 58, 62*
Jordan: R in Palestine, flowing into Dead Sea. *Pp. 1, 2, 20*
Jubayl *see* Byblos
Judah: Reg, W of Dead Sea. *P. 1 Inset*
Jumna: Tributary of Ganges R, N cen. India. *P. 62*
Jutes, The. *P. 12*
Jutland: Reg, N Denmark. *P. 21*

Kabul: On Alexander's route, Afghanistan. *Pp. 5, 51, 62*
Kadesh: Palestine, on upper Orontes R. *Pp. 1, 2*
Kaffa: S Russia, in E Crimea. *P. 23*
Kalahari Desert: W cen. S Africa. *P. 57*
Kalinin (Tver): Russia in Europe, NW of Moscow. *P. 51*
Kaliningrad *see* Königsberg
Kalmar: On SE coast of Sweden. *P. 21*
Kalmar, Union of. *P. 28*
Kaluga: Russia, SW of Moscow. *P. 45*
Kama: E tributary of Volga R. *P. 45*
Kamchatka: Russia in Asia, penin. between Sea of Okhotsk & Bering Sea. *P. 59*
Kamenets-Podolsk: SW Russia, on Dniester R. *P. 45*
Kandahar *see* Alexandria Arachosiorum
Kano: N cen. Nigeria. *P. 56*
Karachi: W Pakistan, near mouth of Indus R. *Pp. 62, 64*
Karaganda: USSR, NW of L Balkhash. *P. 58*
Karakoram Mts: In W cen. Asian mountain mass. *P. 62*
Karakorum: Mongolia, S of L Baikal. *Pp. 25, 31*
Karelo-Finnish SSR: NW. USSR in Europe. *P. 58*
Kariba Gorge: Fed. of Rhodesia & Nyasaland, on Zambezi R. *P. 57*
Karlovy Vary *see* Carlsbad
Karlsruhe: E of Rhine R, N of Black Forest. *P. 51 Inset*
Kars: NE Turkey. *P. 45*
Kasai: Tributary of Congo R, cen. Africa. *P. 56*
Kashgar: W China, near Russian border. *P. 62*
Kashmir: Reg, N India, between India & Pakistan. *P. 62*
Kasserine: Cen. Tunisia, SW of Tunis. *P. 50*
Kathiawar: Penin, W coast of India. *P. 62*
Katmandu: Nepal. *P. 63*
Kattegat: Arm of North Sea, between Sweden & Denmark. *P. 21*
Katyn: On upper Dnieper R, SW of Moscow. *P. 51*
Kaunas (Kovno): USSR, cen. Lithuanian SSR. *P. 58*
Kavalla: Greece, on N coast of Aegean Sea. *P. 43*
Kazakh SSR: USSR, NE of Aral Sea & Caspian Sea. *P. 58*
Kazakhstan: Reg. in Russia, NE of Caspian Sea. *P. 45*
Kazan: On Volga R. *Pp. 45, 58.*
Keijo *see* Seoul
Kénitra *see* Port Lyautey
Kent: Co, SE England. *P. 33*
Kenya: Reg, E Africa. *Pp. 47, 56, 62*
Kenya, Mt: E Africa, E of L Victoria. *P. 56*
Kerak: SE of Dead Sea. *P. 20*
Kerch: E Crimea. *P. 45*
Khabarovsk: E. USSR on Amur R. *P. 59*
Khanaqin: E of Tigris R, NE of Baghdad. *Pp. 56,62*
Kharkov: Russia, near Donets R. *Pp. 45, 51, 58*
Khartoum: Cen. Sudan, on Nile R. *Pp. 56, 62*
Kherson: S Russia, on Dnieper R. *P. 45*
Khiva: USSR, E of Caspian Sea, S of Aral Sea. *P. 58*
Khyber: Pass between cen. Afghanistan & N Pakistan. *P. 62*
Kiaochow Bay: E China, on Yellow Sea. *P. 47*
Kiel: Germany, on W Baltic coast. *Pp. 21, 48, 50*
Kiel Canal: Germany, between Baltic Sea & North Sea. *Pp. 48, 54.*
Kiev: Russia, on Dnieper R. *Pp. 14, 23, 45, 51*
Kilimanjaro, Mt: E Africa, SE of L Victoria. *P. 56*

Kilindini: On E coast of Africa, N of Zanzibar. *P. 56*
Killarney: SW Ireland. *P. 54*
Kimberley: S Africa, on Vaal R. *P. 57*
King's Lynn: E England, S of The Wash. *P. 54*
Kirghiz SSR: USSR, S cen. Asia. *P. 58*
Kir-haraseth: E of Dead Sea. *P. 1*
Kirk-Kilisse (Kirklareli): NW of Sea of Marmora. *P. 43*
Kirkwall: Orkney Is, N of Scotland. *P. 54*
Kirov: USSR, W of Ural Mts. *P. 58*
Kishinev: Russia, W of lower Dniester R. *Pp. 43, 45, 58*
Kiska: SW of Alaska, Aleutian Is. *P. 52*
Kistna: R in S India, flowing E to B of Bengal. *P. 62*
Kisumu: E Africa, on L Victoria. *P. 56*
Kiuchuan *see* Suchow
Kivu, Lake: Cen. Africa, W of L Victoria. *P. 56*
Klaipeda *see* Memel
Kodok (Fashoda): Sudan, on White Nile R. *P. 56*
Kolbatz Monastery: At mouth of Oder R. *P. 21*
Köln *see* Cologne
Kolozsvar: Between Tisza R & Carpathian Mts. *P. 43*
Kolyma: R in NE. USSR, flowing into Arctic Ocean. *P. 59*
Komsomolsk: E. USSR, on Amur R. *P. 59*
Königgratz *see* Sadowa
Königsberg (Kaliningrad): E of mouth of Vistula R. *Pp. 21, 23, 34, 42, 44, 48*
Korcë *see* Koritza
Korea: Reg, E coast of Asia. *Pp. 47, 52*
Korea: 38th Parallel. *Pp. 59, 63*
Koritza (Korcë): SE Albania. *Pp. 43, 50*
Kortrijk (Courtrai): NW Belgium, W of Scheldt R. *P. 54*
Kostroma: Russia, NE of Moscow, on Volga R. *P. 45*
Kovno (Kaunas): Russia, cen. Lithuania, on confluences of Niemen R & Viliya R. *P. 45*
Kra, Isthmus of: SW Siam. *P. 52*
Kragujevac: Serbia. *P. 43*
Kraków (Cracow): S Poland, on Vistula R. *Pp. 48, 58*
Krasnodar: S. USSR, on Kuban R. *P. 51*
Krasnovodsk: USSR, on E coast of Caspian Sea. *P. 58*
Krasnoyarsk: USSR, on upper Yenisei R. *P. 59*
Krefeld: Germany, between Maas R & Rhine R. *P. 51 Inset*
Kremenchug: USSR, on Dnieper R. *P. 51*
Krivoi Rog: USSR, N of mouth of Dnieper R. *P. 51*
Kronshtadt (Kronstadt): USSR, E end of G of Finland. *P. 58*
Kronstadt (Kronshtadt): Russia, E end of G of Finland. *P. 45*
Kronstadt: At E end of Transylvanian Alps. *P. 43*
Kuban: R flowing into Black Sea, N of Caucasus Mts. *Pp. 45, 58*
Kuibyshev (Samara): Russia, on cen. Volga R. *Pp 51, 58*
Kulm: Poland, on Vistula R. *P. 21*
Kumanovo: Near upper Vardar R. *P. 43*
Kumasi: Gold Coast. *P. 56*
Kunlun Mts: NW of cen. Asian mountain mass. *P. 62*
Kunming: SE China, on Burma Road. *P. 63*
Kunming (Reg) *see* Yunnan
Kura: R in Transcaucasia, flowing into Caspian Sea. *P. 45*
Kurile Is: USSR, E of Sea of Okhotsk. *P. 59*
Kursk: Cen. Russia, N of Sea of Azov. *Pp. 45, 51*
Kutais: S of Caucasus Mts. *P. 45*
Kuwait: Reg. & city, NW end of Persian G. *Pp 56, 58, 62*
Kwajalein I: W Pacific, Marshall Is. *P. 52*
Kwangchowan: Penin, SE China. *P. 63*
Kwantung Peninsula *see* Liaotung Peninsula
Kweilin: S China, N of Hong Kong. *P. 52*
Kyoga, Lake: E Africa, N of L Victoria. *P. 56*
Kyongsong *see* Seoul
Kyoto: Japan, S cen. Honshu. *Pp. 59, 63, 64*
Kyushu: S island of Japanese Group. *Pp. 52, 63*

Labrador: Reg, NE Canada. *Pp. 26, 39*
Lachish: Palestine, W of Dead Sea. *P. 1*
Laconia: Reg. SE Peloponnesus. *P. 7 Inset*
Ladoga, Lake: Russia, E of G of Finland. *Pp. 45, 51, 58*
Ladysmith: S Africa. *P. 57*
Lagny-sur-Marne: E of Paris. *P. 22*
Lagos: On coast of Nigeria. *P. 56*

Lahn: R joining Rhine R at Coblenz. *P. 51 Inset*
Lahore: NW India. *P. 62*
Laibach (Ljubljana): On upper Sava R. *Pp. 42, 44*
Lancashire: Co, NW England. *P. 33*
Lancaster: On NW coast of England, E of I of Man. *Pp. 33, 54*
Land's End: Extremity of SW England. *P. 54*
Langres: NE France, E Champagne, in upper valley of Marne R. *Pp. 17, 22*
Laodicaea: S of mouth of Orontes R. *P. 20*
Laon: N France, NE of Paris. *Pp. 14, 17, 22, 55*
Laos: Reg, cen. Indo-China. *P. 63*
La Réole: SW France, on Garonne R. *P. 17*
Larissa: Greece, Diocese of Macedonia, E Thessaly. *Pp. 11, 43*
Larne: On NE coast of N Ireland. *P. 54*
La Rochelle: France, on B of Biscay. *P. 55*
Larsa: S Babylonia, on Euphrates R. *P. 3*
Lascaux: SW France, near Dordogne R. *P. 55*
Lashio: E cen. Burma, NE of Mandalay. *Pp. 52, 63*
Las Navas de Tolosa (*battle 1212*): S cen. Spain. *P. 24*
La Spezia: On NW coast of Italy. *P. 50*
Latium: Reg, cen. Italy, on Tyrrhenian Sea. *P. 6*
Latvia: Reg, on E Baltic Sea. *Pp. 50, 60, 61*
Latvian SSR: USSR, on Baltic Sea. *P. 58*
Laurium, Mt: SE Greece, overlooking Saronic G. *P. 5a*
Lausanne: W Switzerland, on N shore of L Geneva. *Pp. 22, 48, 55*
Lebanon: Reg, on E Mediterranean Sea. *Pp. 51, 56, 58, 62*
Lebanon Mts: W of upper Orontes R. *Pp. 1, 2*
Lech: Tributary of upper Danube R. *P. 22*
Lechfeld (*battle 955*): S Germany, on Lech R. *P. 18*
Le Creusot: E cen. France, between Loire R & Saône R. *P. 55*
Leeds: N cen. England. *Pp. 33, 54*
Leghorn (Livorno): Near mouth of Arno R. *Pp. 32, 49*
Legnano (*battle 1176*): Lombardy. *P. 19*
Le Havre: N France, on English Channel. *Pp. 39, 55*
Leicester: Cen. England. *Pp. 16, 33, 54*
Leicestershire: Co, cen. England. *P. 33*
Leinster: Reg, SE Ireland. *P. 33*
Leipzig: Cen. Germany, W of Elbe R. *Pp. 21, 23, 42, 48, 50*
Leman *see* Geneva
Le Mans: N cen. France, on tributary of Loire R. *P. 17*
Lemberg (Lvov): Russia, N of upper Dniester R. *Pp. 23, 42, 44, 45*
Lemnos: I in N Aegean Sea, off W coast of Anatolia. *Pp. 5a, 7*
Lena: R in USSR, flowing into Arctic Ocean. *P. 59*
Leningrad (St Petersburg): USSR, at E end of G of Finland. *Pp. 51, 58, 64*
León: NW Spain. *P. 24*
León, Kingdom of Castile and. *P. 24*
Leontini: E Sicily. *P. 5a*
Leopold II, Lake: Cen. Africa, E of Congo R. *P. 56*
Leopoldville: Africa, near mouth of Congo R. *P. 56*
Lepanto *see* Naupactus
Leptis: N African coast, S of Sicily. *P. 4*
Le Puiset: Cen. France, N of Orléans. *P. 17*
Lerida: NE Spain, W of Barcelona. *P. 24*
Lesbos: I in E Aegean Sea, off NW coast of Anatolia. *Pp. 4a, 7*
Les Eyzies: France, in valley of Dordogne R. *P. 55*
Leuctra (*battle 371* B.C.): E cen. Greece, N of G of Corinth. *Pp. 5a, 7 Inset*
Lewes: S England. *P. 16*
Leyte: I in Philippine Is. *Pp. 52, 63*
Lhasa: Tibet. *P. 63*
Liaotung Peninsula (Kwantung): S Manchuria, on Yellow Sea. *P. 63*
Libau: On E coast of Baltic Sea. *P. 23*
Liberia: Reg, W Africa. *P. 56*
Libya (Libia): Reg, N Africa, between Tunis & Egypt. *Pp. 47, 50, 56*
Libyan Desert (Libian): N Africa, W of Nile R. *P. 56*
Lichfield: W cen. England. *P. 16*
Lidice: Czechoslovakia, near Prague. *P. 50*
Liechtenstein: Reg, between Switzerland & Austria. *P. 48*
Liége: E Belgium, on Meuse R. *Pp. 16, 50, 51 Inset*
Liguria: Reg, on coast of NW Italy. *P. 6*
Lille: N France, W of Scheldt R. *Pp. 22, 48, 50, 54*

Lima: S America, Peru. *P. 26*
Limerick: Ireland, on Shannon R. *Pp. 33, 54*
Limoges: W cen. France, on tributary of Loire R. *Pp. 17, 55*
Limpopo: R in SE Africa, flowing into Indian O. *P. 57*
Lincoln: E England. *Pp. 16, 22, 33, 54*
Lincolnshire: Co, E England. *P. 33*
Linz: Austria, on upper Danube R. *P. 42*
Lions, Gulf of: Inlet of Mediterranean Sea, on S coast of France. *P. 55*
Lippe: Tributary of Rhine R, Germany. *P. 51 Inset*
Lisbon: W coast of Portugal, on Tagus R. *Pp. 22, 24, 27, 39, 50*
Litani: R, SE of Lebanon Mts. *Pp. 1, 2*
Lithuania: Reg, on E Baltic Sea. *Pp. 21, 28, 45, 48, 50, 60, 61*
Lithuanian SSR: USSR, on E Baltic Sea. *P. 58*
Little Russia (Ukraine): Reg, N of Black Sea. *P. 45*
Liverpool: NW England. *Pp. 50, 54*
Livingstone: Fed. of Rhodesia & Nyasaland, on Zambezi R. *P. 57*
Livonia: Reg, E of Baltic Sea, near G of Riga. *P. 21*
Livorno *see* Leghorn
Ljubljana *see* Laibach
Locarno: SE cen. Switzerland, on N shore of L Maggiore. *P. 48*
Loches: Touraine, on tributary of Loire R. *P. 17*
Locris: Reg, Greece, N of G of Corinth. *P. 7 Inset*
Lodi (*battle 1796*): N Italy on tributary of Po R. *P. 32*
Łódź: Cen. Poland, SW of Warsaw. *Pp. 48, 50, 58*
Loire: R in W cen. France, flowing into B of Biscay. *Pp. 8, 10, 17, 22, 48, 55*
Lomami: Tributary of Congo R. *P. 56*
Lombards, The. *Pp. 12, 13*
Lombards, Kingdom of. *P. 14*
Lombardy: Reg, N Italy, valley of Po R. *Pp. 19, 41*
Londinium (London): S England, on Thames R. *P. 8*
London (Londinium): S England, on Thames R. *Pp. 14, 16, 21, 22, 33, 39, 50, 54, 64*
Londonderry: NW. N Ireland. *Pp. 33, 54*
Lopez, Cape: W Africa, S of G of Guinea. *P. 56*
Lop Nor: L in cen. Asia. *P. 63*
L'Orient (Lorient): W France, on B of Biscay. *Pp. 39, 55*
Lorraine: Reg, valleys of Meuse R, Moselle R & Rhine R. *P. 34*
Lorraine, Lower: Reg, between Rhine R & Scheldt R. *Pp. 16, 18*
Lorraine, Upper: Reg, upper Meuse R & Moselle R. *Pp. 17, 18*
Los Angeles: On SW coast of USA. *P. 64*
Lostwithiel: England, S Cornwall. *P. 33*
Lotharingia: Reg, W Europe, W of Rhine R. *P. 15*
Louisbourg: Canada, SE Cape Breton I. *P. 38*
Lourdes: France, N of Pyrenees. *P. 55*
Lourenço Marques: On coast of E Africa, Mozambique. *P. 57*
Louvain: Lower Lorraine. *P. 18*
Lowlands: Hills in S Scotland. *Pp. 16, 33*
Lualaba: Tributary of Congo R. *P. 56*
Luanda: On coast of Angola. *P. 56*
Lübeck: Germany, on coast of Baltic Sea. *Pp. 18, 21, 22*
Lublin: Cen. Poland. *P. 50*
Lucania: Reg, S Italy, between Tyrrhenian Sea & Tarentum G. *P. 6*
Lucca: Reg, on NW coast of Italy. *Pp. 37, 40, 41*
Lucknow: N India, SE of Delhi. *P. 62*
Lugdunensis: Reg, Gaul. *P. 8*
Lugdunum (Lyons): In valley of Rhône R. *P. 6*
Lüle Burgas (*battle 1912*): Ottoman Empire in Europe. *P. 43*
Lund: SW Sweden. *P. 21*
Lüneburg: N Germany, inland port in valley of Elbe R. *P. 21*
Lusaka: Fed. of Rhodesia & Nyasaland. *P. 57*
Lusignan: W cen. France. *P. 17*
Lusitania: Reg, W Spain & Portugal. *P. 8*
Lutetia (Paris): NW France, on Seine R, just below confluence with Marne R. *P. 8*
Luxemburg: Reg. & city, between SE Belgium & W Germany. *Pp. 37, 41, 42, 44, 48, 50, 51 Inset, 55, 60, 61*
Luzon: I among N Philippine Is. *Pp. 52, 63*
Lvov (Lemburg): USSR, N of upper Dniester R. *Pp. 50, 58*
Lycaonia: Reg, S Anatolia. *P. 4*
Lycia: Reg, S coast of Anatolia, near I of Rhodes. *P. 4*
Lydia: Reg, W Anatolia, on Aegean Sea. *Pp. 4a, 7*

Lynn (King's Lynn): E England, near The Wash. *Pp. 16, 21, 22*
Lyons: E cen. France, at confluence of Rhône R & Saône R. *Pp. 10, 12, 14, 17, 19, 22, 48, 50, 55*

Mass (Meuse): R flowing NW from N France to North Sea near mouth of Rhine R. *P. 51 Inset*
Maastricht: SE Netherlands, on Maas (Meuse) R. *P. 54*
Macao (*1520*): On SE coast of China near Hong Kong. *Pp. 25, 31, 63*
Macassar Strait: Between E Borneo & Celebes. *P. 25*
Macedonia: Reg, cen. Balkan Penin, N of Greece. *Pp. 4, 4a, 5a, 8, 43*
Macedonia, Diocese of. *P. 10*
Mackinac I: N America, in Great Lakes. *P. 38*
Mâcon: E cen. France, on Saône R, N of Lyons. *Pp. 17, 55*
Madagascar (*1500*): W Indian O, E of S Africa. *Pp. 25, 27, 31, 47, 57, 62*
Madeira Is (*1418*): E Atlantic, W of Morocco. *Pp. 26, 30, 39, 56*
Madras: SE India, on B of Bengal. *Pp. 27, 62, 64*
Madrid: Cen. Spain, on tributary of Tagus R. *Pp. 24, 27, 39, 50, 64*
Maeander (Menderes): Large R in W Anatolia—not stream near Ilium (Troy). *P. 7*
Mafeking (*battle 1903*): S Africa, W of Pretoria. *P. 57*
Magadan: E. USSR, on Sea of Okhotsk. *P. 59*
Magdeburg: Cen. Germany, on Elbe R, SW of Berlin. *Pp. 18, 23, 34*
Magellan, Strait of (*1520*): Near S extremity of S America. *Pp. 26, 30*
Maggiore, Lake: N Italy & S Switzerland. *P. 32*
Magnitogorsk: USSR, S Ural Mts. *P. 58*
Magyars, The. *P. 14*
Mahanaim: Palestine, E of Jordan R, between Sea of Galilee & Dead Sea. *P. 1*
Mahon: On Minorca I. *P. 24*
Maikop: S. USSR, near Caucasus, NE of Black Sea. *P. 51*
Main: R in W cen. Germany, joining Rhine R at Mainz. *Pp. 22, 48, 54*
Maine: Reg, NW France. *P. 17*
Mainz (Mayence): Germany, on Rhine R, at confluence with Main R. *Pp. 10, 18, 34, 48, 51 Inset, 54*
Majorca: Largest of Balearic Is, in W Mediterranean Sea. *Pp. 19, 24, 49*
Malabar Coast: SW coast of India. *P. 62*
Malaca (Malaga): S Spain. *P. 4*
Malacca: SE Asia, W coast of S Malay Penin. *Pp. 25, 31, 63*
Malaga (Malaca): S Spain. *P. 24*
Malaya: Reg, SE Asia, lower portion of Malay Penin. *Pp. 47, 52, 63*
Malay Peninsula: SE tip of mainland of Asia. *P. 25*
Malindi (*1498*): On E coast of Africa, N of Zanzibar. *Pp. 25, 27, 31, 56*
Malmédy: Belgium, near border with Germany. *P. 51 Inset*
Malmö: SW Sweden, opposite Copenhagen. *Pp. 21, 42, 48*
Malta (Melita): I in Mediterranean Sea, S of Sicily. *Pp. 37, 49, 50, 60, 61*
Man, Isle of: In N Irish Sea, between England & Ireland. *Pp. 21, 54*
Manchester: N cen. England. *P. 54*
Manchukuo (Manchuria): E Asia, NE of China. *P. 52*
Manchuria (Manchukuo): E Asia, NE of China. *Pp. 59, 63*
Mandalay: Cen. Burma. *Pp. 52, 63*
Manila: Philippine Is, on Luzon I. *Pp. 52, 63, 64*
Mannheim: W Germany, on Neckar R, near Rhine R. *Pp. 48, 51 Inset, 55*
Mantinea (*battle 418* B.C.): S Greece, cen. Peloponnesus. *Pp. 5a, 7 Inset*
Mantua: N Italy, near Po R. *Pp. 19, 32*
Manzi: Reg, S China. *P. 25*
Manzikert (*battle 1071*): E Anatolia, on upper Euphrates R. *Pp. 15, 20*
Maracanda: On Alexander's route, N of Oxus R. *P. 5*
Marathon (*battle 490* B.C.): E Greece, NE of Athens. *P. 7 Inset*
Marathon, Plain of: E Greece, NE of Athens. *P. 4a*
Mareth: near coast of Tunisia. *P. 50*
Mari: Mesopotamia, on upper Euphrates R. *P. 3*

Marianas Is: W Pacific, E of Philippine Is. *P. 52*
Marienburg: N Poland, near mouth of Vistula R.
P. 21
Marienwerder: N Poland, S of Marienburg. *P. 21*
Marignano: N Italy, Duchy of Milan. *P. 32*
Maritza (Hebrus): R in SE Europe, flowing into
N Aegean Sea. *P. 43*
Marmora, Sea of (Propontis): Between Europe
& Asia Minor; with Dardanelles (Hellespont)
& Bosporus links Aegean Sea & Black Sea.
Pp. 35, 43
Marne: Tributary of Seine R, NE France.
Pp. 17, 22, 48, 55
Maros (Mures): R in SE Europe, flowing W to
Danube R. *P. 43*
Marrakech: NW Africa, W cen. Morocco. *P. 56*
Marseilles (Massilia): SE France, on NE shore
of G of Lions. *Pp. 10, 13, 17, 19, 22, 32, 49,*
50, 55
Marshall Is: W Pacific. *P. 52*
Marston Moor (*battle 1643*): N England, W of
York. *P. 33*
Massif Central: Plateau, SE cen. France. *Pp. 17,*
22, 55
Massilia (Marseilles): SE France, on NE shore
of G of Lions. *Pn. 4, 6, 8*
Matadi: Africa, near mouth of Congo R. *P. 56*
Matapan, Cape: S Greece. *P. 50*
Matruh *see* **Mersa-Matruh**
Matzu: I between China & Formosa. *P. 63*
Mauretania: Reg, NW Africa. *P. 8*
Mauritania: Reg, NW Africa. *P. 56*
Mauritius: I in Indian O, E of Madagascar. *P. 62*
Mayence (Mainz): Germany, on Rhine R, at
confluence with Main R. *P. 16*
Meaux: N France, NE of Paris. *P. 17*
Mecca: W Arabia, near Red Sea. *Pp. 15, 25, 27,*
31, 56, 62
Mecklenburg: Reg, N Germany. *Pp. 40, 41, 44*
Media: Reg. between Mesopotamia & Caspian
Sea. *Pp. 3, 5*
Medina (al-Madina): W Arabia. *Pp. 15, 56, 62*
Mediolanum (Milan): N Italy. *Pp. 6, 8*
Mediterranean Sea. *Pp. 2, 8, 10, 14, 22, 27, 49,*
50, 56
Megara: Greece, on coast W of Athens.
P. 7 Inset
Megiddo: N Palestine, SW of Sea of Galilee. *P. 1*
Mekong: R in SE Asia, flowing into S China Sea.
P. 63
Melbourne: On SE coast of Australia. *Pp. 52, 64*
Melita *see* **Malta**
Melrose: S Scotland, on Tweed R. *P. 16*
Memel (Klaipeda): On E coast of Baltic Sea, N
of mouth of Niemen R. *Pp. 21, 23, 48*
Memphis (Menofer): Lower Egypt, on W bank of
Nile R. *Pp. 2, 4, 9*
Menderes *R see* **Maeander R**
Menofer *see* **Memphis**
Merionethshire: Co, NW Wales. *P. 33*
Mersa-Matruh: On W coast of Egypt. *P. 50*
Mesopotamia: Reg, lower valleys of Tigris R &
Euphrates R. *Pp. 3, 5*
Messenia: Reg, Greece, SW Peloponnesus.
P. 7 Inset
Messina: On NE coast of Sicily. *Pp. 19, 23*
Messina, Strait of: Between S Italy & NE Sicily.
P. 6
Metapontum: S Italy, on NW shore of Tarentum
G. *P. 6*
Metz: NE France, on Moselle R. *Pp. 12, 34, 48,*
51 Inset, 55
Meuse (Maas): R flowing NW from France to
North Sea near mouth of Rhine R. *Pp. 8, 16,*
42, 44, 48
Mexico: Central America. *P. 53*
Mexico, Gulf of: SE coast of North America.
Pp. 26, 38, 53
Mexico City (*1519*). Cen. Mexico. *Pp. 26, 30, 64*
Mézières: NE of Paris, on Meuse R. *P. 55*
Micale, Cape: On W coast of Anatolia. *P. 4a*
Middlesbrough: On NE coast of England. *P. 54*
Middlesex: Co, S cen. England. *P. 33*
Midia (Midye): NE Turkey in Europe, on Black
Sea. *P. 43*
Midway Is: In N cen. Pacific, NW of Honolulu.
P. 52
Midye *see* **Midia**
Mikindani: E Africa, SE Tanganyika. *P. 56*
Milan (Mediolanum): N Italy. *Pp. 10, 12, 14,*
19, 22, 28, 29, 32, 34, 42, 49, 50, 64
Milan, Duchy of. *P. 32*
Miletus: W coast of Anatolia. *Pp. 4a, 5a, 7*
Milford Haven: On S coast of Wales. *P. 54*
Mimizan: SW France. *P. 55*
Mindanao: Southernmost I in Philippine Is.
Pp. 52, 63
Mindoro: I, cen. Philippine Is. *P. 52*

Minhow (Foochow): On E coast of China, NW of
Formosa. *P. 63*
Minorca: I in Balearic Is, W Mediterranean Sea.
Pp. 19, 24, 36
Minsk: W cen. Russia, between Niemen R &
Dnieper R. *Pp. 45, 50, 58*
Miram, Waters of *see* **Huleh, Lake**
Mirandola: Italy, lower valley of Po R. *P. 32*
Mississippi: R in N America. *P. 38*
Mitanni: Reg, upper valley of Tigris R. *P. 3*
Mitrovica (Mitrovitza): Ottoman Empire, near
Serbian frontier. *P. 43*
Mitrovica *see* **Sirmium**
Mitumba Mts: Africa, W of L Tanganyika. *P. 56*
Mitilini *see* **Mytilene**
Moab: Reg, SE of Dead Sea. *Pp. 1, 2*
Modena: N Italy, S of Po R. *Pp. 9, 22, 32, 37,*
41, 49
Modena, Duchy of. *P. 32*
Moesia: Reg, lower valley of Danube R. *P. 9*
Mogadiscio (Mogadishu): On E coast of Africa,
in Somalia. *Pp. 56, 62*
Mogador: NW Africa, SW Morocco. *P. 56*
Mogilev: Russia, upper valley of Dnieper R.
P. 45
Möhne Dam: Germany, on Ruhr R. *P. 51 Inset*
Moldau: Tributary of Elbe R. *Pp. 23, 42*
Moldavia: Reg, SE Europe, N of Danube R.
Pp. 28, 35, 43
Moldavian SSR: Portion of USSR bordering on
Romania. *P. 58*
Molotov *see* **Perm**
Moluccas: Is between Celebes & New Guinea.
Pp. 25, 63
Mombasa: On E coast of Africa, N of Zanzibar.
Pp. 56, 62
Monaco: On SE coast of France. *P. 49*
Monastir *see* **Bitolj**
Mongolia: Reg, E cen. Asia, N of China. *Pp. 25,*
31
Mongolia, Inner: Reg, between Mongolian
People's Republic & N China. *P. 63*
Mongolian People's Republic (Outer Mongolia):
E cen. Asia. *Pp. 59, 63*
Monmouth: Co, NW shore of Bristol Channel.
P. 33
Monrovia: On coast of Liberia. *P. 56*
Mons: SW Belgium. *P. 54*
Mont Blanc: Between France & Italy. *P. 55*
Mont Cenis: Pass over the Alps. *Pp. 19, 22*
Monte Carlo: Extreme SE coast of France. *P. 55*
Monte Cassino: Cen. Italy, N of Naples. *Pp. 10, 14*
Montenegro: Reg, E coast of Adriatic Sea.
Pp. 41, 43, 60
Montmorency: N France, near Paris. *P. 17*
Montpellier: S France, near coast of Mediter-
ranean Sea. *Pp. 17, 19, 22, 55*
Montreal: E Canada, on St Lawrence R. *Pp. 20,*
38, 64
Mont-St-Michel: On coast of W Normandy.
P. 17
Morava: R in cen. Europe, flowing S to Danube
R. *Pp. 8, 23, 42, 44, 48*
Morava: R in Yugoslavia, flowing N to Danube
R. *P. 49*
Moravia: Reg, W of Carpathian Mts. *Pp. 18, 34,*
42, 44
Moray Firth: NE coast of Scotland. *P. 54*
Morea *see* **Peloponnesus**
Morocco: Reg, NW Africa. *Pp. 46, 56, 60, 61*
Mortain: SW Normandy. *P. 17*
Moscow: W cen. Russia. *Pp. 45, 51, 58, 64*
Moselle: R in France & Germany, in confluence
with Rhine R at Coblenz. *Pp. 16, 22, 48,*
51 Inset, 54
Mostar: Dalmatia. *P. 43*
Mosul: On upper Tigris R. *Pp. 20, 51, 58*
Motya: Near W extremity of Sicily. *P. 4*
Moulins: France, on Loire R, N of Massif
Central. *P. 55*
Mountains are listed under their names
Mozambique (*1498*): Reg. & city, SE Africa.
Pp. 27, 31, 47, 57, 62
Mozambique Channel: Strait between Mada-
gascar & SE Africa. *P. 57*
Mtwara: On extreme S coast of Tanganyika.
P. 57
Mukden (Shenyang): S Manchuria. *Pp. 59, 63, 64*
Mulhouse: NE France, near Rhine R. *Pp. 48, 55*
Munich (München): S Germany, Bavaria, on
Isar R. *Pp. 23, 32, 42, 48, 50*
Munster: NW Germany, between Weser R &
ower Rhine R. *Pp. 34*
Muqaiyir *see* **Ur**
Mura (Mur): Tributary of Drava R. *Pp. 42, 48*
Murcia: SE Spain. *P. 24*
Mures R *see* **Maros R**
Murmansk: On NW coast of Russia. *Pp. 51, 58*

Muscat: SE Arabia, on S coast of G of Oman.
P. 2
Muscovy: Reg, W cen. Russia. *P. 2*
Mweru, Lake: Cen. Africa. *P. 56*
Mycale (*battle 479* B.C.): W Anatolia, N c
mouth of Maeander R. *P.*
Mycenae: NE Peloponnesus, Greece, N of Argos
P. 7
Mysia: Reg, NW Anatolia. *P. 5*
Mysore: S India. *P. 6*
Mytilene (Mitilini): On I of Lesbos, E Aegea
Sea, near Anatolia. *P. 5*

Nablus *see* **Shechem**
Nagasaki: On SW coast of Japan. *Pp. 52, 6*
Nagoya: Cen. Japan, SW of Tokyo. *Pp. 59, 63, 6*
Nairobi: E Africa, S cen. Kenya. *Pp. 56, 6*
Namsos: On N cen. coast of Norway. *P. 5*
Namur: Belgium, on Maas R. *P. 51 Inse*
Nancy: NE France, in upper valley of Moselle R
Pp. 48, 51 Inset, 5
Nanking: E China, on Yangtze R. *Pp. 52, 59, 63*
6
Nan Shan Mts: N cen. China. *P. 6*
Nantes: France, at mouth of Loire R. *Pp. 17, 22*
50, 5
Nanumea: I in W Pacific, N of Fiji Is. *P. 5*
Naples (Neapolis, Parthenope): On SW coast o
Italy. *Pp. 14, 19, 28, 32, 35, 43, 49, 6*
Naples, Kingdom of. *Pp. 37, 4*
Narbada: R in cen. India, flowing W int
Arabian Sea. *P. 6*
Narbo (Narbonne): S France, on G of Lions. *P.*
Narbonensis: Reg, S France. *P.*
Narbonne: S France, on G of Lions. *Pp. 10, 13*
17, 22, 5
Narva: On G of Finland. *P. 5*
Narva: R flowing into G of Finland. *P. 5*
Narvik: N Norway. *P. 5*
Naseby (*battle 1645*): Cen. England, in North
amptonshire. *P. 3*
Nassau: Reg, on Rhine R. *P. 4*
Nassau, Duchy of. *P. 4*
Naucratis: Egypt, in Nile Delta. *P.*
Naumburg: Germany, on Saale R. *P. 1*
Naupactus (Lepanto, *sea battle 1571*): coast o
cen. Greece, on G of Corinth. *P. 5*
Navarre: Reg, NE Spain. *Pp. 24, 2*
Naxos: NE Sicily. *P.*
Naxos: I in S Aegean Sea. *Pp. 4, 4a, 7, 2*
Nazareth (En Nasira): W of Sea of Galilee. *Pp.*
2
Ndola: Fed. of Rhodesia & Nyasaland, nea
Congo panhandle. *P. 5*
Neapolis (Naples, Parthenope): On SW coast o
Italy. *Pp. 5a, 6,*
Neckar: Tributary of Rhine R, SW German
P. 4
Negeb: Reg, S Palestine. *P.*
Negrais, Cape (Pagoda Point): Burma, SW c
Rangoon. *P. 6*
Negropont *see* **Chalcis and Euboea**
Neisse: Tributary of Oder R. *P. 4*
Neman (Niemen): R in W Russia, flowing int
Baltic Sea. *P. 5*
Nemausus (Nîmes): S France, in valley of Rhôn
R *Pp. 6,*
Nepal: Reg, NE of India. *Pp. 52, 6*
Netherlands: NW Europe, on North Sea. *P. 3*
42, 48, 54, 58, 60, 6
Netherlands, Kingdom of the. *P. 4*
Netherlands East Indies. *P. 5*
Neuchâtel, Lake: W Switzerland, N of L Geneva
P. 5
Neuhäusel: NW Ottoman Empire, near Bud
Pest. *P. 3*
Neustria: Reg, NW Europe. *P. 14 Inse*
Nevers: Cen. France, on upper Loire R. *Pp. 17, 5*
New Amsterdam (New York): North Americ
P. 3
Newark: Cen. England, on Trent R. *P. 1*
Newburn (*battle 1640*): NE England. *P. 3*
Newbury (*battles, 1642, 1644*): S cen. Englanc
P. 3
New Caledonia: I in SW Pacific, E of Australia
P. 5
New Carthage (Cartagena): S coast of Spain. *P.*
Newcastle: On NE coast of England. *Pp. 10, 14*
21, 22, 33, 5
Newchwang (Yingkow): S Manchuria, at base o
Liaotung Penin. *P. 6*
Newfoundland: I in N Atlantic, E of Canada
Pp. 26, 3

New Granada (*1536*): NW. S America. *P. 26*
New Guinea: I, E Malay Archipelago, N of Australia. *Pp. 47, 52*
New Hebrides: Is. in SW Pacific, NE of Australia. *P. 47*
New Orleans: Near G of Mexico, on Mississippi R. *P. 38*
Newport: On N shore of Bristol Channel. *P. 54*
New York (New Amsterdam): NE. USA. *Pp. 53, 64*
New Zealand: S Pacific. *Pp. 47, 52*
Niamey: Africa, on Niger R. *P. 56*
Nicaea: E of Sea of Marmora. *Pp. 11, 14, 20*
Nicaea (Nice): On SE coast of Gaul. *P. 10*
Nicaea, Empire of. *P. 20 Inset*
Nicaragua: Central America. *Pp. 26, 53*
Nice (Nicaea): SE France, on Mediterranean coast. *Pp. 32, 49, 50, 55*
Nicomedia (Izmit): NW Anatolia, on E arm of Sea of Marmora. *Pp. 7, 9*
Niemen (Neman): R in Russia, flowing into Baltic Sea. *Pp. 21, 23, 44, 45, 48*
Niger: R in W Africa, flowing into G of Guinea. *P. 27*
Nigeria: Reg, W Africa. *Pp. 47, 56*
Nijmegen (Nimwegen): E Netherlands, on lower Rhine R. *P. 51 Inset*
Nikopol: USSR, Ukraine, on lower Dnieper R. *P. 58*
Nile: R in NE Africa, flowing N into Mediterranean Sea. *Pp. 2, 4, 9, 11, 14, 20, 25, 56, 62*
Nile Delta: mouth of Nile R. *P. 20*
Nilgiri Hills: S India. *P. 62*
Nimes (Nemausus): S France, in valley of lower Rhône R. *Pp. 17, 55*
Nimwegen *see* Nijmegen
Nineveh: Assyria, on Tigris R. *P. 3*
Ninghsien (Ningpo): E China, S of Shanghai. *P. 63*
Nish (Nis): N Balkan penin, S of Danube R. *Pp. 12, 43*
Nizhni Novgorod (Gorki, Gorky): Cen. Russia, on upper Volga R. *P. 45*
Nizh.-Tagil: USSR, on E slope of Ural Mts. *P. 58*
Norcia *see* Nursia
Norfolk: Co, E England. *P. 33*
Noricum: Reg, S of upper Danube R. *P. 8*
Norilsk: N. USSR, near mouth of Yenisei R. *P. 59*
Normandy: Reg, NW France. *P. 17*
Northamptonshire: Co, S cen. England. *P. 33*
North Dvina: R in NW Russia flowing into White Sea. *P. 45*
Northern Ireland. *Pp. 54, 58*
North Frisian Is: North Sea, along coast between Zuider Zee & mouth of Weser R. *P. 54*
North Korea *see* Korea
North Sea: Arm of Atlantic, between Great Britain & Scandinavia. *Pp. 14, 16, 21, 22, 44, 48, 50, 54*
Northumberland: Co, NE England. *P. 33*
Norway. *Pp. 16, 21, 28, 29, 36, 50, 58, 60, 61*
Norwich: E England, in Norfolk. *Pp. 16, 33, 54*
Notium: On W coast of Anatolia. *P. 5a*
Nottingham: Cen. England. *Pp. 16, 33, 54*
Nottinghamshire: Co, cen. England. *P. 33*
Nova Lisboa: W cen. Angola. *P. 57*
Novara: NW Italy, in upper valley of Po R. *P. 32*
Nova Scotia: Reg, SE Canada. *Pp. 26, 38*
Novgorod: NW Russia, S of L Ladoga. *Pp. 21, 45*
Novi Bazar: Ottoman Empire, near border of Serbia. *P. 43*
Novocherkassk: S Russia, on lower Don R. *P. 45*
Novorossiisk: Russia, on NE coast of Black Sea. *P. 45*
Novosibirsk: USSR, on upper Ob R. *Pp. 51, 59*
Noyon: N France, on upper Oise R. *Pp. 17, 22*
Nubian Desert: E of Nile R. *Pp. 56, 62*
Nuremberg: Germany, NW Bavaria, S of upper Main R. *Pp. 18, 22, 44*
Nursia (Norcia): Italy, in cen. Apennines. *P. 6*
Nyasa, Lake: SE Africa. *P. 57*
Nyasaland: Reg, SE Africa. *P. 47*

Ob: R in USSR, E of Ural Mts, flowing into Arctic Ocean. *P. 58*
Ochrida: on L at head of Drin R. *P. 43*
Oder (Odra): R in cen. Europe, flowing N to Baltic Sea. *Pp. 8, 10, 21, 23, 34, 42, 44, 48, 50*
Odessa: S Russia, on W coast of Black Sea. *Pp. 45, 51, 58*
Odessus: On W coast of Black Sea. *P. 4*
Odoacer, Kingdom of. *P. 12*
Odra R *see* Oder R

Ogooué (Ogowe): R in W Africa, flowing into G of Guinea near C Lopez. *P. 56*
Oise: Tributary of Seine R, N France. *P. 17*
Okhotsk, Sea of: Arm of Pacific, E of Russia in Asia. *P. 59*
Okinawa: Largest I in Ryukyu group, SE of Japan, in W Pacific. *Pp. 52, 63*
Olbia: On Mediterranean coast, E of Massilia. *P. 4*
Olbia: On NE coast of Sardinia. *P. 4*
Oldenburg: Reg, NW Germany, on North Sea. *P. 41*
Oléron, Ile d': W of France, near La Rochelle. *Pp. 17, 55*
Olmütz (Olomouc): On upper Morava R. *Pp. 42, 48*
Olympia: NW Peloponnesus. *Pp. 5a, 7 Inset*
Olympus, Mt: NE Greece. *P. 7*
Olynthus (*battle 348 B.C.*): Macedonia, NE Greece. *P. 7*
Oman: Reg, SE Arabian penin. *P. 62*
Oman, Gulf of: Arm of Arabian Sea, extending between Oman & Iran. *P. 62*
Ommiads, Emirate of. *P. 14*
Omsk: USSR, E of Ural Mts, on Trans-Siberian Railway. *P. 59*
Onega, Lake: N Russia, E of L Ladoga. *Pp. 45, 58*
Opis: On Tigris R. *P. 5*
Oporto: NW Portugal, on Douro R. *Pp. 24, 27*
Oradour: France, W of Masif Central. *Pp. 50, 55*
Oran: NW Africa, SW of Algiers. *Pp. 50, 56*
Orange: R in S Africa. *P. 57*
Ordos Plateau: N cen. China. *P. 63*
Orel: Cen. Russia, N of upper Donets R, S of Moscow. *Pp. 45, 51, 58*
Orenburg (Chkalov): Russia, on Ural R. *P. 45*
Orkney Is: NE of Scotland. *Pp. 16, 21, 33, 54*
Orléans: N cen. France, on Loire R. *Pp. 12, 17, 18, 22, 55*
Ormuz (*1515*): On coast at entrance to Persian G. *Pp. 25, 27, 31*
Orontes: R in Syria, flowing N & W to Mediterranean Sea. *Pp. 1, 2, 20*
Orsk: At S extremity of Ural Mts. *P. 58*
Orvieto: Cen. Italy, in Papal States, W of L Bolsena. *P. 32*
Osaka: S coast of Japan, W of Nagoya. *Pp. 59, 63, 64*
Oslo: On SE coast of Norway. *Pp. 21, 50, 58*
Osnabrück: NW Germany, between Weser R & lower Rhine R. *P. 34*
Ostend: Belgium, on North Sea. *P. 54*
Ostia: Italy, at mouth of Tiber R. *Pp. 6, 8, 10, 32*
Ostrogoths, The. *Pp. 12, 13*
Oświęcim *see* Auschwitz
Otranto: SE tip of S Italy. *P. 32*
Otranto, Strait of: Between SE Italy & W Albania. *P. 43*
Ottoman Empire. *Pp. 28, 29, 35, 36, 37, 40, 41, 43, 47, 60*
Outer Mongolia: E cen. Asia, between China & USSR. *P. 52*
Oxford: S cen. England. *Pp. 16, 33, 54*
Oxfordshire: Co, S cen. England. *P. 33*
Oxus: R, flowing from cen. Asian mountain mass into Aral Sea. *P. 5*

Pacific Ocean. *Pp. 25, 46, 52, 53*
Padua: NE Italy, NW of Venice. *P. 32*
Padus R *see* Po R
Paestum *see* Poseidonia
Pagoda Point *see* Negrais, Cape
Pakistan: Regions, NW India & NE India. *Pp. 62, 63*
Palatinate: Reg, on upper Rhine R. *Pp. 41, 44*
Palermo (Panormus): On NW coast of Sicily. *Pp. 19, 23, 32*
Palestine: E of Mediterranean Sea. *Pp. 9, 51*
Palma: Majorca. *P. 24*
Palmyra (Tadmor): Syria, NE of Damascus. *Pp. 9, 11*
Palos: On S coast of Spain. *P. 27*
Pamirs: Mts, extreme W of Asian mountain mass. *P. 62*
Pampeluna (Pamplona): NE Spain. *P. 24*
Pamphylia: Reg, on S coast of Anatolia. *P. 4*
Pamplona *see* Pampeluna
Panama (*1519*): S Central America. *Pp. 26, 53*
Panama Canal: Cen. America between Atlantic & Pacific. *P. 53*
Panama Canal Zone: Central America. *P. 46*
Pannonia: Reg, between E end of Alps & upper Danube R. *Pp. 6, 8*

Panormus (Palermo): On NW coast of Sicily. *P. 4*
Panticapaeum: Caucasus, on Black Sea, opposite Crimea. *P. 5*
Papal States: Cen. Italy. *Pp. 19, 28, 29, 32, 36, 37, 40, 41*
Paphlagonia: Reg, N cen. Anatolia. *P. 4*
Paraguay: Cen. S America. *P. 53*
Parentis: SW France. *P. 55*
Paris (Lutetia): NW France, on Seine R, just below confluence of Marne R. *Pp. 13, 14, 17, 18, 22, 42, 48, 50, 55, 58, 64*
Parma: Reg. & city, N Italy, in cen. valley of Po R. *Pp. 32, 37, 41, 49*
Parthenope (Neapolis, Naples): On SW coast of Italy. *P. 4*
Parthia: Reg, SE of Caspian Sea. *P. 5*
Parthian Empire. *P. 9*
Pasargadae: On Alexander's route, S Plateau of Iran. *P. 5*
Patagonia: Reg, at S end of S America. *P. 26*
Patna: N India, on Ganges R. *P. 63*
Patras: Greece, NW Peloponnesus. *P. 43*
Pattala: On Alexander's route, India, on Indus R. *P. 5*
Pau: France, N of Pyrenees. *P. 55*
Pavia: N Italy, on Po R. *Pp. 14, 22, 32*
Pearl Harbor: Inlet on S coast of Oahu I, W of Honolulu, mid-Pacific. *P. 53*
Pechora: R in Russia, flowing NW from Ural Mts into Arctic O. *Pp. 45, 58*
Pécs *see* Fünfkirchen
Peenemünde: Germany, on Baltic coast, opposite Sweden. *P. 50*
Peiping (Peking): NE China. *Pp. 59, 63, 64*
Peking: NE China. *Pp. 25, 31*
Peipus, Lake: Estonia, S of G of Finland. *Pp. 21, 45, 50*
Pella: Macedonia. *P. 7*
Peloponnesus (Morea): S part of Greece. *Pp. 5a, 7, 43*
Pembroke: SW Wales. *P. 33*
Pembrokeshire: Co, SW Wales. *P. 33*
Pennines: Mts in cen. England. *P. 33*
Penza: Cen. Russia, on tributary of Volga R. *Pp. 45, 58*
Penzance: Extreme SW England. *P. 54*
Perekop: S. USSR, at isthmus between Crimea & mainland. *P. 51*
Pergamum (Bergama): W Anatolia. *Pp. 4, 7, 9*
Périgueux: France, W of Massif Central. *Pp. 17, 55*
Perm (Molotov): E cen. Russia, E of Ural Mts. *P. 45*
Pernambuco (*1500*): E Brazil. *P. 26*
Perpignan: France, N of E Pyrenees. *P. 55*
Persepolis: On Alexander's route, S of Plateau of Iran. *P. 5*
Persia (Iran). *Pp. 3, 7, 25, 58*
Persian Empire. *P. 4a*
Persian Gulf: Arm of Arabian Sea, between Arabia & Iran (Persia). *Pp. 3, 5, 15, 25, 27, 56, 62*
Persis: Reg, NW of Persian G. *P. 5*
Perth: Cen. Scotland. *Pp. 16, 33, 54*
Peru: W coast of S America. *P. 53*
Perugia: Cen. Italy, on upper Tiber R. *Pp. 32, 49*
Peruvian Andes: Mt range, W. S America, S of Equator. *P. 26*
Pescadores: Is, off E coast of China. *P. 63*
Peshawar: W Pakistan, near Khyber Pass. *P. 62*
Pest (Budapest): Cen. Hungary, on Danube R. *Pp. 23, 34*
Peterborough: Cen. England, SW of The Wash. *Pp. 16, 54*
Petra (Sela): Between Dead Sea & G of Aqaba. *P. 1*
Petrozavodsk: N Russia, on W shore of L Onega. *P. 45*
Petsamo: On NW coast of Russia (Finland) on Arctic O. *Pp. 51, 58*
Pevensey: On S coast of England, W of Hastings. *P. 16*
Phanagoria: W Caucasus, opposite Crimea. *P. 5*
Pharpar: R flowing into desert E from Mt Hermon. *P. 1*
Pharsalus: On mainland of Greece. *P. 7*
Phasis: Extreme E shore of Black Sea. *Pp. 5, 9*
Philadelphia: NE. USA. *Pp. 38, 64*
Philiphaugh: S cen. Scotland. *P. 33*
Philippi (*battle 42 B.C.*): S Macedonia, N of Thasos I. *Pp. 7, 9*
Philippine Is: W Pacific, E of S China Sea. *Pp. 25, 47, 52, 63*
Philippine Sea: Part of W Pacific, E of Philippine Is. *P. 63*
Philippopolis (Plovdiv): S Balkan penin, on Maritza R. *Pp. 20, 43*

Philistia: Reg, on coast, W of Dead Sea.
P. 1 Inset
Phocaea: W Anatolia, on Aegean Sea. *P. 7*
Phocis: Reg, cen. Greece. *P. 7a*
Phoenicia: Reg, on E coast of Mediterranean Sea. *Pp. 1, 5*
Phra (Prophthasia): On Alexander's route, NE of Plateau of Iran. *P. 5*
Phrygia: Reg, W cen. Anatolia. *Pp. 4, 7*
Piacenza: NW Italy, on Po R. *P. 32*
Piave: R in N Italy, flowing into Adriatic Sea. *P. 42*
Picts, The. *Pp. 12, 13*
Piedmont: Reg, NW Italy. *P. 29*
Pilsen: Bohemia, Czechoslovakia. *Pp. 42, 48*
Pindus Mts: NW Greece. *Pp. 35, 43*
Piraeus: Greece, on Saronic G, harbor for Athens. *Pp. 7 Inset, 43*
Pirot: SE Serbia. *P. 43*
Pisa: Cen. Italy, on Arno R. *Pp. 19, 22, 32, 50*
Pisidia: Reg, S Anatolia. *P. 4*
Pistoia: Italy, Republic of Florence, E of Apennines. *P. 32*
Pithom: NE Egypt. *P. 2*
Plataea (*battle 479* B.C.): E cen. Greece, S of Thebes. *Pp. 4a, 7 Inset*
Plevna: Cen. Bulgaria. *P. 43*
Ploeşti: SE cen. Romania. *Pp. 43, 50*
Plovdiv *see* Philippopolis
Plymouth: On SW coast of England. *Pp. 33, 39, 54*
Po (Padus): R in N Italy, flowing E to Adriatic Sea. *Pp. 6, 8, 10, 14, 17, 22, 32, 34, 49*
Podgorica: Montenegro. *P. 43*
Poissy: N France, on Seine R. *P. 17*
Poitiers (*battle 1356*): W cen. France, SE of Nantes. *Pp. 14, 17, 55*
Pola: On NE coast of Adriatic Sea. *Pp. 23, 42, 49*
Poland. *Pp. 18, 21, 28, 29, 36, 45, 48, 50, 58, 60, 61*
Poland, Government General of. *P. 61*
Poland, Kingdom of. *Pp. 34, 37, 41*
Poltava (*battle 1709*): Russia, between Donets R & Dnieper R. *P. 45*
Pomerania: Reg, NE Germany, on Baltic Sea. *P. 18*
Pomerania, Eastern: Reg, NE Germany, on Baltic Sea. *P. 34*
Pomerania, Western: Reg, NE Germany, on Baltic Sea. *P. 34*
Pomerelia: Reg, on Baltic Sea, W of Vistula R. *P. 21*
Pompeii: S Italy, SE of Neapolis (Naples). *Pp. 6, 8*
Pondicherry: On E coast of India, S of Madras. *Pp. 25, 62*
Pontus: NE Anatolia, along shore of Black Sea. *Pp. 5, 9*
Pontus: Diocese of. *P. 11*
Poona: W India. *P. 62*
Port Arthur: S Manchuria, S end of Liaotung Penin. *Pp. 59, 63*
Port Darwin: On coast of N cen. Australia. *P. 52*
Port Elizabeth: on S coast of S Africa. *P. 57*
Port Harcourt: W Africa, E of Niger R. *P. 56*
Port Lyautey (Kénitra): NW Africa, on coast of Morocco. *P. 56*
Port Moresby: On SE coast of New Guinea. *P. 52*
Port Nolloth: On NW coast of S Africa, near mouth of Orange R. *P. 57*
Porto Bello: Central America, on Caribbean coast of Panama. *P. 26*
Port Said: NE Egypt, on Mediterranean Sea, N end of Suez Canal. *Pp. 51, 56, 62*
Portsmouth: On S coast of England, near I of Wight. *Pp. 33, 50, 54*
Port Sudan: NE Sudan, on Red Sea. *Pp. 56, 62*
Portugal: W extremity of Europe, W of Spain. *Pp. 24, 28, 29, 36, 37, 50, 60, 61*
Poseidonia (Paestum): On SW coast of Italy. *P. 4*
Posen (Poznań): Between Oder R & Vistula R. *Pp. 42, 44*
Potidaea: On SE coast of Macedonia. *Pp. 5a, 7*
Poznań (Posen): Between Oder R & Vistula R. *Pp. 48, 58*
Prague: Cen. Europe, on Moldau R. *Pp. 18, 23, 34, 42, 44, 48, 50, 58, 64*
Prato: N Italy, between Arno R & Apennines. *P. 32*
Pressburg (Bratislava): At confluence of Danube R & Morava R. *Pp.. 34, 42, 44*
Preston: NW England. *Pp. 33, 54*
Prestwick Airport: W cen. Scotland. *P. 54*
Pretoria: S cen. Transvaal, S Africa. *P. 57*
Principe: I in G of Guinea. *P. 56*
Pripet: Tributary of Dnieper R, W Russia. *See Front Endpaper*
Pripet Marshes: E Poland & W Russia. *P. 50*
Prizrend: Ottoman Empire, E of Drin R. *P. 43*

Prophthasia *see* Phra
Propontis (Sea of Marmora): Between Europe & Anatolia; with Dardanelles (Hellespont) & Bosporus, links Aegean Sea & Black Sea. *Pp. 4a, 7*
Provence: Reg, SE of Rhône valley. *P. 17*
Provins: N France, between Seine R & Marne R. *Pp. 17, 22*
Prussia: Reg, N & E Germany. *Pp. 18, 21, 28, 36, 37, 42, 44*
Prussia, Duchy of. *P. 34*
Prussia, Kingdom of. *Pp. 40, 41*
Prut (Pruth): Tributary of Danube R. *Pp. 9, 23, 43, 45*
Pskov: SE of L Peipus. *P. 45*
Puerto Rico (*1493*): I in W Indies. *P. 26*
Punjab: Reg, NW India. *Pp. 5, 62*
Pusan: E Asia, on SE coast of Korea. *P. 59*
Pylos (Pylus): On SW coast of Peloponnesus. *Pp. 5a, 7 Inset*
Pyongyang: N Korea. *P. 59*
Pyrenees: Mts in SW Europe, from B of Biscay to coast of G of Lions. *Pp. 8, 14, 17, 24, 55*

Quebec (Stadacona): SE Canada, on St. Lawrence R. *P. 38*
Quelimane: Africa, on E coast of Mozambique. *P. 57*
Quemoy: I off coast of China, W of Formosa. *P. 63*
Quito: W S America. *P. 26*

Rabat: NW Africa, NW Morocco. *P. 56*
Rabaul: NE New Britain I, Bismarck Archipelago, W Pacific. *P. 52*
Rabbath-ammon (Amman): NE of Dead Sea, on headwaters of Jabbok R. *P. 1*
Radnorshire: Co, cen. Wales. *P. 33*
Raetia: Reg, S of Danube R. *P. 8*
Ragusa (Dubrovnik): On cen. coast of Adriatic Sea. *Pp. 23, 32, 43*
Ragusa, Republic of. *P. 35*
Ramoth-gilead: SE of Sea of Galilee, in valley of Yarmuk R. *P. 1*
Rangoon: S Burma, on Irrawaddy R. *Pp. 52, 62*
Rann of Cutch: Marshy area, NW India. *P. 62*
Rapallo: On NW coast of Italy. *P. 49*
Ratisbon (Regensburg, Castra Regina): S Germany, on Danube R. *P. 10*
Ravenna: NE Italy, SW of mouth of Po R. *Pp. 6, 10, 12, 13, 14, 19, 23, 32, 49*
Ré, Ile de: Off W coast of France, in B of Biscay. *P. 55*
Reading: S England, W of London. *Pp. 33, 54*
Red (Yuan): R in China & Indo-China, flowing into G of Tonkin. *P. 63*
Red Sea: Between W Arabia & NE Africa. *Pp. 2, 9, 15, 25, 27, 56, 62*
Regensburg (Ratisbon, Castra Regina): S Germany, on Danube R. *Pp. 18, 34, 48*
Reggio *see* Rhegion (Rhegium)
Reims: NE France, Champagne, N of Marne R. *Pp. 13, 14, 17, 18, 22, 48, 50, 55*
Remagen: W Germany, on Rhine R, NW of Coblenz. *Pp. 50, 51 Inset*
Rennes: NW France, Brittany. *P. 55*
Resina *see* Herculaneum
Rethel: NE France, on tributary of Oise R. *P. 17*
Réunion: I in Indian O, E of Madagascar. *P. 62*
Reval (Revel): On G of Finland. *Pp. 21, 4a*
Rhegion (Rhegium, Reggio): S Italy, on Strait of Messina. *Pp. 4, 5a*
Rhine: R in W Europe, flowing N to North Sea. *Pp. 8, 10, 16, 22, 34, 42, 44, 48, 50, 51 Inset, 55*
Rhine, Confederation of the. *Pp. 37, 40, 41*
Rhine, Palatinate of the. *P. 34*
Rhineland: Reg, W Germany. *P. 48*
Rhodes: I in SE Aegean Sea, off SW coast of Anatolia. *Pp. 4, 4a, 7, 9, 11, 20, 23, 50*
Rhodesia: SE cen. Africa. *P. 57*
Rhodope Mts: Between Aegean Sea & Balkan Mts. *Pp. 35, 43*
Rhône: R flowing from Switzerland through France to Mediterranean Sea. *Pp. 8, 10, 17, 22, 32, 42, 49, 55*
Rhuddlan: N Wales. *P. 16*
Riblah: NE of Lebanon Mts, on Orontes R. *P. 1*
Richmond: N cen. England. *P. 16*
Riga: On S coast of Baltic Sea at mouth of W Dvina R. *Pp. 21, 23, 45, 50, 58*
Rijeka *see* Fiume
Rimini: NE coast of Italy. *Pp. 32, 50*

Rio de Janeiro (*1555*): On SE coast of Brazil *Pp. 26, 30, 64*
Rio de la Plata (*1501*): R in S America flowing into S Atlantic. *Pp. 26, 30*
Rio de Oro (Ouro): Reg, on NW coast of Africa *Pp. 26, 46*
Riom: S cen. France, in N Massif Central. *P. 55*
Rio Muni: Reg, W Africa, E of G of Guinea. *P. 47*
Risley: NW cen. England. *P. 54*
Rochester: On SE coast of England, near mouth of Thames R. *Pp. 16, 54*
Rodez: S cen. France, on tributary of Garonne R. *P. 17*
Roer: Tributary of Maas R, Germany & France. *P. 51 Inset*
Romania: Reg, SE Europe. *Pp. 43, 44, 45, 50, 58, 60, 61*
Rome: Italy, on Tiber R. *Pp. 6, 8, 10, 12, 13, 14, 19, 23, 27, 32, 35, 43, 49, 50, 58, 64*
Rome, Diocese of. *P. 10*
Roncaglia: N Italy, on Po R. *P. 19*
Roncesvalles: Spain, pass over Pyrenees to France. *Pp. 14, 17*
Rosslare: On SE coast of Ireland. *P. 54*
Rostock: On SW coast of Baltic Sea. *P. 21*
Rostov: Russia, near mouth of Don R. *Pp. 45, 51, 58*
Rotterdam: W Netherlands, near mouth of Rhine R. *Pp. 48, 50, 54*
Roubaix: NE France, near Belgian border. *P. 54*
Rouen: N France, on Seine R. *Pp. 17, 22, 55*
Roum, Sultanate of. *Pp. 20, 20 Inset*
Roussillon: Reg, E end of Pyrenees. *P. 24*
RSFSR *see* Russian Soviet Federated Socialist Republic
Rubicon: R in N cen. Italy, flowing E into Adriatic Sea. *P. 6*
Rudolf, Lake: E Africa, N Kenya. *P. 56*
Ruhr: Reg, in W Germany. *Pp. 22, 50, 51 Inset*
Ruhr: Tributary of lower Rhine R, W Germany. *Pp. 48, 54*
Rukwa, Lake: SW Tanganyika. *P. 56*
Rumelia: Reg, N & W of Aegean Sea. *P. 35*
Rumelia, Eastern: Between Ottoman Empire & Bulgaria on Black Sea. *P. 43*
Runnymede: On S bank of Thames R, S England. *P. 16*
Ruschuk (Ruse): Bulgaria, on Danube R. *P. 43*
Russia. *Pp. 21, 28, 29, 40, 41, 45*
Russian Soviet Federated Socialist Republic (RSFSR). *Pp. 58, 59*
Rutland: Co, cen. England, SW of The Wash. *P. 33*
Ruvuma: R in E Africa, border of Tanganyika & Mozambique. *P. 57*
Ryazan: Cen. Russia, SE of Moscow. *P. 45*
Ryukyu Is: SW of Japan, between E China Sea & Pacific. *Pp. 52, 63*

Saale: Tributary of Elbe R, cen. Germany. *Pp. 23, 48*
Saar: Reg, between Moselle R & Rhine R. *Pp. 48, 51 Inset, 55, 60*
Saarbrücken: Between Moselle R & Rhine R. *Pp. 48, 51 Inset, 55*
Sadowa (Königgratz, *battle 1866*): Bohemia, on upper Elbe R. *P. 42*
Safi: NW Africa, W cen. Morocco. *P. 56*
Sagami Bay: Japan, E coast of Honshu, S of Yokohama. *P. 52*
Sagres: On SW coast of Portugal, near C St Vincent. *Pp. 24, 27*
Sahara Desert. *P. 56*
Saigon: Indo-China, on Saigon R. *P. 52*
Saigon-Cholon: SE Asia. *P. 64*
St Albans: S cen. England. *P. 16*
St Andrews: On E coast of Scotland. *Pp. 33, 54*
St Augustine (*1565*): NE Florida, on Atlantic. *P. 26*
St Bernard, Great: Pass over the Alps. *Pp. 19, 22, 55*
St Bernard, Little: Pass over the Alps. *P. 19*
St Bernardino: Pass over the Alps. *P. 18*
St David's: On SW coast of Wales. *P. 16*
St Etienne: SE cen. France, between upper Loire R & Rhône R. *Pp. 49, 55*
St Gall: In valley of upper Rhine R. *P. 19*
St George's Channel: Strait between Wales & Ireland. *P. 54*
St Gotthard (*battle 1664*): W Hungary, on tributary of Danube R. *P. 34*
St Gotthard: Pass over the Alps. *P. 32*
St Helena: I in S Atlantic. *P. 57*
St Ives: S cen. England. *P. 22*

St Jean d'Angély: France, W of Massif Central. *P. 17*

St Lawrence: R in Canada. *Pp. 26, 38*

St Louis: W Africa, N of Dakar. *P. 56*

St Louis (*1764*): On Mississippi R. *P. 38*

St Malo: On NW coast of France. *Pp. 17, 27*

St Nazaire: NW France, at mouth of Loire R. *Pp. 50, 55*

St Petersburg (Leningrad): At E end of G of Finland. *P. 45*

St Quentin: N France, on Somme R. *P. 22*

St Vincent, Cape: Extreme SW Portugal. *P. 24*

Saipan: S cen. Marianas Is, W Pacific. *P. 52*

Sakarya (Sangarius): R in NW Anatolia. *See Front Endpaper*

Sakhalin: I in W Okhotsk Sea, N of Japan. *Pp. 47, 59*

Salamanca: W cen. Spain. *Pp. 24, 55*

Salamis (*battle 480* B.C.): I in Saronic G, near Athens. *Pp. 4a, 7 Inset*

Salamis: E coast of Cyprus. *P. 4*

Salem: Massachusetts. *P. 38*

Salerno: On SW coast of Italy, SE of Naples. *Pp. 32, 50*

Salisbury: S cen. England. *Pp. 16, 33, 54*

Salisbury: Fed. of Rhodesia & Nyasaland. *P. 57*

Salla: Reg, N Finland. *P. 50*

Salonika (Thessalonica): S cen. Macedonia, near mouth of Vardar (Axius) R. *Pp. 11, 35, 43*

Saluzzo: NW Italy, on tributary of Po R. *P. 32*

Salween: R in SE Asia, flowing through China & Burma. *P. 63*

Salzburg: Austria, between Inn R & Danube R. *Pp. 14, 18, 42, 44, 48*

Samara (Kuibyshev): Russia, on eastward loop of Volga R. *P. 45*

Samaria (Sebastye): Reg, W of Jordan R. *P. 1*

Samarkand: Asia, SE of Aral Sea. *Pp. 25, 62*

Samoa: Is. in SW cen. Pacific, NE of Fiji Is. *P. 52*

Samogitia: Reg, on coast of Baltic Sea, between Niemen R & W Dvina R. *P. 21*

Samos: I in E Aegean Sea, off W coast of Anatolia. *Pp. 4, 4a, 5a, 7*

Sancerre: Cen. France, on Loire R. *P. 17*

Sandwich: On SE coast of England. *Pp. 16, 22*

San Francisco: On cen. W coast of U.S.A. *P. 53*

Sangarius R *see* Sakarya R

Sanjak of Novibazar: Reg, Ottoman Empire, between Montenegro & Serbia. *P. 43*

Sankuru: Tributary of Kasai R, cen. Africa. *P. 56*

San Marino: Reg, E cen. Italy. *Pp. 32, 49*

San Salvador (*1492*): W North Atlantic. *Pp. 26, 38*

San Stefano: Near Constantinople *P. 43*

Santa Catalina: I in Atlantic, off SW coast of S America. *P. 26*

Santander: N Spain, on B of Biscay. *Pp. 17, 24, 55*

Santarem: Cen. Portugal, on Tagus R. *P. 24*

Santiago: Chile. *Pp. 26, 64*

Santiago de Compostella: NW Spain. *Pp. 22, 24*

Saône: Tributary of Rhône R, E France. *Pp. 17, 22, 42, 48, 55*

São Paulo: On E coast of S America. *P. 26*

São Tomé: I in G of Guinea, W Africa. *Pp. 27, 56*

Saragossa: NE Spain, on Ebro R. *Pp. 14, 17, 24, 55*

Sarai: W Asia, on Volga R. *P. 27*

Sarajevo: Bosnia, SW of Belgrade. *Pp. 35, 43, 44*

Saratoga: N America, on Hudson R. *P. 38*

Saratov: Russia, on Volga R. *Pp. 45, 58*

Sarawak: NW Borneo. *P. 63*

Sardinia: I in Mediterranean Sea, W of Italy. *Pp. 6, 8, 14, 19, 22, 32, 49, 50*

Sardinia, Kingdom of. *Pp. 36, 37, 40, 41*

Sardis: W Anatolia. *P. 4a*

Sarmatia: Reg, N of Black Sea. *P. 11*

Saronic Gulf (G of Aegina): Inlet of Aegean Sea, on SE coast of Greece. *Pp. 5a, 7*

Sarreguemines: NE France, between upper Moselle R & Rhine R. *P. 55*

Saudi Arabia: Arabian penin. *Pp. 51, 56, 62*

Sava: Tributary of Danube R. *Pp. 8, 23, 34, 43, 49*

Saverne: Between Moselle R & Rhine R. *P. 51 Inset*

Savo: I in SE Solomon Is, W Pacific. *P. 52*

Savoy: Reg, SE France & NW Italy. *Pp. 17, 28, 29, 34*

Savoy, Duchy of. *Pp. 12, 13, 14*

Saxons, The. *P. 32*

Saxony: Reg. on lower Elbe R. *Pp. 16, 18*

Saxony: Reg. on upper Elbe R. *Pp. 36, 40, 41, 44*

Saxony, Electorate of. *P. 34*

Scandinavia: N Europe. *See Front Endpaper*

Scania: Reg, extreme S of Sweden. *P. 21*

Scapa Flow: Orkney Is, off N coast of Scotland. *P. 54*

Scheldt: R in W Europe, flowing into North Sea. *Pp. 16, 22, 48, 54*

Schleswig: Reg, NW Germany. *P. 44*

Schwerin: S of Wismar, near coast of Baltic Sea. *P. 21*

Scotland: N part British Is. *Pp. 16, 21, 28, 29,54*

Scots, The. *Pp. 12, 13*

Scutari (Üsküdar): Ottoman Empire, near Constantinople. *P. 43*

Sebastye *see* Samaria

Sedan: NE France, on Meuse R. *Pp. 51 Inset, 55*

Segesta: NW Sicily. *P. 5a*

Seilun *see* Shiloh

Seine: R in N France, flowing NW into English Channel. *Pp. 8, 17, 22, 42, 48, 55*

Sela (Petra): S Palestine, between Dead Sea & G of Aqaba. *Pp. 1, 2*

Selby: N cen. England. *P. 33*

Seleucia: On Tigris R. *P. 11*

Selinus: SW Sicily. *P. 4*

Semipalatinsk: On tributary of Ob R, NE of L Balkhash. *P. 58*

Senegal: W Africa. S of Senegal R. *P. 56*

Seoul (Keijo, Kyongsong): Cen. Korea. *Pp. 59, 63, 64*

Serbia (Servia): Reg, in cen. Balkan penin. *Pp. 19, 43, 44, 60*

Sète: France, on G of Lions. *P. 55*

Setúbal: On W coast of Portugal, S of Lisbon. *Pp. 22, 24*

Sevastopol: Russia, on N coast of Black Sea. *Pp. 45, 51, 58*

Severn: R in W England, flowing S into Bristol Channel. *Pp. 16, 22, 33, 54*

Seville: SW Spain, on Guadalquivir R. *Pp. 10, 12, 24, 39*

Seychelles: Is. in Indian O, NE of Madagascar. *P. 62*

Sfax: N Africa, E Tunisia. *P. 56*

Shanghai: E China, S of mouth of Yangtze R. *Pp. 59, 63, 64*

Shannon: R in Ireland, flowing SW into Atlantic. *Pp. 33, 54*

Shannon Airport: W cen. Ireland. *P. 54*

Shantung: Reg. & penin, NE China. *P. 63*

Shechem (Nablus): W of Jordan R. *P. 1*

Sheffield: N cen. England. *P. 54*

Shenyang *see* Mukden

Shetland Is: N of Scotland, N of Orknev Is. *P. 21*

Shikoku: I, Japan, SW of Honshu. *P. 63*

Shiloh (Seilun): Cen. Palestine, W of Jordan R. *P. 1*

Shimonoseki: Japan, SW extremity of Honshu. *P. 63*

Shrewsbury: W England, on Severn R. *Pp. 16, 33, 54*

Shropshire: Co, England, W of Severn R. *P. 33*

Shumla (Shumen): E Bulgaria, W of Varna. *P. 43*

Shush *see* Susa

Si: R in SE China, flowing into S China Sea, near Hong Kong. *P. 63*

Siam (Thailand): SE Asia, N of Malay Penin. *Pp. 25, 52*

Siam, G of: Arm of S China Sea. *Pp. 52, 63*

Sian (Changan): N cen. China on Wei R. *P. 63*

Siberia: Russia in Asia. *See Front Endpaper*

Sicilies, Kingdom of the Two. *Pp. 19, 32, 36, 37, 41*

Sicily: I, W of extreme SW Italy. *Pp. 4, 5a, 6, 8, 14, 23, 49, 50*

Sicily, Kingdom of. *Pp. 37, 40*

Sicyon: S Greece, NE Peloponnesus. *P. 7 Inset*

Sidon: On E coast of Mediterranean Sea, S of mouth of Litani R. *Pp. 1, 2, 5, 20*

Sidra, Gulf of: Mediterranean Sea, N of Libya. *P. 56*

Sieg: Tributary of Rhine R. *P. 51 Inset*

Siena: Cen. Italy, S of Arno R. *Pp. 19, 23, 32*

Siena, Republic of. *P. 32*

Sierra Leone: Reg, on W coast of Africa. *Pp. 46, 56*

Sigeum: NW Anatolia, near Ilium (Troy). *P. 7*

Sikkim: Reg, NE India, E of Nepal. *P. 63*

Silesia: Reg, along Oder R. *P. 44*

Silesia, Duchy of. *P. 34*

Silistra: Romania, on Danube R. *P. 43*

Simbirsk (Ulyanovsk): Russia, SE of Moscow, on Volga R. *P. 45*

Simla: NW India, N of Delhi. *P. 62*

Simonstown: On S coast of S Africa. *P. 56*

Sinai: Reg. & penin, between Egypt & Arabia. *P. 2*

Sinaia: Romania, SE Transylvanian Alps, near frontier of Hungary. *P. 43*

Singapore: Extreme SE of Asia, at end of Malay penin. *Pp. 25, 52, 63, 64*

Sinigaglia: On E coast of Italy. *P. 32*

Sinkiang: Reg, cen. Asia, NW China. *P. 63*

Sinop (Sinope): N cen. Anatolia, on coast of Black Sea. *Pp. 5, 59*

Sirmium (Mitrovica): Illyricum, near confluence of Danube R & Sava R. *Pp. 7, 8*

Siwa Oasis: NW Egypt. *P. 4*

Skagerrak: Strait between Norway & Denmark. *Pp. 21, 50, 54*

Skagway: S Alaska. *P. 53*

Skoplje: N cen. Balkan penin. *P. 50*

Skye: I off W coast of Scotland. *P. 54*

Slavs, The. *Pp. 12, 13, 14*

Slesvig *see* Schleswig

Slivnitza: Bulgaria, near frontier of Serbia. *P. 43*

Slovakia: Reg. between Morava R & Carpathians, N of Hungary. *Pp. 42, 61*

Smolensk: Russia, W of Moscow, on upper Dnieper R. *Pp. 45, 51, 58*

Smyrna (Izmir): On W coast of Anatolia. *Pp. 7, 11, 35, 43*

Socotra: I, S of Arabian penin. *P. 62*

Sodom & Gomorrah: Palestine, possibly now beneath Dead Sea. *P. 1*

Sofia: W Bulgaria. *Pp. 35, 43, 50, 58*

Sogdiana: Reg, on middle Oxus R. *P. 5*

Soissons: N France, on Aisne R. *Pp. 12, 13, 14*

Sokoto: W Africa, NW Nigeria. *P. 56*

Sollium: On W cen. coast of Greece. *P. 5a*

Solomon Is: Group in SW Pacific, E of New Guinea. *P. 52*

Solway Firth: Inlet of Irish Sea, between England & Scotland. *P. 54*

Somalia: Reg, E Africa, between Equator & G of Aden. *Pp. 56, 62*

Somaliland: Reg, E coast of Africa. *Pp. 47, 56, 62*

Somerset: Co, SW England. *P. 33*

Somme: R in N France, flowing NW to English Channel. *Pp. 16, 22, 48, 54*

Southampton: S England, N of I of Wight. *Pp. 16, 21, 22, 33, 50, 54*

South China Sea: Between S China, Indo-China, Philippine Is & Borneo. *P. 63*

South Korea *see* Korea

South Sea: Another name of Pacific Ocean. *Pp. 26, 30*

South-West Africa: Reg. *P. 57*

Sovetsk *see* Tilsit

Sozopol *see* Apollonia

Spain: SW Europe. *Pp. 28, 29, 36, 37, 49, 50, 55, 60, 61*

Spain, Diocese of. *P. 10*

Spalato (Split): On Dalmatian coast of Adriatic Sea. *Pp. 10, 43*

Spanish Main: N coast of S America. *Pp. 26, 30*

Spanish March: Reg, NE Spain. *P. 14*

Sparta: Reg. & city, Peloponnesus, Greece. *Pp. 4a, 5a, 7 Inset*

Speyer (Spires): W cen. Germany, on Rhine R. *P. 18*

Sphacteria: I in SW Peloponnesus, near Pylos. *P. 5a*

Spires *see* Speyer

Spitsbergen: I, N of Norway, in Arctic O. *P. 58*

Split *see* Spalato

Splügen: Pass over the Alps. *Pp. 18, 32*

Spoletium (Spoleto): Cen. Italy, SE of Tiber R. *P. 6*

Spoleto (Spoletium): Cen. Italy, SE of Tiber R. *Pp. 14, 19*

Spratly: I in cen. S China Sea. *P. 63*

Spree: Tributary of Elbe R, E cen. Germany. *Pp. 23, 48*

Srinagar: In Kashmir, between India & W Pakistan. *P. 62*

Stadacona: On St. Lawrence R, now part of Quebec. *P. 38*

Staffordshire: Co, W cen. England. *P. 33*

Stalingrad: USSR, on W loop of lower Volga R. *Pp. 51, 58*

Stalinsk: USSR, on tributary of Ob R. *P. 59*

Stamford Bridge (*battle 1066*): N England, NE of York. *P. 16*

Stavanger: On SW coast of Norway. *P. 21*

Stavropol: Russia, N of Caucasus Mts. *P. 45*

Stettin (Szczecin): Near mouth of Oder R. *Pp. 18, 21, 23, 34, 42, 48*

Stirling: Cen. Scotland. *Pp. 16, 33, 54*

Stockholm: SE Sweden, on Baltic Sea. *Pp. 21, 50, 58*

Stoke on Trent: W cen. England. *P. 54*

Stornoway: In Hebrides, off NW Scotland. *P. 54*

Stourbridge: E cen. England. *P. 22*

Stralsund: N Germany, on SW coast of Baltic Sea. *P. 21*

Strasbourg: E France, on Rhine R. *Pp. 10, 14, 17, 18, 48, 51 Inset, 55*

Stratford on Avon: Cen. England. *P. 54*

Stresa: NW Italy, W shore of L Maggiore. *P. 49*

Struma (Strymon): R flowing from Bulgaria S into Aegean Sea. *P. 43*

Strymon (Struma): R flowing S through Macedonia into Aegean Sea. *Pp. 4a, 7*

Stuttgart: SW Germany, on upper Neckar R. *P. 48*

Styria: Reg, cen. & SE Austria. *P. 34*
Suchow (Kiuchuan): N cen. China, between Hwang R & Grand Canal. *P. 63*
Sudan: NE Africa. *Pp. 56, 62*
Sueves, The. *Pp. 12, 13*
Suez: NE Egypt, at N end of G of Suez. *Pp. 27, 51, 56, 62*
Suez Canal: NE Africa, between NW end of Red Sea & Mediterranean Sea. *P. 51*
Suffolk: Co, E England. *P. 33*
Sulina: Romania, on Black Sea. *P. 43*
Sulu Sea: SW of Philippine Is. *P. 63*
Sumatra: I, S of Malay Penin. *Pp. 25, 52, 63*
Sumer: Reg, in lower valleys of Tigris R & Euphrates R. *P. 3*
Sunium Promontory: On E cen. coast of Greece. *P. 4a*
Surat: On W coast of India. *Pp. 25, 27*
Surrey: Co, S England. *P. 33*
Susa (Shush): Between Mesopotamia & Plateau of Iran. *Pp. 3, 5*
Susia: On Alexander's route, N of Plateau of Iran. *P. 5*
Sussex: Co, S England. *P. 33*
Sutlej: Tributary of Indus R, Pakistan. *P. 62*
Sverdlovsk (Yekaterinburg): Russia, in E cen. Ural Mts. *P. 58*
Swabia: Reg, S Germany. *P. 18*
Swansea: On S coast of Wales. *P. 54*
Swaziland: Reg, SE Africa. *P. 57*
Sweden: NW Europe. *Pp. 21, 28, 29, 36, 37, 40, 41, 48, 50, 58, 60, 61*
Swindon: S cen. England. *P. 54*
Swiss Confederation. *Pp. 37, 40, 41*
Switzerland: Cen. Europe. *Pp. 28, 29, 36, 42, 48, 50, 55, 58, 60, 61*
Syagrius, Kingdom of: N France. *P. 12*
Sybaris: On SE coast of Italy. *P. 4*
Sydney: On SE coast of Australia. *Pp. 52, 64*
Syracuse: On SE coast of Sicily. *Pp. 4, 5a, 6, 8, 23, 32, 50*
Syr Darya: R in USSR, flowing NW into Aral Sea. *P. 62*
Syria: Reg, E end of Mediterranean Sea. *Pp. 2, 5, 9, 51, 56, 58, 60, 61, 62*
Szczecin *see* **Stettin**
Szechwan: Reg, W cen. China. *P. 63*
Szeged: S Hungary, near confluence of Tisza R & Maros R. *P. 43*
Szeming *see* **Amoy**

Taanach: Palestine, SW of Sea of Galilee. *P. 1*
Tabor, Mt: Between Kishon R & Sea of Galilee. *Pp. 1, 2*
Tabriz: NW Iran (Persia), between Caspian Sea & upper valley of Tigris R. *Pp. 25, 56, 62*
Tadmor *see* **Palmyra**
Tadzhik SSR: USSR, bordering on Afghanistan & China. *P. 58*
Taganrog: Russia, NE coast of Sea of Azov, near mouth of Don R. *Pp. 45, 51*
Tagus: R in W cen. Spain & Portugal, flowing into Atlantic near Lisbon. *Pp. 8, 22, 24*
Taillebourg: France, W of Massif Central. *P. 17*
Taiwan *see* **Formosa**
Takla Makan: Desert in Sinkiang prov, W China. *P. 62*
Takoradi: On W coast of Africa, Gold Coast. *P. 56*
Tallin: On G of Finland. *P. 58*
Tambov: Cen. Russia, W of upper Don R. *Pp. 45, 58*
Tana, Lake: E Africa, source of Blue Nile R. *Pp. 56, 62*
Tanais: NE of Crimean penin, at mouth of Don R. *P. 5*
Tananarive: Madagascar. *P. 57*
Tanga: E Africa, near Zanzibar. *P. 56*
Tanganyika, Lake: E Africa, boundary between Tanganyika & Belgian Congo. *P. 56*
Tangier: International Zone, extreme NW Africa, on Strait of Gibraltar. *Pp. 50, 56, 60, 61*
Tangier *see* **Tingis**
Tannenberg (*battle 1410, Grunwald 1914*): E Prussia, S of Königsberg. *Pp. 21, 48*
Tannu-Tuva: Reg, S. USSR, NW of Mongolia. *P. 59*
Tantura *see* **Dor**
Taranto (Tarentum): SE coast of Italy, on G of Taranto. *Pp. 19, 49, 50*
Tarawa: I, W cen. Pacific, in Gilbert Is group. *P. 52*
Tarentum (Taranto): SE coast of Italy, on G of Tarentum (Taranto). *Pp. 4, 6*

Tarentum, Gulf of: Inlet of Ionian Sea, SE of Italy. *Pp. 5a, 6*
Tarim: R in W China, flowing E. *P. 62*
Tarraco *see* **Tarragona**
Tarraconensis: Reg, Spain. *P. 8*
Tarragona (Tarraco): E coast of Spain. *Pp. 10, 24*
Tarsus: S Anatolia, NE of Cyprus. *Pp. 2, 5, 11, 15, 20*
Tartu *see* **Dorpat**
Tashkent: USSR, SE of Aral Sea. *P. 58*
Taunton: SW England. *Pp. 33, 54*
Taurus Mts: S Anatolia. *See Front Endpaper*
Taxila: Between Indus R & Hydaspes R. *P. 5*
Tbilisi (Tiflis): USSR, S of Caucasus Mts. *P. 58*
Tehran: Iran, S of Caspian Sea *Pp. 51, 56, 62, 64*
Tell Beit Mirsim: W of Dead Sea. *P. 1*
Tell el Amarna: On Nile R. *P. 2*
Tell Qasileh: On coast of cen. Palestine. *P. 1*
Temesvar: Austria-Hungary, between Maros R & Transylvanian Alps. *P. 43*
Tempe, Vale of: NE Greece. *P. 4a*
Tende: SE France, near Italian border. *P. 55*
Teos: W Anatolia. *P. 4*
Testry: Carolingian Empire, NW France. *P. 14*
Tetuán: NW Africa, near Strait of Gibraltar. *P. 56*
Teutonic Knights, The. *P. 28*
Thailand (Siam): SE Asia, N of Malay Penin. *P. 63*
Thames: R in S England. *Pp. 14, 16, 22, 33, 54*
Thanet, I of: Reg, NE portion of Kent, SE England. *P. 16*
Thapsacus: Mesopotamia, on Euphrates R. *P. 5*
Thar Desert (Indian Desert): NW India, E of lower Indus R. *P. 62*
Thasos: I, N Aegean Sea, S of Thrace. *Pp. 4a, 5a, 7*
Thebes: Greece, NW of Athens. *Pp 4a, 5a, 7 Inset, 20*
Thebes, Duchy of Athens and. *P. 20 Inset*
Theiss R *see* **Tisza R**
Theodosia: On SE coast of Crimea. *P. 5*
Thermopylae: Pass in E Greece. *P. 4a*
Thessalonica (Salonika): On E coast of Greece. *P. 20*
Thessalonica, Kingdom of. *P. 20 Inset*
Thessaly: Reg, N Greece. *Pp. 4a, 5a, 7, 43*
Thorn: N Poland, on Vistula R. *P. 21*
Thourout: Flanders, between Scheldt R & sea coast. *P. 22*
Thrace: Reg, SE Europe, NE of Greece. *Pp. 4, 4a, 7, 9, 43*
Thrace, Diocese of. *P. 11*
Three Points, Cape: W Africa, SW Gold Coast. *P. 56*
Thuringia: Reg, cen. Germany. *Pp. 18, 44*
Thuringians, The. *Pp. 12, 13*
Tiber: R in cen. Italy, flowing W. *Pp. 6, 23, 32, 49*
Tiberias: Palestine, W shore of Sea of Galilee. *P. 20*
Tibet: Reg, cen. Asia, N of India. *Pp. 25, 31, 63*
Tibetan Plateau (Chang Tang): Cen. Asia. *P. 62*
Ticino (Ticinus): Tributary of Po R, N Italy. *P. 32*
Ticinus (Ticino): Tributary of Po R, N Italy. *P. 6*
Tien Shan: Mts in USSR & W China. *P. 62*
Tientsin: NE China, near Peiping (Peking). *Pp. 59, 63, 64*
Tierra del Fuego: Off S extremity of S America. *P. 26*
Tiflis (Tbilisi): Russia, S of Caucasus. *P. 45*
Tignes Reservoir: In French Alps, on Isère R. *P. 55*
Tigris: R in SE Asia, flowing into Persian G. *Pp. 3, 5, 9, 11, 15, 20, 56, 62*
Tikhvin: USSR, E of Leningrad. *P. 51*
Tilsit (Sovetz): E Prussia, on Niemen R. *P. 48*
Timbuktu (Tombouctou): Cen. W Africa, near upper Niger R. *Pp. 27, 56*
Timor: I in S Malay Archipelago, N of Australia. *P. 52*
Tingis (Tangier): Extreme NW Africa, on Strait of Gibraltar. *Pp. 4, 8*
Tirana (Tiranë): On extreme SE coast of Adriatic Sea. *Pp. 43, 49, 50*
Tirnovo: N of Balkan Mts, Bulgaria. *Pp. 35, 43*
Tiryns: Greece, E Peloponnesus. *P. 7 Inset*
Tisza (Theiss): Tributary of Danube R. *Pp. 8, 10, 23, 35, 43, 44*
Tivoli: Cen, Italy, S of Tiber R. *P. 32*
Tobolsk: USSR, on Ob R. *P. 58*
Tobruk: On coast of Libya. *P. 50*
Togoland: Reg, W Africa, near Gold Coast. *Pp. 46, 56*
Tokyo: Japan. *Pp. 52, 63, 64*
Toledo (Toletum): Cen. Spain, on Tagus R. *Pp. 22, 24*
Toletum (Toledo): Cen. Spain, on Tagus R. *P. 8*

Tombouctou *see* **Timbuktu**
Tomsk: USSR, on upper Ob R. *P. 59*
Tonkin, Gulf of: Arm of S China Sea, W of Hainan I. *P. 63*
Tordesillas, Line of. *Pp. 25, 26, 31*
Torgau: Germany, on Elbe R. *P. 50*
Toronto: Canada. *P. 64*
Tortosa: On coast of Syria, off Cyprus. *P. 20*
Toul: NE France, on Moselle R. *Pp. 17, 18, 34*
Toulon: SE France, on Mediterranean Sea. *Pp. 49, 50, 55*
Toulouse: S France, on upper Garonne R. *Pp. 12, 17, 22, 24, 55*
Touraine: Reg, NW cen. France. *P. 17*
Tournai: On Scheldt R, between Flanders & Lorraine. *Pp. 10, 18, 54*
Tours: NW cen. France. *Pp. 10, 14, 17, 22, 55*
Trabzon *see* **Trebizond (Trapezus)**
Transcaucasia: Reg, S of Caucasus Mts, between Black Sea & Caspian Sea. *P. 45*
Transjordan: Reg, E of Jordan R. *P. 51*
Transjordan Plateau: E of Jordan R. *P. 51*
Transylvania: Reg, SE Europe. *Pp. 35, 43, 44, 45*
Transylvanian Alps: Mts in Hungary & Romania. *P. 43*
Trapezus (Trebizond): NE Anatolia, on Black Sea. *P. 5*
Trebia: Tributary of Po R. *P. 6*
Trebizond (Trabzon, Trapezus): NE Anatolia, on Black Sea. *Pp. 11, 15*
Trent: R in E cen. England, flowing NE. *P. 54*
Trent *see* **Trento**
Trentino: Reg, NE Italy, on upper Adige R. *P. 42*
Trento (Trent): NE Italy, on Adige R. *Pp. 42, 48*
Trèves (Trier): W Germany, on Moselle R. *Pp. 12, 16*
Treviso: NE Italy. *P. 32*
Trier (Trèves): W Germany, on Moselle R. *Pp. 10, 18, 34, 48, 51 Inset, 54*
Trieste: NE Italy, at head of Adriatic Sea. *Pp. 42, 44, 49, 50*
Trinidad (*1498*): I in West Indies, off NE coast of Venezuela. *Pp. 26, 38*
Tripoli: N Africa, on Mediterranean Sea, S of Malta. *Pp. 10, 15, 50, 56*
Tripolis: Reg. & city on coast of Palestine. *P. 20*
Tripolitania: Reg, on N coast of Africa. *P. 56*
Troezen: Near coast of S Greece. *P. 4*
Trondheim: On cen. coast of Norway. *Pp. 21, 50*
Troy *see* **Ilium**
Troyes: NE France, on upper Seine R. *Pp. 12, 17, 18, 22, 55*
Truk: I in cen. Caroline Is, W Pacific. *P. 52*
Tsaritsyn: Russia, on Volga R. *P. 45*
Tsinan: E China, on Yellow R, S of Peiping. *P. 63*
Tsingtao: NE China, SE shore of Kiaochow B. *P. 63*
Tula: Cen. Russia, near head of Don R. *Pp. 45, 51*
Tungting, Lake: SE cen. China. *P. 63*
Tunis (Carthage): On cen. coast of N Africa. *Pp. 10, 19, 22, 49, 50, 56*
Tunisia: Reg, N Africa. *Pp. 47, 49, 50, 56, 60, 61*
Turfan Depression: E Sinkiang, W China. *P. 63*
Turin: NW Italy, on Po R. *Pp. 19, 22, 32, 49, 50, 55*
Turkey. *Pp. 51, 58, 60, 61*
Turkistan: Reg, cen. Asia, in Russia & China. *P. 62*
Turkmen SSR: USSR, E of Caspian Sea. *P. 58*
Turtucaia: on lower Danube R. *P. 43*
Tuscany: Reg, N cen. Italy. *Pp. 19, 29, 36, 37, 41*
Tver (Kalinin): Russia, on upper Volga R. *P. 45*
Tweed: R in S Scotland. *P. 33*
Tyre (Es Sur): On E coast of Mediterranean Sea, S of mouth of Litani R. *Pp. 1, 2, 5, 9, 20*
Tyrol: Reg, W Austria. *Pp. 34, 42, 44*
Tyrrhenian Sea: SW of Italy. *Pp. 6, 8, 32, 49*

Ubangi: Tributary of Congo R, cen. Africa. *P. 56*
Ubangi-Shari: Reg, cen. Africa, N of Ubangi R. *P. 56*
Udine: NE Italy, W of Isonzo R. *P. 42*
Uganda: Reg, E Africa, N of L Victoria. *Pp. 47, 56*
Ugarit: On NE coast of Mediterranean Sea, W of Orontes R. *P. 2*
Ujiji: E Africa, on E shore of L Tanganyika. *P. 56*
Ukraine *see* **Little Russia**
Ukrainian SSR: SW. USSR. *P. 58*
Ulan Bator: Mongolia, S of L Baikal. *P. 59*
Ulan-Ude: USSR S of L Baikal. *P. 59*

Ulm: S Germany, on Danube R. *P. 48*
Ulster: Reg, N Ireland. *P. 33*
Ulyanovsk *see* Simbirsk
Union of South Africa. *Pp. 47, 57*
Union of Soviet Socialist Republics. *Pp. 51, 52, 58, 59, 60, 61, 62*
United Netherlands. *Pp. 29, 36*
United States of America. *Pp. 46, 53*
Upsala: E Sweden, NW of Stockholm. *P. 21*
Ur (Muqaiyir): In lower valley of Euphrates R. *P. 3*
Ural: R in Russia, flowing from Ural Mts to Caspian Sea. *Pp. 45, 58*
Ural Mts: NW Asia. *Pp. 45, 58*
Uralsk: Russia, on Ural R. *P. 45*
Urbino: NE cen. Italy, between Apennines & N Adriatic Sea. *P. 32*
Uruguay: Reg, E coast of S America. *P. 53*
Usküb (Skoplje): Ottoman Empire, on upper Vardar R. *P. 43*
Usküdar *see* Scutari
USSR *see* Union of Soviet Socialist Republics
Utrecht: Cen. Netherlands, near mouth of Rhine R. *Pp. 16, 54*
Uzbek SSR: USSR, SE of Aral Sea. *P. 58*
Užice: Serbia, near headwaters of Drina R. *P. 43*

Valais: Reg, S of Swiss Confederation. *P. 40*
Valence: France, on Rhône R. *P. 55*
Valencia (Valentia): On E coast of Spain. *P. 24*
Valenciennes: NE France, near Belgian border. *P. 54*
Valentia (Valencia): On E coast of Spain. *P. 8*
Valladolid: NW cen. Spain. *Pp. 24, 55*
Valona (Vlone): Ottoman Empire, Albania, near Strait of Otranto. *P. 43*
Valparaiso: On W coast of S America. *P. 26*
Vandals, The. *Pp. 12, 13*
Vardar: R in Ottoman Empire, flowing through Macedonia into Aegean Sea. *P. 43*
Varna: On NW coast of Black Sea, Bulgaria. *Pp. 35, 43*
Velikie Luki: USSR, N of upper W Dvina R. *P. 50*
Venetia: Reg, NE Italy. *Pp. 6, 41*
Venetian Republic. *P. 32*
Venezuela: Reg, N. S America. *Pp. 26, 53*
Venice: Reg, & city, NE Italy, on Adriatic Sea. *Pp. 10, 14, 19, 23, 27, 28, 29, 32, 34, 36, 42, 44, 49*
Venlo: Netherlands, on Maas R. *P. 51 Inset*
Ventimiglia: NW Italy, near French border. *P. 55*
Veracruz: E Mexico, on G of Mexico. *P. 26*
Verde, Cape (Vert): W Africa. *Pp. 26, 30*
Vézelay: E cen. France, in Burgundy. *P. 18*
Viborg: N cen. Denmark. *P. 58*
Vicenza: NE Italy, N of Adige R. *P. 32*
Vichy: Cen. France, in N Massif Central. *Pp. 50, 55*
Victoria, Lake: E cen. Africa. *P. 56*
Victoria Falls: Cen. Africa, on Zambezi R. *P. 57*
Vidin: Bulgaria, on Danube R. *Pp. 35, 43*
Vienna: Cen. Europe, on Danube R. *Pp. 10, 18, 23, 34, 42, 44, 48, 50, 58, 64*
Vienne: France, on Rhône R. *P. 17*
Vietnam: SE Asia. *P. 63*
Viliya: Tributary of Niemen (Neman) R, W Russia. *P. 45*
Vilna (Wilno): W Russia, between Viliya R & Niemen R. *Pp. 45, 50, 58*
Vindhya Range: Mts in cen. India. *P. 62*
Visigoths, The. *Pp. 12, 13*
Vistula: R in NE Europe, flowing N to Baltic Sea near Danzig. *Pp. 8, 10, 21, 23, 34, 42, 44, 48*
Vitebsk: Russia, on upper W Dvina R. *Pp. 45, 50*
Vladikavkaz (Dzau Dzhikau): Russia, on N edge of Caucasus Mts. *P. 45*
Vladimir: Cen. Russia, on tributary of upper Volga R. *P. 45*
Vladivostok: Extreme E. USSR, on Sea of Japan. *Pp. 52, 59*
Vlone *see* Valona

Volga: R in E Russia, flowing S & E into Caspian Sea. *Pp. 11, 27, 45, 51, 58*
Volkhov: R in N Russia, flowing N into L Ladoga. *P. 45*
Volo (Volos): Greece, E Thessaly, on gulf N of Euboea. *P. 43*
Vologda: Russia, N of upper Volga R. *P. 45*
Volos *see* Volo
Volta: R in W Africa, flowing into G of Guinea. *P. 56*
Volterra: W cen. Italy, in Republic of Florence. *P. 32*
Volturno (Volturnus): R in S cen. Italy, N of Naples. *P. 49*
Volturnus (Volturno): R in S cen. Italy. *P. 6*
Vorkuta: N. USSR, N of Ural Mts on tributary of Pechora R. *P. 58*
Voronezh: S cen. Russia, on Don R. *P. 45*
Voroshilovgrad: S. USSR, in valley of Donets R, N of Rostov. *P. 45*
Vosges Mts: NE France, W of upper Rhine R. *P. 34*
Vouillé: S cen. France. *P. 13*
Vyatka: On Vyatka R, W of Ural Mts. *P. 45*
Vyatka: Tributary of Kama R, Russia. *P. 45*
Vyborg: NW Russia, between G of Finland & L Ladoga. *P. 45*

Wadi Halfa: On Nile R, N of Khartoum. *P. 56*
Wake I: W Pacific, N of Marshall Is. *P. 52*
Wales: Reg, W of England. *Pp. 16, 54*
Walfish Bay *see* Walvis Bay
Wallachia: Reg, between Danube R & Transylvanian Alps. *Pp. 35, 43*
Walvis Bay (Walfish): On cen. coast of SW Africa. *P. 57*
Warsaw: Cen. Poland, on Vistula R. *Pp. 23, 34, 42, 45, 48, 50, 58*
Warsaw, Duchy of. *P. 37*
Warwickshire: Co, W cen. England. *P. 33*
Wash, The: Inlet of North Sea, E coast of England. *P. 54*
Washington: Eastern USA. *P. 53*
Waterford: On SE coast of Ireland. *P. 54*
Wei: R in N China. *P. 63*
Weihaiwei: NE China, N shore of Shantung Penin. *P. 63*
Weimar: Cen. Germany, W of upper Saale R. *P. 48*
Wellington: New Zealand. *P. 52*
Wells: SW England. *Pp. 16, 33*
Wesel: Germany, on Rhine R. *P. 51 Inset*
Weser: R in W Germany, flowing N into North Sea. *Pp. 21, 42, 44, 48, 54*
West Dvina: R in N Europe, flowing into Baltic Sea at Riga. *Pp. 23, 45, 58*
Western Ghats: Mts on W coast of India. *P. 62*
West Indies: In Caribbean Sea. *P. 38*
Westmorland: Co, NW England. *P. 33*
Wexford: On SE coast of Ireland. *P. 54*
White Mountain (*battle 1620*): Bohemia. *P. 34*
White Nile: R in cen. E Africa, flowing N from L Albert, to confluence with Blue Nile R at Khartoum. *P. 56*
White Sea: Inlet of Barents Sea, on N coast of Russia. *Pp. 45, 51, 58*
Wiener Neustadt: Austria, near border of Hungary. *P. 50*
Wiesbaden: W Germany, on Rhine R. *P. 48*
Wight, Isle of: Off S coast of England. *P. 54*
Wilhelmshaven: Germany, on coast of North Sea. *Pp. 48, 50*
Wilmington: North Carolina. *P. 38*
Wilno *see* Vilna
Wiltshire: Co, S cen. England. *P. 33*
Winchester: S England. *Pp. 16, 22, 33, 54*
Windhoek: On coast of SW Africa, E of Walvis Bay. *P. 57*
Windsor: S England, on Thames R. *P. 16*
Wisby: On Gotland I, in Baltic Sea. *Pp. 21, 23*
Wismar: Germany, on SW coast of Baltic Sea. *P. 21*
Witwatersrand: Plateau in cen. Transvaal, S Africa. *P. 57*

Wolverhampton: W cen. England. *P. 54*
Worcester: W cen. England, on Severn R. *Pp. 16, 33, 54*
Worcestershire: Co, W England. *P. 33*
Worms: W Germany, on Rhine R. *Pp. 12, 18*
Wrath, Cape: Extreme NW Scotland. *P. 54*
Wrocław *see* Breslau
Wuppertal: Germany, on tributary of Rhine R. *P. 51 Inset*
Württemberg: Reg, S Germany. *Pp. 18, 44*
Württemberg, Kingdom of. *Pp. 40, 41*
Yakutsk: E. USSR, on Lena R. *P. 59*
Yalta: Russia, S coast of Crimea, on Black Sea. *Pp. 45, 51, 58*
Yalu: R between SE Manchuria & Korea. *P. 63*
Yangtze: R in China, flowing E to East China Sea, near Shanghai. *Pp. 25, 63*
Yap: NW Caroline Is, W Pacific. *P. 52*
Yarmouth (Great Yarmouth): On E coast of England. *P. 21*
Yarmuk: Tributary of Jordan R, Palestine. *Pp. 1, 2*
Yaroslavl: Russia, on Volga R. *Pp. 45, 58*
Yekaterinburg (Ekaterinburg, Sverdlovsk): Russia, E cen. Ural Mts. *P. 45*
Yekaterinodar (Ekaterinodar, Krasnodar): S Russia, on Kuban R. *P. 45*
Yekaterinoslav (Ekaterinoslav, Dnepropetrovsk): Russia, E cen. Ukraine, on Dnieper R. *P. 45*
Yellow Sea: Inlet of Pacific, between NE China & Korea. *Pp. 59, 63*
Yemen: Reg, on SW coast of Arabian penin. *Pp. 56, 62*
Yenan (Fushih): NE cen. China. *P. 63*
Yenisei: R in USSR, W cen. Asia, flowing N into Arctic O. *P. 59*
Yerevan: USSR, near border of Turkey. *P. 58*
Yeu, Ile d': I off W coast of France, in B of Biscay. *P. 55*
Yingkow *see* Newchwang
Yokohama: On SE coast of Honshu, Japan. *Pp. 52, 63*
York (Eburacum): N England. *Pp. 10, 14, 16, 22, 33, 54*
Yorkshire: Co, NE England. *P. 33*
Yorktown: SE Virginia. *P. 38*
Ypres: NW Flanders. *Pp. 16, 22*
Yuan (Red): R in SE cen. China, flowing into G of Tonkin. *P. 63*
Yucatan: Penin. in Central America, projecting into G of Mexico. *P. 26*
Yugoslavia. *Pp. 49, 50, 58, 60, 61*
Yunnan (Kunming): Reg, S China, bordering Burma & French Indo-China. *P. 52*

Zacynthus (Zante): & city off W coast of Greece. *P. 4*
Zadar *see* Zara
Zadracarta: On Alexander's route, SE Caspian Sea. *P. 5*
Zagreb: Yugoslavia, near upper Sava R. *P. 49*
Zalaca: W cen. Spain, between Tagus R & Guadiana R. *P. 24*
Zama (*battle 202 B.C.*): N Africa, SW of Carthage. *P. 6*
Zambezi: R in S cen. & SE Africa. *P. 57*
Zante *see* Zacynthus
Zanzibar: I & city, off E coast of Africa. *Pp. 27, 56*
Zara (Zadar): On E cen. Adriatic coast, Dalmatia. *Pp. 43, 49*
Zered: R flowing W into S end of Dead Sea. *Pp. 1, 2*
Zhitomir: SW Russia, between upper Bug R & Dnieper R. *P. 45*
Zinder: S Sahara Desert, N of Nigerian border. *P. 56*
Zuider Zee (Ijsselmeer): NW Europe, inlet of North Sea. *Pp. 21, 54*
Zürich: W of L Constance, N Switzerland. *Pp. 32, 42, 48*
Zweibrücken: W Germany, near borders of France & Saar. *P. 55*

ERRATA

Maps

Page 7.   **Ainos** and **Nicomedia** have been transposed.

Page 8.   For **Mediolanium** read **Mediolanum.**

Page 22.   **Augsburg** and **Ulm** have been transposed.

Page 60.   **Europe:** 1924, the area of **East Prussia** enclosed by the
black line should be red, belonging to **Germany.**

Back Endpaper.   The name of the **Amazon R** is alongside one of its tributaries (Madeira R).

EXERCISES FOR THE

FOX

ATLAS OF EUROPEAN HISTORY

SUGGESTIONS FOR MAP EXERCISES

The following suggestions are offered as much to illustrate a technique as to provide actual assignments. They are based on the assumption that if the educated reader is obligated to bring at least a minimum of solid geographic knowledge to the study of history, he is under no obligation to commit to memory intricate details of transitory territorial developments. The suggested assignments, therefore, are usually divided into two sections: the *first* containing lists of topographical features and cities which are to be learned and the *second*, of historical developments to be plotted on blank outline maps.

The items to be learned, it will be noticed, are those geographic features and place names which play the most important parts and recur the most frequently in accounts of European history. The initial assignment may, therefore, appear obvious and the subsequent ones repetitious. This repetition, however, is intentional with the purpose of reinforcing the student's knowledge of the most important aspects of historical geography.

Although systematic use of an atlas will undoubtedly increase the student's familiarity with geography, there is no substitute for frequent map quizes; only by continually testing his progress is he likely to acquire the desired knowledge and self-assurance. Similarly, if a conscientious student can develop his ability to read complicated geographic descriptions by constant use of the atlas, he will, nevertheless, find that the regular requirement of plotting important boundaries and routes on blank outline maps will help materially both to increase his skill and to fix the habit of using it.

I. EUROPE

(see Front Endpaper)

Locate on blank outline map and learn:

1. Seas & Straits

Adriatic Sea; Aegean Sea; Baltic Sea; Black Sea; Bosporus; Caspian Sea; English Channel; Mediterranean Sea; North Sea; Persian Gulf; Strait of Gibraltar.

2. Peninsulas & Islands

The Scandinavian, Iberian, Italian, Balkan and Anatolian peninsulas. The Crimea.
Balearic Is.; Corsica; Crete; Cyprus; Sardinia; Sicily.

3. Mountains

Alps; Apennines; Atlas; Carpathians; Caucasus; Pyrenees; Taurus; Urals.

4. Rivers

Danube; Dnieper; Euphrates; Loire; Nile; Po; Rhine; Rhône; Tiber; Tigris; Vistula; Volga.

II. ANCIENT NEAR EAST

(see pp. 1, 2–3)

A. Locate on outline map and learn:

1. Rivers, Seas, etc.

Jordan; Nile; Orontes; Gulf of Aqaba; Dead Sea; Sea of Galilee; Red Sea.

2. Mountains, Deserts, etc.

Lebanon Mtns.; Sinai Peninsula; Arabian Desert; Mesopotamia.

3. Cities

Babylon; Damascus; Ezion-geber; Jerusalem; Memphis; Sidon; Tyre.

B. On outline map show:

Empire of David and Solomon and indicate location of: Edom; Israel; Judah; Moab; Philistia; Phoenicia.

III. ANCIENT GREECE

(see pp. 4–5, 6–7)

A. Locate on outline map and learn:

1. Seas, etc.

Bosporus; Hellespont; Strait of Messina; Indus River; Aegean Sea; Black Sea; Ionian Sea; Gulf of Corinth; Propontis; Saronic Gulf.

2. Islands & Peninsulas

Crete; Cyprus; Rhodes; Salamis; Sicily; Peloponnesus; The Crimea.

3. Areas

Epirus; Lydia; Macedonia; Persia; Phrygia; Thrace.

4. Cities

Athens; Ilium; Sparta; Syracuse.

B. On outline map show:

1. Route of Alexander.

2. Extent of the Athenian Empire and alliances (431 B.C.).

3. Extent of Greek and Phoenician colonization (by locating four colonies of each).

IV. ROME

(see pp. 6–7, 8–9)

A. Locate on outline map and learn:

1. Rivers, Seas, etc.

Danube; Nile; Po; Rhine; Rhône; Tiber; Adriatic Sea; Ionian Sea; Tyrrhenian Sea; Alps.

2. Cities

Actium; Alexandria; Antioch; Athens; Brundisium; Byzantium; Cannae; Carthage; Massilia; Neapolis; Rome.

3. Areas

Cisalpine Gaul; Dacia; Illyricum; Macedonia; Mauretania; Thrace.

B. On outline map show:

Empire under Trajan (including three great walls).

V. LATER EMPIRE AND BARBARIANS

(see pp. 10–11, 12–13)

A. Locate on outline map and learn:

1. Cities

Adrianople; Athens; Constantinople; Hippo; Lyons; Milan; Monte Cassino; Nicaea (in Pontus); Ravenna; Rome; Trier; York.

2. Rivers

Danube; Ebro; Loire; Rhine.

B. On outline map show:

1. Empire of Vandals (mid 5th century).
2. Empire of Justinian (565).

VI. BYZANTINE, ISLAMIC AND FRANKISH EMPIRES

(see pp. 14–15)

A. Locate on outline map and learn:

1. Rivers

Douro; Ebro; Elbe; Indus; Loire; Meuse; Oder; Rhône; Scheldt; Weser.

2. Cities

Aix-la-Chapelle; Baghdad; Cairo; Constantinople; Cordova; Mecca; Medina; Monte Cassino; Paris; Ravenna; Reims; Saragossa; Tours; Venice.

B. On outline map show:

1. Extent of Byzantine, Islamic and Frankish Empires.

2. Division of Frankish Empire by the Treaties of Verdun and Mersen.
   (Show later political units formed from Lotharingia: Holland; Belgium; Luxembourg; Switzerland; Alsace; Burgundy; Savoy; Lombardy.)

VII. FEUDAL MONARCHIES

(see pp. 16–17, 18–19)

A. Locate on outline map and learn:

1. Rivers

Elbe; Garonne; Loire; Main; Meuse; Oder; Rhône; Saône; Scheldt; Seine; Severn; Thames.

2. Principal French provinces

Aquitaine; Artois; Brittany; Burgundy; Champagne; Flanders; Ile de France; Normandy.

3. Stem Duchies of the Holy Roman Empire

Bavaria; Bohemia; Franconia; Lorraine; Saxony; Swabia.

4. Cities

Bordeaux; Canossa; Canterbury; Hastings; Legnano; London; Orléans; Palermo; Reims; Vienna.

B. On outline map show:

1. The maximum continental holdings of the kings of England.

2. The western boundary of the Holy Roman Empire, naming the rivers that it follows.

VIII. GROWTH OF TRADE

(see pp. 21, 22–23)

A. Locate on outline map and learn:

1. Rivers

Danube; Elbe; Garonne; Loire; Marne; Meuse; Moselle; Oder; Po; Rhine; Rhône; Scheldt; Seine; Saône; Thames; Vistula; Weser.

2. Cities

Amsterdam; Augsburg; Basle; Bordeaux; Cologne; Genoa; Leipzig; London; Lübeck; Lyons; Marseilles; Milan; Narbonne; Nuremberg; Paris; Rouen; Toulouse; Troyes.

3. Mountains and Passes

Alps; Apennines; Pyrenees; Massif Central; Brenner Pass; St. Bernard Pass.

B. On outline map show:

Four overland trade routes from the Mediterranean to the Atlantic, English Channel or the Baltic labeling the names of rivers, passes and principal cities through which they pass, for example: (i) Venice to Lübeck, (ii) Genoa to London via Basle, (iii) Marseilles to London, (iv) Narbonne to London.

IX. EMERGENCE OF NATIONAL MONARCHIES

(see pp. 16–17, 21, 24, 28–29)

A. Locate on outline map and learn:

1. Cities

Copenhagen; Königsberg; Lisbon; London; Madrid; Paris; Stockholm; Vienna.

B. On outline map show:

1. Religious situation, *c.* 1560.

2. Monarchies of England, France, Spain, Portugal, territories of Austrian Hapsburgs, Hohenzollerns and the boundaries of the Holy Roman Empire.

X. EXPANSION OF EUROPE OVERSEAS

(see pp. 20, 25, 26–27, 30–31)

A. Locate on outline map and learn:

1. Cities

Aden; Bombay; Cairo; Ceuta; Constantinople; Damascus; Mozambique; Samarkand; Venice.

2. Capes

Bojador; Good Hope; Horn; Verde.

3. Islands

Azores; Canary Is; Cape Verde Is; Ceylon; Hispaniola; Madagascar; Madeira Is; Newfoundland; Puerto Rico.

4. Seas, etc.

Indian Ocean; Persian Gulf; Red Sea; Strait of Magellan.

B. On outline map show:

1. Line of Tordesillas (1494).
2. Routes of three great expeditions of exploration.
3. Overseas Empires of Spain and Portugal (1600).

XI. THE SEVENTEENTH CENTURY

(see pp. 29, 33, 34–35)

A. Locate on outline map and learn:

1. Rivers

Danube; Elbe; Oder; Severn; Thames; Tisza; Vistula.

2. Mountains

Balkan; Carpathian.

3. Areas

Bohemia; Moldavia; Rumelia; Silesia; Transylvania; Wallachia.

4. Cities

Belgrade; Berlin; Buda; Pest; Cracow; Marston Moor; Naseby; Prague; Pressburg; Preston; Sofia; Vienna.

B. On outline map show:

1. Principal European states after the Treaty of Westphalia.
2. Greatest extent of Turkish conquest.

XII. THE EIGHTEENTH CENTURY

(see pp. 36, 38–39)

A. Locate on outline map and learn:

1. Rivers

Drava; Dniester; Dvina; Oder; Sava; Vistula.

2. Areas

Newfoundland; Nova Scotia.

3. Cities

Annapolis (Nova Scotia); Louisbourg; Fort Duquesne; Plymouth (England); Stadacona.

B. On outline map show:

Principal states in Europe 1789, name rivers and mountains which serve as major boundaries, and locate and name capital cities.

XIII. THE FRENCH REVOLUTION

(see pp. 36–37, 40–41)

A. Locate on outline map and learn:

1. Rivers

Bug; Elbe; Main; Oder; Niemen (Neman); Po; Rhine; Weser.

2. Islands & Capes
Corsica; Trafalgar.

B. On outline map show:

1. The Empire of the French and the Allied States (1812).

2. Central Europe after the Congress of Vienna.

XIV. CENTRAL AND EASTERN EUROPE IN THE NINETEENTH CENTURY

(see pp. 42–43, 44, 45)

A. Locate on outline map and learn:

1. Rivers

Dnieper; Dniester; Don; Drava; Elbe; Main; Moldau; Sava; Tisza; Volga.

2. Mountains

Balkan; Carpathian; Transylvanian Alps.

3. Areas

Bessarabia; Bosnia; Crimea; Dalmatia; Dobruja; Eastern Rumelia; Galicia; Macedonia; Sanjak of Novi Bazar; Schleswig; Transylvania; Venetia.

4. Cities

Belgrade; Bucharest; Cracow (Kraków); Moscow; Prague; Salonika; St. Petersburg; San Stefano; Sarajevo; Sevastopol; Trieste.

B. On outline map show:

1. States created from former Turkish territory, 1815–1881.
2. Boundaries and principal provinces of the Austro-Hungarian Empire in 1878.

XV. THE NINETEENTH CENTURY INDUSTRIAL AND COLONIAL DEVELOPMENT

(see pp. 45, 46–47, 56–57, 58–59, 62–63)

A. Locate on outline map and learn:

1. Rivers & Seas

Amur; Congo; Nile; Yangtze; Caspian Sea; Red Sea.

2. Areas

Korea; Manchuria; Tibet.

3. Cities

Barcelona; Berlin; Danzig; Florence; Glasgow; London; Moscow; Paris; St. Petersburg; Stockholm; Trieste; Vienna.

B. On outline map show:

The British Empire on the eve of the First World War.

XVI. THE FIRST WORLD WAR AND THE PEACE SETTLEMENT

(see pp. 48–49, 60)

A. Locate on outline map and learn:

1. Rivers

Danube; Drava; Elbe; Marne; Niemen; Oder; Rhine; Ruhr; Somme; Vistula.

2. Areas

Bosnia; Saar; Serbia; Silesia.

3. Cities

Belgrade; Budapest; Danzig; Fiume; Gdynia; Memel; Munich; Prague; Trieste; Vienna; Warsaw.

B. On outline map show:

Europe 1914; 1924.

XVII. THE SECOND WORLD WAR

(see pp. 50–51, 52–53)

A. Locate on outline map and learn:

1. Rivers, etc.

Don; Volga; Yangtze; Gulf of Aden; Red Sea.

2. Areas & Islands

Ethiopia; Manchuria; Mongolia; Leyte; Malta; Okinawa; Solomon Is.

3. Cities

Canton; Chungking; El Alamein; Hong Kong; Leningrad; Moscow; Mukden; Singapore; Stalingrad; Tokyo; Vladivostok; Yalta.

B. On outline map show:

1. The boundaries established as a result of the First World War affecting territory that had been subject to German and Hapsburg rule in 1914.

2. The greatest extent of German and Japanese Conquest 1939–45.

XVIII. USSR AND SATELLITES AFTER SECOND WORLD WAR

(see pp. 58–59)

A. Locate on outline map and learn:

1. Rivers, Lakes, etc.

Oder; Vistula; Volga; Amur; Ob; Lena; Lake Balkhash; Lake Baikal; Ural Mtns.

2. Areas

Ukraine; Georgia; Siberia.

3. Cities

Baku; Bucharest; Gorky; Moscow; Prague; Sofia; Stalingrad; Warsaw.

B. On outline map show:

Boundaries of the USSR and the satellite states.

XIX. THE FAR EAST AFTER THE SECOND WORLD WAR

(see pp. 62–63)

A. Locate on outline map and learn:

1. Rivers, etc.

Indus; Ganges; Yangtze; Persian Gulf; Yellow Sea; Bay of Bengal.

2. Areas

Korea; Pakistan; Tibet; Vietnam.

3. Cities

Colombo; Delhi; Hanoi; Hong Kong; Karachi; Peiping; Seoul; Yokohama.

B. On outline map show:

Boundaries of China, India.

XX. EUROPE: MID-TWENTIETH CENTURY

On outline map show:

1. **Europe:** National boundaries as they existed in 1955.

2. **World:** Principal groups of powers; NATO, Soviet States, Arab States.

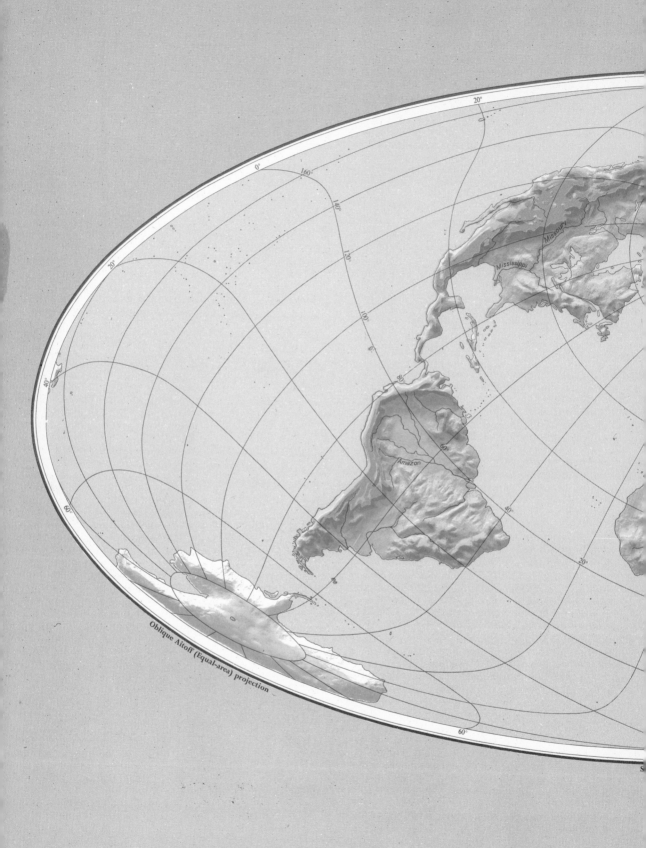

Oblique Aitoff (Equal-area) projection